The Catholic Calumet

EARLY AMERICAN STUDIES

SERIES EDITORS
Daniel K. Richter, Kathleen M. Brown,
Max Cavitch, and David Waldstreicher

Exploring neglected aspects of our colonial, revolutionary, and early national history and culture, Early American Studies reinterprets familiar themes and events in fresh ways. Interdisciplinary in character, and with a special emphasis on the period from about 1600 to 1850, the series is published in partnership with the McNeil Center for Early American Studies.

A complete list of books in the series is available from the publisher.

The Catholic Calumet

Colonial Conversions in French and Indian North America

Tracy Neal Leavelle

PENN

UNIVERSITY OF PENNSYLVANIA PRESS

PHILADELPHIA

Copyright © 2012 University of Pennsylvania Press

Published by
University of Pennsylvania Press
Philadelphia, Pennsylvania 19104-4112
www.upenn.edu/pennpress

Printed in the United States of America on acid-free paper
10 9 8 7 6 5 4 3 2 1

Library of Congress Cataloging-in-Publication Data

Leavelle, Tracy Neal.
 The Catholic calumet : colonial conversions in French and Indian North America / Tracy Neal Leavelle. — 1st ed.
  p. cm. — (Early American studies)
 Includes bibliographical references and index.
 ISBN 978-0-8122-4377-2 (hardcover : alk. paper)
  1. Jesuits—Missions—New France—History.
2. Indians of North America—Missions—New France—History. 3. Indians of North America—New France—Religion. I. Title. II. Series: Early American studies.
 F1030.7.L43 2012
 299.7—dc23
                                           2011024364

For Aaron and Noah, sons and brothers

Theologians
They don't know nothing
About my soul
About my soul
From "Theologians" by Wilco

I'm talking about people here . . .
Chucho Montoya in *Lone Star*, directed by John Sayles

Contents

Chapter 1

Spiritual Gifts

Conversion as Cross-Cultural Practice

A delegation of Illinois Indians on a diplomatic mission astonished the residents of New Orleans in 1730 with their ardent participation in the Catholic ritual life of the colonial capital. The Jesuit missionary Mathurin le Petit observed that during their three-week stay "[the Illinois] charmed us by their piety, and by their edifying life. Every evening they recited the rosary . . . and every morning they heard me say Mass." People crowded into the church to witness the spectacle of "savage" Indians worshiping and singing before the altar. The highlight for the audience was a responsive Gregorian chant in which Ursuline nuns "chanted the first Latin couplet . . . and the Illinois continued the other couplets in their language in the same tone." The Illinois appeared to be very well educated in Catholic practice, pausing during their daily activities to recite a variety of prayers. "To listen to them," concluded the priest, "you would easily perceive that they took more delight and pleasure in chanting these holy Canticles, than the generality of the Savages." Le Petit was correct in a sense. The inhabitants of some of the Illinois villages had developed a strong attachment to Christianity through years of interaction and exchange with the French.[1]

Illinois leaders Chicagou and Mamantouensa arrived in the city at the head of the delegation to show solidarity with their French allies who were embroiled in deadly conflicts with Native nations in the lower Mississippi valley. In an audience with the French governor, Chicagou presented two calumets, or ceremonial pipes, one symbolizing the shared French-Illinois attachment to Christianity and the other the diplomatic and military alliance between them. The Illinois had since the middle of the seventeenth century engaged the

French in calumet ceremonies to sustain friendly relations. In the 1690s, the Illinois converted in large numbers to Catholicism, adding a significant new dimension to the relationship. The connection now required two calumets, and one of these thoroughly Native ritual objects represented the religious traditions introduced by the French. This "Catholic" calumet seems an apt symbol for the ways in which the Illinois incorporated Catholicism into their lives. The calumet was an indigenous cultural vessel that now carried new meaning, just as the Catholic prayers the Illinois chanted in the New Orleans church in their own Native language contained Illinois cultural concepts.[2]

Indeed, the Illinois defined themselves as Christians through the ritual of prayer, through religious practice. Le Petit commented that "the Illinois . . . were almost all 'of the prayer' (that is, according to their manner of expression, that they are Christians)."[3] The Illinois term was *araminatchiki*, for "those who pray." *Araminatchiki* spoke, sang, and chanted Illinois words in a new Christian order and context, but these words could never be emptied entirely of their indigenous meaning. Ambiguity reigned in the volatile colonial world the Indians and French made together in the seventeenth and eighteenth centuries. Effective navigation of this swiftly changing world required the kind of cultural creativity on vivid display in the houses of worship and colonial offices of New Orleans. The appearance of a "Catholic" calumet in 1730 represented the results of many decades of encounter and cultural translation, a particularly compelling example of the exchange of spiritual gifts.

A well-known early encounter between the Illinois and the French revealed the importance of these gifts in establishing and maintaining relationships. On 17 May 1673, the Jesuit Jacques Marquette embarked on his famous exploration of the Mississippi with the French trader Louis Jolliet and a small group of men. It took the travelers a month of hard work to make their way from the mission of Saint Ignace at Michilimackinac to Green Bay and, finally, into the mighty river itself. The party paddled down the Mississippi for a week without seeing any other people. Finally, on 25 June, they spotted a path leading inland from the water's edge. Alone, Marquette and Jolliet followed the trail and approached a group of villages near a river. They shouted to announce their presence and waited for the villagers to greet them.

Marquette recounted that four old men walked slowly toward the two Frenchmen. Two of the men carried calumets, beautiful ceremonial pipes "finely ornamented and Adorned with various feathers."[4] Silently, they raised the pipes to the sun. Marquette was relieved to see the calumet ceremony because he knew the Indians reserved such treatment for friends and potential allies. He also noted that the men wore cloth, which indicated that they had traded in French goods. The men stopped before the explorers, and Marquette asked who they were. They replied that they were Illinois and then offered the calumets for the Frenchmen to smoke. The four Illinois men invited Marquette and Jolliet to enter the village, where the rest of the people waited impatiently to greet their foreign guests.

A long series of formal ceremonies followed. At the door of a cabin, an old man, entirely nude according to the missionary, extended his hands toward the sun and said, "How beautiful the sun is, O frenchman, when thou comest to visit us! All our village awaits thee, and thou shalt enter all our Cabins in peace." Marquette and Jolliet entered the cabin, where a crowd of people watched them carefully. The priest heard some people say quietly, "How good it is, My brothers, that you should visit us." The Frenchmen smoked the calumet again and then accepted an invitation from a "great Captain" to visit his nearby settlement for a council.[5] Many curious Illinois who had never seen the French before lined the path to the village. The Illinois leader greeted them at his cabin flanked by two old men. All three were nude, and they held a calumet toward the sun. The two explorers smoked again and entered the cabin.

Marquette reciprocated, using four gifts to speak to the assembly. By the first, he informed the Illinois that the party explored the river and contacted its peoples with peaceful intentions. "By the second, I announced to them that God, who had Created them, had pity on Them, inasmuch as, after they had so long been ignorant of him, he wished to make himself Known to all the peoples; that I was Sent by him for that purpose; and that it was for Them to acknowledge and obey him."[6] The third present announced that the French monarch had subdued the Iroquois and would restore peace throughout the land. Finally, the fourth gift asked the Illinois to share their information about the river and the lands and peoples to the south.

The Illinois leader responded with a speech that welcomed the French explorers and requested that Marquette return to teach them about the great spirit. He then gave Marquette and Jolliet three gifts: a young Indian slave, an esteemed calumet, and a third unnamed gift that was part of a plea that the explorers go no farther. After the council, the hosts fed Marquette and Jolliet a ceremonial meal of four courses. The leader placed bites of boiled corn meal (*sagamité*), fish, and buffalo in their mouths as if the Frenchmen were children, but the visitors refused the dog that was offered as the third course. After the feast, an orator led them around the village to all the cabins, calling the people out to greet the visitors. Marquette explained that "everywhere we were presented with Belts, garters, and other articles made of the hair of bears and cattle, dyed red, Yellow, and gray. These are all the rarities they possess. As they are of no great Value, we did not burden ourselves with Them." The tired travelers slept in the captain's cabin and the following day pushed their canoes back into the water in front of a crowd that Marquette estimated at almost 600 people. Pleased with their reception, the missionary promised to return the next year to instruct the Illinois, a people who had in his view "a gentle and tractable disposition."[7]

In this detailed journal, Marquette documented a voyage of exploration and discovery that marked the arrival of the French in the heart of the continent and the establishment of dynamic new relationships with Native peoples. The Jesuit superior in New France, Claude Dablon, applauded the success of the expedition. He noted the geographic significance of the river systems that Jolliet and Marquette traveled and declared the potential of the rich and beautiful lands that awaited colonization in the *pays d'en haut*, the upper country that lay above and to the west of the Saint Lawrence River valley. Dablon also viewed the waterways as key routes into a promising new field for evangelization. French officials responded quickly to the opportunity and by the early eighteenth century had created a colonial empire that stretched from the Saint Lawrence, through the Great Lakes, to the mouth of the Mississippi. This grand empire was more fragile than it appeared on maps of European territorial claims, however. The French relied on the cooperation of Native peoples in sophisticated diplomatic alliances and elaborate commercial networks to maintain the interior colonies. Without cooperation, they were virtually powerless in a vast region that remained, in many ways, Indian country. Neither the French nor the diverse Native nations that lived in the region were able to impose their visions of stability on the region.[8]

The familiarity of Marquette's account and the larger-scale concerns of French empire building all too easily obscure the complexity of what was really happening in the kind of close encounter the missionary described. There was an intimacy, intensely spiritual in nature, in the interaction. Not unexpectedly, Marquette framed the entire enterprise in religious terms. The missionary reflected in the first lines of his journal that when he received his orders to accompany Jolliet, "I found myself in the blessed necessity of exposing my life for the salvation of all these peoples." The idea of death in service to God brought him joy. The planned journey seemed that much more auspicious in that the instructions arrived on the feast of the Immaculate Conception of

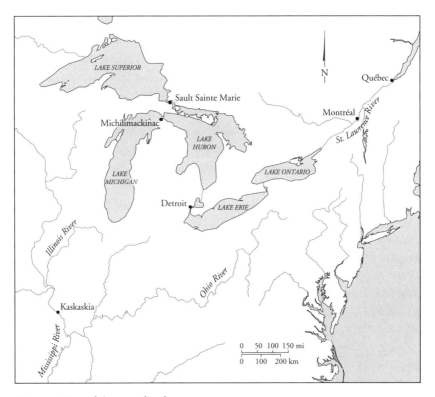

Figure 1. Map of the *pays d'en haut*, or upper country

the Blessed Virgin, with whom he always claimed a special relationship. In the final section of the account, Marquette described the baptism of a dying child in a different Illinois village and concluded, "Had this voyage resulted in the salvation of even one soul, I would consider all my troubles well rewarded, and I have reason to presume that such is the case." The baptism represented a moment of spiritual encounter that fit into the pattern already established through the ritual greetings, sharing of food, exchange of gifts, and problematic attempts at communication.[9]

For the Illinois, too, the spiritual dimension of the encounter was important, although for very different reasons. In their case, unknown beings and strange events sometimes embodied or communicated *manet8a*, or "power" in the Illinois language, and therefore they required special attention and analysis. Reimagine for a moment the encounter from the Illinois perspective. It was midsummer, and the days were long, hot, and humid. The corn was well established in the fields so carefully tended by women. Someone heard shouting from the main path to the river, and two strangers appeared. What did these men want? Clearly, they were French, for the Illinois had seen and traded with them in the Great Lakes region to the north. Four elders went to greet the visitors, two of them carrying *ap8aganaki*, or calumets, which they raised to the sun as a sign of welcome and honor. The black-robed stranger asked who they were, a question difficult to understand because he did not speak well. "*Inoki,*" they replied, which meant "we are the people" in Illinois. The Frenchmen put the *ap8aganaki* to their lips, and the soothing smoke from the sacred herb drifted into the air, the first sign of a potential relationship. Together, the six men entered the village to continue the ceremonial greetings.[10]

"How good it is, My brothers, that you should visit us," the people said. Two more times the visitors shared the *ap8aganaki* before they sat in the cabin of a prominent man to talk. The black-robed one offered gifts as he spoke; he seemed to know how to behave as a guest. He talked about peace and friendship and of spiritual things, too. He spoke with reverence about *kichemanet8a*, a great spirit, but the listeners could not discern the true nature of this being. When the man finished speaking, the Illinois leader presented a series of valuable gifts to show his respect and to signal his positive response to the offer of friendship and alliance. An Indian slave would accompany them down the river and the calumet would ensure a peaceful journey. Women delivered generous bowls of food to the cabin, and the host fed his visitors. They accepted most of the food in the carefully scripted ritual but refused the dog. Why? And why on the way out did they fail to take the intricately designed gifts offered by the people? Many things remained unclear, but the Illinois knew that these men, or others like them, would return. Hopefully, they would bring more gifts and items for trade. Maybe, with more men, they could help them fight their enemies in this tumultuous time. Perhaps the one who talked of *manet8aki*—spirits—had access to new rituals and valuable spiritual powers.[11]

Encounters like these initiated a complicated process of cultural translation and mutual conversion that lasted for a century in the *pays d'en haut*, the great expanse of land and water that encompassed the Great Lakes and Illinois country. Marquette understood that diplomatic protocol demanded that he present gifts to Indian leaders, but he probably did not fully appreciate the immense power in some of the gifts. If he had, the missionary likely would have gratefully accepted the finely crafted and vibrantly colored objects the Illinois pressed into his hands. It was precisely items like these that men carried into battle for protection and strength. A gift was not just a thing, a mute object. Gifts could speak, and some contained great power. Even the exchange of seemingly mundane items established potentially lasting relationships with mutual obligations.[12]

Although the value of these smaller gifts failed to translate clearly, Marquette easily recognized the calumet, *ap8agana* in Illinois, as a very special gift. As Marquette expressed it, the calumet "seems to be the God of peace and of war, the Arbiter of life and of death." Marquette described the calumet: "It is fashioned from a red stone, polished like marble, and bored in such a manner that one end serves as a receptacle for the tobacco, while the other fits into the stem; this is a stick two feet long, as thick as an ordinary cane, and bored through the middle." He continued, "It is ornamented with the heads and necks of various birds, whose plumage is very beautiful. To these they also add large feathers,—red, green, and other colors,—wherewith the whole is adorned." Birds were powerful other-than-human beings, and their feathers possessed useful power. Dablon commented in his report on the expedition that "this gift has almost a religious meaning among these peoples."

The spiritually potent pipes commanded great respect throughout the region and beyond, among many Native peoples. The Illinois used the calumet and its related ceremonies "to put an end to Their disputes, to strengthen their alliances, and to speak to Strangers," as well as to demonstrate respect toward the *manet8aki*, the spirits who populated their world. The calumet communicated the sincerity and identity of its carrier. It served as a translator of peaceful intent. Marquette gladly accepted the priceless gift, and he later used it to avoid dangerous confrontations with wary Indians to the south. The exchange of gifts in the Illinois village represented the establishment of a respectful, reciprocal relationship with the two Frenchmen. They were no longer strangers. Participation in these rituals reflected a major adaptation to Native customs for Marquette and Jolliet, a kind of conversion. The Illinois had started to incorporate these men into an Indian world, even as the two visitors looked forward to a time when the French would rule a commercial empire populated by Christian Indians.[13]

Religious encounters in the *pays d'en haut* brought people together in ways that promoted exchange across cultural borders, but not in a simple or straightforward fashion. Colonialism and its effects—the appearance of colonial officials, traders, and missionaries; the movements of Native peoples responding to pressures and to opportunities; the establishment and desertion of villages, forts, trading posts, and missions; the impact of warfare, disease, and alcohol—created unsteady formations on which to build new relationships. In the seventeenth and eighteenth centuries, a confluence of diverse peoples in a complex colonial environment contributed to the social and cultural transformation of the upper Great Lakes and Mississippi valley.

It seems somehow appropriate that this transformation occurred in a place defined by its rivers and lakes, by swift currents and quiet coves, by rhythmic waves and sudden tempests. French missionaries paddled into this changing world to lead its transformation. On lakeshores and riverbanks, on long portage trails, and on high bluffs with golden prairie views, they tried to persuade Native people to accept them as teachers, ceremonial specialists, and political allies. In Indian lodges and wooden chapels, the missionaries urged their listeners to recognize the new manitous, the spirits that offered the only true path to paradise. The shared space of Native villages and Indian missions left ample room for a variety of responses. The priests delivered their message and conducted their rituals using Native languages. Cultural influences flowed in many directions, influencing the expression of missionary spirituality and the emergence (and the rejection) of Native Christianities. Ultimately, generations of encounter produced a series of colonial conversions, the creation of hybrid cultural forms and religious practices that reflected simultaneously the movement and the persistence of boundaries. These interactions gave birth to the "Catholic" calumet the Illinois presented to their French friends.

Singular definitions of conversion that depend on the idealized renovation of imperial subjects from "savages" to "Christians" are insufficient to explain the complicated processes that unfolded in this colonial world. The experiences of Native peoples and missionaries argue instead for the adoption of a plural, dynamic, and flexible concept of conversion that accounts for the changes in all participants. Such a perspective requires an analysis of religious action—orientation and movement, song and speech, ritual and relationships—more than it does a simple delineation of faith and doctrine. Ritual activity and social relations remained the basis for Native religious life even for those who adopted Christianity, the *araminatchiki*.[14]

The classic definition of conversion emphasizes the abandonment of indigenous religious practices for faith in a Christian God and "orthodox" Christian ritual, but such a view is too limited for the diverse religious changes that occurred in the *pays d'en haut*. Missionaries participated actively in these movements, seeking as they did their own spiritual transformation as they labored to bring others to Christ. Rarely was conversion a simple movement

Figure 2. Captain of the Illinois nation, with his calumet and lance. [Louis Nicolas], *Codex Canadensis* (ca. 1700). Courtesy of the Gilcrease Museum, Tulsa, Okla.

away from one settled identity or set of practices toward another equally stable identity or ritual regime. Rather, the movement itself represented a significant element of conversion, a substantive engagement with difference that left none of the participants unchanged. A broader analysis of multiple conversions—French and Indian—more clearly articulates varied responses to cultural and religious differences and avoids the many problems that arise when trying to measure the supposed sincerity of Native neophytes. Conversions of all kinds in French and Indian North America took place in a colonial context notable for its shifting and often highly localized and deeply personal power relations. These plural transformations reflected the emergence of complicated and unstable cross-cultural religious practices.

A primary definition of conversion is "turning in position, direction, destination." In this sense, cultural encounters that involved any authentic exchange across lines of difference required a reorientation, a turn toward or away from the other, the identification of a new direction of travel. This metaphorical movement is apparent in the meeting of Marquette and Jolliet with the Illinois. The French explorers left the flow of the Mississippi to follow a path into an uncertain new world. The Illinois in turn shifted their gaze from the interior life of the village to the visitors from the outside. Marquette and Jolliet later returned to the river with a tangible expression of the relationship they had formed there.[15]

Religious studies scholar Thomas Tweed emphasizes "movement, relation, and position" in his theoretical reflections on religion. Tweed argues that two "orienting metaphors are most useful for analyzing what religion is and what it does: spatial metaphors (*dwelling* and *crossing*) signal that religion is about finding a place and moving across space, and aquatic metaphors (*confluences* and *flows*) signal that religions are not reified substances but complex processes." He explains that dwelling "allows devotees to map, build, and inhabit worlds. It is homemaking. In other words, as clusters of dwelling practices, religions orient individuals and groups in time and space, transform the natural environment, and allow devotees to inhabit the worlds they construct." Homemaking involves the construction of physical and cultural boundaries and is, therefore, an expression of power. The emphasis on crossing is recognition of the inherent instability of boundaries over time. "Religions," Tweed contends, "are not only about being in place but also about moving across. They employ tropes, artifacts, rituals, codes, and institutions to mark boundaries, and they prescribe and proscribe different kinds of movements across those boundaries."[16]

Tweed's use of the terms *confluences* and *flows* acknowledges the mixing of cultural and social streams within and between communities, a metaphor that works well for a region traveled most efficiently by water. The colonial setting of the *pays d'en haut* encouraged both crossing and dwelling. Missionaries arrived to redraw boundaries and reform communities, but like Marquette in the Illinois village, they often found themselves drawn into complex spiritual worlds that they did not entirely understand. Crossing and dwelling constituted a form of remapping the world, a way of enlarging the Christian homeland to incorporate others. The experience also offered opportunities for personal spiritual development. This exterior process of itinerant movement through space was closely connected to the interior movement from sin to sanctification, the translation of cross-cultural encounters into a sometimes radical spiritual transformation.

Missionaries often waited impatiently to participate in this communal and individual endeavor. Marquette was writing to the general of the Society of Jesus requesting a post in the foreign missions as early as the 1650s, before he had even finished his theological studies. In 1665, he wrote again and indicated that he had been set on service in the foreign missions since childhood. In that same year, his colleague, Claude Allouez, prepared to leave the French settlement of Trois-Rivières to reestablish the Jesuit mission in the upper Great Lakes, recently vacant because of the death of the previous missionary. Allouez had spent seven years working and studying to get ready for the challenge and to fulfill his dreams of Christian devotion. On 20 July 1665, he said a votive mass in honor of Saint Ignatius and Saint Francis Xavier to promote his plan for the mission to the primarily Algonquian-speaking peoples of the region, but Catholic saints alone could not grant the missionary's wish. Allouez needed the cooperation and assistance of Native peoples. A little over two weeks after the mass, Allouez finally convinced a party of reluctant Native traders to carry him in their bark canoes on their return trip into the lakes.[17]

Allouez turned again to Xavier for inspiration and guidance a few years later, when Allouez started a journey to open another Jesuit mission farther into the country. He and his two companions invoked the missionary saint in prayer twice each day during the difficult winter journey in 1669. The month-long trip ended in early December at a Native village on Green Bay that was home to people from several Native nations. Allouez celebrated a mass to mark the occasion on Xavier's feast day, 3 December, and asked the Jesuit saint to be the patron of the new mission that Allouez named after him.

"The thought of saint François-Xavier moves my spirit," Allouez recorded in some personal writings about the missionary vocation. "If men of the world expose themselves to as many perils and undertake such great works to win goods that will only perish, how difficult could it be for the servants of God to accept suffering and danger in order to win souls purchased in the precious blood of Jesus Christ!" Allouez saw in his hard labor for the missions, his encounters pleasant and otherwise with Native peoples, and the baptisms and conversions that he gained an incomparable path to the saintliness modeled by his missionary hero Saint Francis Xavier.[18]

In April of the following year, Allouez visited a village of Mascouten, Miami, and Illinois Indians west of Lake Michigan. At a feast, a Native elder stood with a bowl of tobacco and addressed his visitor: "This is well, black Gown, that thou comest to visit us. Take pity on us; thou art a Manitou; we give thee tobacco to smoke. . . . We are often ill, our children are dying, we are hungry. Hear me, Manitou; I give thee tobacco to smoke. Let the earth give us corn, and the rivers yield us fish; let not disease kill us any more, or famine treat us any longer so harshly!" Allouez responded that "it was not I to whom their vows must be addressed; that in our necessities I had recourse to Prayer to him who is the only and the true God; that it was in him that they ought to place their trust; I told them that he was the sole Master of all things, as well as of their lives, I being only his servant and envoy."[19]

Allouez's encounter reveals some of the challenges of navigating a world in motion. He believed that the Indians greeted him as a god, but he misunderstood his welcome. The translation was poor in this early encounter. The term *manitou* in Algonquian languages referred to spirits, the other-than-human persons that populated the landscape, as well as to the power that could influence the world and its inhabitants. In this case, the people in the village showed respect for Allouez, not yet knowing the extent of his power or how he might use it. Jacques Marquette acknowledged this understanding when he referred to manitous at one point as "persons of consequence." The elder, sprinkling sacred tobacco, requested that the Jesuit priest, a person of consequence, share his power for their benefit. The Algonquian-speaking peoples of the region constantly cultivated ritual bonds with the manitous around them, for manitous offered essential access to the power that made life possible. Allouez recognized the strength of these traditions and hoped to turn the people away from their honored spirits and toward his own. French missionaries adapted Native religious terminology and ideas so that they could explain Christianity in comprehensible terms. In the Illinois language, God became *kichemanet8a*, or the great spirit, the ultimate source of power in the world. The priests tried to introduce a vertical orientation in communities defined largely by horizontal relationships. The challenge of translation and the confluence of cultures limited the priests' ability to produce such a dramatic reorientation. Some Native peoples rejected the proposed transformation, while others translated concepts and practices into creative new expressions of indigenized Christianities.[20]

In the years after Marquette's encounter with the Illinois, Jesuit missionaries often encountered resistance to their teachings, especially among the Peoria band of the Illinois. Some Peoria leaders explicitly made the connection between rejection of the missionaries and maintenance of Peoria identity. One, for example, argued that Jesuit teachings were simply useless in the Illinois country. Religious traditions could not, in this view, be conveniently transported from one territory to another. Peoria identity required Peoria religion. A Peoria leader suggested to a man flirting dangerously with Christianity that the community stage a public presentation by the nation's elders and chiefs about the continuing relevance and power of Peoria religious traditions compared to the unwelcome ideas from afar. The established map of the Peoria homeland made little space available for the missionaries and their religious practices.[21]

By the eighteenth century, however, many Illinois communities had adapted to the presence of Christianity, some enthusiastically. The Illinois described conversion as a change of heart or a rebirth.[22] This internal reorientation also involved the remapping of boundaries and the translation of cultures, but it did not mean giving up a Native identity. In 1725, five years before he appeared to acclaim in New Orleans, Chicagou traveled to Paris to defend Illinois autonomy and claims to land. "We have ceded to [the French] the land we formerly occupied at Kaskaskia [a village near the Mississippi]," he said; "that is fine, but it is not good that they come mingle with us and put themselves in the middle of our village and our surrounding lands. I believe you who are the great chiefs, you must leave us masters of the land where we have placed our fire." Chicagou refused to accept further displacement, especially given the attachment of his people to the French and to Christian practice. The delivery of the calumets to the French governor in New Orleans strengthened the connection. The two episodes together, separated by five years and two long journeys by water, demonstrated the effects of crossing and dwelling and the confluence of cultures.[23]

These colonial conversions represented a range of emergent cross-cultural religious practices explored here through attention to a series of critical interpretive issues. Our voyage into this world starts well before Marquette's arrival on the Mississippi or the dramatic Illinois appearance in New Orleans. It begins instead with an examination of Jesuit and Ottawa origins, both mythic and historical. In the middle of the seventeenth century, the Ottawa confederacy responded to vicious colonial and intertribal conflicts by reorganizing around key sites in their ancient homeland at the center of the Great Lakes region. The resettlement of some Ottawa communities in locations that were both new and old at the same time allowed the Ottawa confederacy to maintain control of strategically important sites and thus retain its place in the evolving systems of alliance and exchange.[24] The eruption of violence and the spread of disease also destroyed many of the Jesuit missions in New France, the most famous of them being the missions to the Hurons. Like the Ottawas, the Jesuits sought a new beginning in the upper Great Lakes.

The stories of Ottawa and Jesuit origins as well as strong memories of the recent past created a dynamic cultural and experiential background for the relationships that developed in the new missions in the Great Lakes area. The stories provided essential statements on moral behavior and interpersonal relations in a changing world. They also contributed to the formation of divergent concepts of human nature, and they influenced attempts to mediate otherness through rituals of exchange. Native peoples like the Ottawas and Illinois viewed the missionaries as potentially powerful outsiders who had not yet formed the social bonds necessary for acceptance in their communities. For their part, the Jesuits certainly perceived Indians as savages in need of salvation, but they also recognized innate spiritual qualities that indicated a connection to the original revelation of God.

The missionaries' desire to restore this lost affiliation attracted them to a much larger project to transform land and people according to an ideal Christian landscape centered spiritually and metaphorically at Jerusalem. The attempted destruction of a savage Babylon and the erection of a new holy kingdom in the North American interior took place in a land already rich in meaning, filled with stories, and alive with power. Indians and missionaries introduced to their encounters competing visions for the creation and maintenance of ordered cultural landscapes that reflected and reinforced notions of the sacred, interpretations of the past, and visions for the future. The geographies of these encounters reveal space as a significant arena for colonial contests over people, place, and meaning. Despite these differences, Jesuit and

Native models of spiritual transformation remained flexible enough to accommodate multiple perspectives at the same time. Priests and Indians identified convergences in their respective traditions that became the basis for the creative reexpression of spiritual experiences and for the redefinition of self, personhood, and community. And Indians were not the only ones transformed by these spiritual encounters. Guided by the example of the *Spiritual Exercises*, the founding document for Jesuit spiritual practice, Catholic priests articulated new identities of their own in what was to them a savage wilderness of frequent affliction, suffering, and martyrdom.

Access to this world of stories and spirits can be difficult. The linguistic material prepared by Jesuit missionaries in the Illinois language therefore provides an important supplement to the standard French sources. These Native-language materials, which scholars are only now beginning to use, show how the intersection of language, culture, and history affected the contours of spiritual life and the course of religious change. Examination of missionary translations of Christian concepts offers significant opportunities to consider how Native peoples might have received and reshaped difficult ideas like grace and sin. The very prayer manuals and dictionaries intended to increase the effectiveness of the missionary enterprise also supply evidence of the limits of translation and the effects of intercultural mediation on the creation of indigenous forms of Christianity.

One of the results of this interpretive journey through the Native villages and missions of the *pays d'en haut* is a more textured description of religious life in these multicultural communities, one that recognizes the humanity of all participants. It has been all too easy for scholars to deny the sincerity of missionaries and to dismiss the genuine engagement of Native peoples with Christianity. Most accounts of French-Indian encounters in the region have not treated religion in detail or have considered religion to be simply another weapon in the arsenal of colonial domination. In their otherwise admirable attempts to counter the hagiographic style and heroic tone of some earlier historical accounts, scholars often dismiss the overt religious elements in missionary literature as formulaic and essentially meaningless constructions or as merely another expression of colonial propaganda. While the connection between missionization and larger colonial systems is undeniable, it is equally important to recognize that missionary literature recounts real efforts to achieve the eternal salvation of Native peoples and of the missionaries who carried the gospel to them. Social, political, and economic issues were important but still secondary to this original purpose. Moreover, the relationship between these additional concerns and the enduring goal of conversion changed through time and from situation to situation.[25]

Unfortunately, the corrective trend toward critical accounts of missionization has generated a strong bias against Christianity as an authentic expression of Indian religiosity. In an analysis of Native Christianity, scholar James Treat observes that "Native Christians have been called heretical, inauthentic, assimilated, and uncommitted; they have long endured intrusive definitions of personal identity and have quietly pursued their own religious visions, often under the very noses of unsuspecting missionaries, anthropologists, agents, and activists."[26] Surveys of Native American religious traditions rarely devote much space to discussions of Christianity despite its importance in Native communities past and present.[27] Christian missionization unquestionably supported colonization, dispossession, and the destruction of Native cultures. Yet the adoption and indigenization as well as the rejection of Christianity represented thoughtful and varied responses to colonization. The essentialist critique of Native Christianities fails to sufficiently recognize human agency and discounts the creative dimensions of encounter.[28]

An episode from a Mascouten and Miami village west of Lake Michigan presents a clear demonstration of substantive engagement across cultures, as well as the uncertainty that always seemed to go along with it. In 1676, the Jesuit Antoine Silvy praised a man he called Joseph for his piety and his dedication to prayer. When Silvy arrived at his mission, few of the several thousand inhabitants of the village claimed to be Christian. By Silvy's count, only 36 adults and 126 children had received baptism. He added only five more children and four adults to this modest number. The chapel was often full, but most people appeared only out of curiosity, not to pray with the missionary. Joseph was an exception. Silvy thought him the most remarkable of all the older Christians. The priest provided his superiors an example in his report. "An accident that greatly surprised me, happened recently to this poor man, while I was saying mass, at which he was very devoutly assisting. For, when I was at the consecration and was elevating the sacred host, he suddenly fell into such convulsions that he seemed like one possessed." "He was," Silvy continued, "Brought to himself; and after mass, when I wished to know the Cause of that accident, I was greatly consoled on learning that it was none other than the respectful Awe that the good christian felt at that august mystery."[29]

According to Silvy, Joseph always requested new prayers to incorporate into his ritual routines. He asked for a brief rosary of seven or eight words and "he said it with such special attention and affection that he inspired me with devotion, and Gave me unequaled pleasure. It would be an exceeding consolation to have many neophytes like him." Joseph seemed particularly concerned with calling down divine protection for his son, who had gone off to war in the conflict-ridden region.[30]

Joseph's assistance alongside the missionary as well as the trance he endured during the mass point toward the very real possibility that Joseph had identified important intersections or convergences between Christianity and indigenous religious practices. Joseph may, in fact, have apprenticed himself to the missionary to become a kind of Christian healer who could operate in both worlds. Silvy perceived him as the ideal neophyte—helpful, enthusiastic, and pious in practice—but Joseph's performance at the mass would have been even more familiar in the large public ceremonies that were common in these Native villages.

The French trader and colonial official Pierre Deliette described these ceremonies among the Miamis and Illinois in a memoir he left after many years of service in the Illinois country. Deliette wrote, "Two or three times in the summer, in the most attractive spot in their village, they plant some poles in the ground, forming a sort of enclosure . . . which they furnish with mats." As people prepared the ceremonial ground, the medicine men and women convened in a cabin to discuss their plans and get themselves ready for the coming rites. At the appointed time, the men and women entered the enclosure and sat down. A leader rose to address the healers and the assembled crowd. "My friends," he instructed, "today you must manifest to men the power of our medicine so as to make them understand that they live only as long as we wish." Shaking their gourd rattles and chanting, the healers called on their manitous in turn. "Immediately," according to Deliette, "three or four men get up as if possessed, among them some who resemble men who are on the point of dying. Their eyes are convulsed and they let themselves fall prostrate and grow rigid as if they were expiring." In the climax of the ceremony, the healers expelled the offending manitous from the ailing men using their own spirits and powers. The power to do so constituted its own kind of spiritual gift, one that had to be handled with care and respect lest the reciprocal relationship between healer and manitou be damaged or severed.[31]

Deliette argued dismissively that these medicine men and women conducted the ceremonies to instill fear and uphold their power and influence in the community. On the other hand, the pattern seems remarkably similar to the mass Silvy described. Such masses typically took place inside a small wooden chapel or in a specially prepared ground with a large wooden cross towering over the scene. Silvy would have arrived to say mass with all his priestly accoutrement and called the assembly to worship. Joseph stood by as his assistant. At a critical moment in the mass, Silvy elevated the sacred host for the consecration, the very moment of transubstantiation, and Joseph fell into a trance, as if possessed. In this case, the body and blood of Jesus Christ induced the trance, and the power of God pulled Joseph out of it so that he could continue his worship. Joseph worked closely with Silvy before and after the spectacular event to add to his repertoire of prayers and then used these acquired rituals to seek protection for his family. Silvy viewed him as the model convert. Joseph and others around him may have been just as impressed with his special access to new manitous and spiritual power.

Such events, with all their ambiguity, became a common feature of the colonial conversions that transformed the religious landscape of the *pays d'en haut* in the seventeenth and eighteenth centuries. The distance traveled from this moment, from this early encounter, to the presentation of a "Catholic" calumet in New Orleans some decades later was indeed a long and difficult journey marked by uncertainty. It was precisely this pervasive element of ambiguity, however, that supported the formation of new relationships and the creative exchange of spiritual gifts—powerful and attractive to some, threatening and still dangerous to others.

Chapter 2

Histories

Origins and Experience

In an entry for August 1660, Jérôme Lalemant, superior of the Society of Jesus in New France, recorded in a journal that an Ottawa trading fleet arrived at the French settlements on the Saint Lawrence River. He reported that sixty canoes made the journey from Lake Superior to Montréal and Trois-Rivières, bringing a large and valuable load of furs. After they completed their transactions and filled their canoes with European goods, the Ottawa traders prepared to make the two-month return trip to the upper Great Lakes. Trade between the Ottawas and the French was not based solely on animal skins and iron implements, however. Human relationships were also an important part of the alliance, and the Ottawas allowed three Jesuits and six other Frenchmen into their canoes for the journey. Fathers René Ménard and Charles Albanel and the *donné* Jean Guerin planned to open a new mission in the upper country, where they would renew Jesuit contacts with peoples dispersed by the wars of the 1640s and 1650s and spread the gospel to other nations that had not yet heard their message of Christian redemption. Albanel never made it past Montréal, kicked out of his canoe and deposited on shore by an angry paddler, but Ménard and Guerin completed the difficult upstream journey and started a mission on the southern shore of Lake Superior.[1]

Ménard established Notre Dame de Bon Secours at a strategically placed Native village on the Bay of Sainte Thérèse, modern Keweenaw Bay. The settlement was composed primarily of Ottawa and Ojibwa bands, but other groups regularly passed through the area, and Ménard hoped to take advantage of this easy access to multiple Native nations. His Jesuit companions on the Saint Lawrence waited anxiously for news of the distant mission. Finally, in the *Jesuit Relation* for 1660 and 1661, editor Paul Le Jeune relayed a message from Ménard that "the harvest is abundant, but the Laborers all too few." "In short," Le Jeune wrote, "the cry is raised on every hand, 'Send aid; save bodies and souls; destroy the Iroquois, and you will plant the Faith throughout a territory of more than eight hundred leagues in extent.'"[2]

Ménard may have been overwhelmed with apostolic work, but Le Jeune exaggerated his report of abundant harvests. In a letter written in June 1661 to his superior Lalemant, Ménard reported that his hard work had attracted only a few converts. His Native hosts politely tolerated his presence, and a few came to learn and pray. The people generously shared their food and frequently invited Ménard and the other French representatives to feasts and celebrations, but most people did not display a strong desire for conversion. The Indians simply accepted Ménard as a necessary part of the alliance with the French. Indeed, prior knowledge of French missionaries caused some people to fear Ménard. The missionary had to baptize children by stealth because fearful parents, hearing from Wendat, or Huron, neighbors that the sacrament might kill them, hid their sick children. Frustrated, Ménard eventually turned his attention to the Tionontatis, also known to the French as the Petuns, and the Wendats settled farther west on Chequamegon Bay. The Tionontati and Wendat refugees still had strong memories of the Jesuits and their teachings from the extensive missionary work the Jesuits conducted on Lake Huron's Georgian Bay from the 1620s through the 1640s. Ménard decided to use this knowledge and experience to build the foundation for a Christian Indian community in the upper Great Lakes.[3]

The fear of baptism and Ménard's approach to his apostolic work show that the relationship between the French and the Native peoples of the Great Lakes already had a complex history by the 1660s, when the Jesuits struggled to rebuild their spiritual empire in the region. Both Ménard and the Ottawas looked to this history to explain how they had arrived at that moment and to intuit the potential of their encounter. They also considered the stories of a more distant past, stories that gave meaning to the world around them. Ottawa myths and oral tradition preserved the fundamental knowledge of their origins, culture, kinship networks, and connections to place.[4] The Jesuits, too, had a rich written and oral tradition, filled with inspiring mythic figures, that explained the origins and culture of the Society of Jesus and that oriented the Jesuits in the world. In both cases, mythology provided a moral compass for action in the world. The recent history of the region provided yet another layer of new experience and meaning. Fifty years of Jesuit mission work in French North America, including the spectacular rise and fall of the Wendat mission, fired the apostolic fervor of Ménard and those who followed him. The missionaries of the past provided attractive spiritual models and practical information on mission operation. For the Ottawas and other Native peoples, trade, cultural exchange, disease, conflict, and migration marked a half century of truly astonishing change. These challenging experiences promoted flexibility and caution among Native peoples, a willingness to experiment as well as a desire for regular and reliable intercultural relationships. The past offered many lessons for those who sought inspiration and guidance.

*   *   *

The French trader and intercultural mediator Nicolas Perrot shared a vivid account of Ottawa origins in his important *Mémoire* of the second half of the seventeenth century. Perrot related that the Ottawas "believe that before the earth was created there was nothing but water; that upon this vast extent of water floated a great wooden raft, upon which were all the animals, of various kinds, which exist on earth; and the chief of these, they say, was the Great Hare." The Great Hare looked around for a place to land, but he saw only water and birds, and he became discouraged. He finally asked the beaver to dive from the raft to bring up some soil from the bottom of the water. "He assured the beaver, in the name of all the animals, that if he returned with even one grain of soil, he would produce from it land sufficiently spacious to contain and feed all of them." Although the beaver hesitated to accept the risk, he finally agreed to try. He was under the water so long that the other animals feared that he had died. Finally, the beaver's motionless body floated to the surface. The animals pulled him from the water and examined his claws, but they found no soil. The animals next placed their hopes in the otter: "They represented to him that he would go down quite as much for his own welfare as for theirs." Although the otter stayed down even longer than the beaver, he emerged from the depths in the same apparently lifeless condition and without any soil.

The situation seemed hopeless when the muskrat volunteered to go to the bottom. The animals doubted the muskrat's strength and power, but they encouraged him to try. "The muskrat then jumped into the water, and boldly dived; and, after he had remained there nearly twenty-four hours he made his appearance at the edge of the raft, his belly uppermost, motionless, and his four feet tightly clenched. The other animals took hold of him, and carefully drew him up on the raft. They unclosed one of his paws, then a second, then a third, and finally the fourth one, in which there was between the claws a little grain of sand." The Great Hare, as promised, took the grain of sand and placed it on the raft, and it began to grow. Scattering it about, the Great Hare increased the amount of soil until it was the size of a mountain. He ordered the fox to inspect the work and to increase it still more. The fox reported that there was enough land to support all the animals, but the Great Hare believed the world remained insufficient to support them all, and he continued to enlarge what he had made, even to the present time. The animals from the raft spread out over the earth, and "when the first ones died, the Great Hare caused the birth of men from their corpses, as also from those of the fishes which were found along the shores of the rivers which he had formed in creating the land."[5]

Although Perrot likely shaped this narrative to meet his goal of explaining Native culture and history in the region, his intimate knowledge of Indian life and culture during the period makes it an invaluable source on seventeenth-century Ottawa oral tradition. Furthermore, while other versions of Ottawa origin myths often differ in detail, they nevertheless reinforce many of the important themes stressed in the Perrot account. Anishinaabe peoples like the Ottawas and the Ojibwas called these sacred tales *aadizookaanag*, or the grandfathers. The events in the stories took place far in the past at an indistinct time, but the locations for many of the most significant episodes were well known to the people who shared them.[6]

One of the premier mythic themes the creation story reveals is the fundamental interconnectedness of life. The animals became the ancestors of men when the Great Hare intervened to transform the corpses of the dead animals into the first men. In the continuation of the tale, the Great Hare, known as Michabou in other stories and recognized as an aspect of the Ottawa trickster-hero Nanabozho, showed these men how to obtain their food and clothing from these animal ancestors. He also formed women to share with men the daily work of living, dividing life's responsibilities between them. The Jesuit Sébastian Rasles noted that the Anishinaabe peoples claimed descent from the Great Hare and other powerful beings like the Carp and the Bear. A prominent Ottawa leader from the nineteenth century, Andrew J. Blackbird, recounted some of this oral tradition and explained that Nanabozho referred to the inhabitants of the earth as "his nephews" and taught them how to live.[7]

A second prominent theme, related to the first, is cooperation. The Great Hare and the animals were partners in creation. The unselfish behavior of the earth divers, willing to risk their lives for others, made the creation of the earth possible. The Great Hare floated on the raft with the animals, powerless to change the world until the muskrat successfully returned with a grain of sand. Power, a third important element in the story, was the creative, transformational energy released through this cooperation. The muskrat appeared weaker than the beaver and the otter but in fact possessed more power than they did in this instance, and he succeeded where the others had failed. Like the muskrat, the Great Hare also used his power for the benefit of others. Recognizing the interconnectedness of life and accepting his own responsibilities, the Great Hare brought order to the world, forming the land, making a place for each animal, creating men and women, and teaching them how to live. Finally, this origin story shows that creation was an ongoing process, that change was a normal and inevitable condition of the world. The Great Hare wandered the earth, continually adding to what he had already formed. Each group of persons, human and other-than-human, had a place in this world.[8]

Perrot's account represents only one version of one tale in a complex, ever-evolving cycle of stories shared in Ottawa and other Native cabins through time. This vital oral tradition presented an indispensable guide to life and the land, an essential social and spatial map of the world and the diverse persons that populated it. In their daily lives, the Ottawas elaborated on the mythic themes of interconnectedness and cooperation, power and transformation expressed in the creation story. Reciprocal kinship obligations and connections to place provided the fundamental Ottawa cultural orientation or worldview. The Ottawas organized the world into successively wider circles of social relations that linked people within and between communities and places.

Basic Ottawa social organization located individuals in a network of relationships that emphasized communal responsibilities and that stressed horizontal ties over vertical or hierarchical relations. The immediate family, related through the father, formed the first in the concentric rings of kinship and provided the closest and most intimate set of social relations. Several larger groupings extending beyond the family maintained a variety of crosscutting connections that are often difficult to untangle in seventeenth- and eighteenth-century sources. The local village or band seems to have been a socioeconomic grouping of families, with a strong territorial dimension. Clan membership, determined by birth and traced through the father, created ties of kinship that linked these largely independent villages and bands.

At the time of contact with the French in the early seventeenth century, the Ottawas were further divided into four major subgroups that controlled the strategically significant water access points into and out of Lake Huron. In the east, the Kiskakons (or "cut-tail people," in reference to the bear) lived on Nottawasaga Bay, not far from their Iroquoian-speaking allies, the Tion-ontatis. The Sinagos (or "black squirrel people") had their main village on Manitoulin Island in northern Lake Huron. This important village was the spiritual center of the Ottawa confederacy and the location of the annual councils that brought the distinct nations together for political discussions, ceremonial activities, and social events. The Kamigas or Sables (the "people of the sandy beach") and the Nassauakuetons (or "people of the fork," perhaps in reference to the fork of a river) maintained their primary summer village on the western end of the lake, at Michilimackinac and to the south along the shores of the lake. Leaders had little coercive authority within these various subgroups but played an important role in relations between them and with outsiders. The Ottawa language, regular cooperation and exchange between groups, and frequent shared residency in larger villages provided yet another wider circle of social relationships. Ottawas viewed people who remained out-side these various connections as socially ill-defined and therefore approached them cautiously. In order to normalize relations with strangers, Ottawas had to form bonds and expand the social network.[9]

Gifts and the ideal of reciprocity created and maintained these necessary ties throughout the web of social relations. Perrot furnished a detailed descrip-tion of the treatment of strangers that highlights the importance of these concepts, a tradition of hospitality that Ménard and many others came to rely on even as they failed sometimes to grasp its larger significance. He wrote that "when any stranger asks it from them, they could not receive him more kindly, no matter how unknown he may be; it is on their side the most friendly of welcomes, and they even go so far as to spend all their means to entertain those whom they receive." The host made the visitor as comfortable as possible in his cabin and offered him the best food that could be found in the village. "While the guest is eating," Perrot continued, "all the leading people come to pay him visits. If he is clad in cloth garments, they take from him his clothing, and instead they give him furs, of their handsomest and most valued, to clothe him from head to foot. He is invited to all the feasts that are given in the village." Finally, Perrot explained, "when the stranger shows a desire to return whence he came, they load him with what is most suitable for his journey." Having established a relationship, the host could then count on similar treatment if he returned the visit.[10]

Ménard became a part of this critical social process soon after he arrived in the Great Lakes. The Indians regularly invited the missionary to their feasts. Ménard praised the generosity of his small band of neophytes, noting that "when they have anything out of the ordinary, either meat or fish, they do not fail to share it with us." At a time when there was very little food and Ménard did not have enough for even another day, he received an invitation to a small feast "where there was a double handful of indian corn. I was given a present of a handful, which we added to our fish; and happy was he who found some in a plate." Ménard worried that he did not have the goods, whether knives, beads, or tobacco, to respond to such generosity properly. He used the few items that he had carried with him as token gifts, and he and the other French provided some services to their hosts. Ménard bled patients with his lancet (perhaps not the most well-chosen gift in the end), while a French companion mended metal weapons. The Jesuit believed that the hospitality he experienced represented "a certain spirit of charity and gratitude" toward the French visitors, but it might be better characterized as one means by which the Indians forged a social bond with the missionary and, more widely, with the French.[11]

These principles also worked in the larger regional network of exchange. In 1662, some Ottawas traveled north from Lake Superior to establish trade with more distant nations. According to Perrot, the goods they carried were old and not very valuable, even worthless from his perspective. Yet "those people declared that they were under great obligations to the Outaoüas for having had compassion upon them and having shared with them the merchandise which they had obtained from the French. In acknowledgment of this," Perrot wrote, "they presented to them many packages of peltries, hoping that their visitors would not fail to come to them every year, and to bring them the like aid in trade-goods."[12]

The Feast of the Dead also cemented ties between peoples in the region. Algonquian-speaking peoples may have borrowed the feast from the Wendats and adapted it to their own ceremonial needs. In the ritual, a nation or nations honored their dead relatives from the past few years by inviting other communities for an intensive period of ceremonial activity, feasting, and exchange that lasted several days. Perrot related that the hosts sent "deputies from their own people into all the neighboring villages that are allied with them, and even as far away as a hundred leagues or more, to invite those people to attend this feast."[13] In a display of mutual respect, the guests arrived with gifts and received even more valuable gifts in return. Feasting and dancing followed. The ritual culminated in the burial of the carefully cleansed bones of the deceased relatives and in certain cases with the bestowal of important clan or family names on the descendents of the deceased. A 1670 Jesuit account claimed that around 1,500 people attended a Feast of the Dead held in honor of an Amikwa chief. Such a large gathering offered unequaled opportunities to establish and maintain ties between widely dispersed communities.[14]

The concept of reciprocity also played an important role in subsistence practices. Fishing and agriculture provided the foundation for the Ottawa diet. Men cast their nets in the rich fisheries of the Great Lakes, while women cultivated corn, beans, and squash in fields near the Ottawa villages. Men also left these villages in summer and winter to hunt, and women gathered seasonal plants and berries, adding additional food resources to a relatively rich and varied diet. Obtaining these foods from the earth involved the cultivation of good relationships with the manitous. Although the Great Hare was one of the most important manitous, there were many others who interacted more personally and directly with the Ottawas than this powerful figure. The manitous, who possessed varying degrees of power, influenced the success or failure of Ottawa subsistence practices. They could fill Ottawa nets with whitefish, make deer impossible to track, or bring rain during the most critical days of the short northern growing season. Ottawas and others made ritual offerings of tobacco and food to these manitous to maintain good relations with them and, therefore, a stable and abundant food supply. Furthermore, most Native individuals in the Great Lakes obtained a personal manitou through fasting and a spiritual quest at adolescence. The personal manitou then shared its power with the individual, affecting his or her success in obtaining food and in social relations, trade, journeys, warfare, healing, and many other areas of life. Ritual and reciprocity helped preserve the essential sacred balance between people and other beings in the world and promoted a good, prosperous, and healthy life. The redistribution of food through the social network also reinforced kinship connections in the larger human community.[15]

When the French arrived in the Great Lakes in the seventeenth century, they introduced new powers and objects to the Ottawa world, presenting fresh opportunities for cooperation and exchange and adding new strands to the existing web of social relations. The Ottawas believed that these new peoples, so different from those they had known before, must have had a creation separate from their own. Ottawa stories and their own deep experience had shown the Ottawas that change was inevitable. This solid cultural foundation prepared the Ottawas to adapt and survive, to search for a new order rooted in ancient tradition during the generations of change that followed their first encounters with the French strangers.[16]

The first recorded encounter with the French occurred in 1615, when Samuel de Champlain, the founder of the French settlement at Québec, met a large group of Ottawa men near the mouth of the French River on Georgian Bay. The following year, Champlain traveled to an Ottawa village in the Bruce Peninsula region, west of the Wendats and Tionontatis. Despite these early encounters with the French colonizer, most contact with the French for the next several decades remained indirect. The Ottawa homeland in the early seventeenth century arced from the Bruce Peninsula in the south to massive Manitoulin Island in the northern waters of Lake Huron. The great distance from the French settlements on the Saint Lawrence and the powerful Wendat confederacy that stood in between them buffered Ottawa relations with the French.[17]

The Ottawas nevertheless developed a strategic position in the Great Lakes region to take advantage of the French presence in North America. Contemporary observers and modern scholars have recognized the Ottawas as powerful middlemen in the trade of furs, European goods, and other items. Trade and gift exchange were without question a critical component of relationships with the French and with other Native nations. It appears, however, that trade was only part of a larger effort to maintain Ottawa control over the access points around the Lake Huron homeland. This position relied on social, political, and economic relationships with the Iroquoian-speaking Tionontatis and Wendats to their east and the other Algonquian-speaking peoples in the Great Lakes region. In the 1610s, the Wendats established a strong trading alliance with the French that thrived for four decades. They gathered furs from the Algonquian-speaking peoples around the eastern Great Lakes and beyond, funneling them to the French in exchange for metal implements and other articles, which they then redistributed. The Ottawas became important partners in this vast trade network. Each summer they met the Wendat traders returning from the Saint Lawrence near the mouth of the French River. There, Ottawa traders exchanged furs, shell beads, pigments, and perhaps copper for valuable European goods. They then passed some of these goods on to more distant nations in the upper Great Lakes and surrounding areas for more of the furs and other Native trade items. The Ottawas eventually controlled extensive travel and trade networks around Lakes Michigan and Superior and earned a widespread reputation as astute traders.[18]

Regional conflicts disrupted these strategic arrangements in the 1640s and destroyed them altogether by the end of the decade as the Five Nations of the Iroquois League, the Haudenosaunee, achieved a dominant position among the Native peoples of northeastern North America. The Saint Lawrence valley and eastern Great Lakes witnessed horrendous violence in the 1640s. Although war and violence had been common in the region, the scale and fury of the new wars seemed to dwarf those of previous conflicts. A complex set of circumstances stimulated a terrible cycle of escalating violence, setting the stage for the series of bloody wars that erupted periodically through the rest of the century. The wars were a product of the colonial world.

The Ottawas discovered some advantage in the injection of European trade goods into the region, but the French-aligned Wendats and the Dutch-aligned Five Nations profited the most from the European trade. The foreign goods, from copper pots to guns and decorative items, attracted Indians because of their usefulness, beauty, novelty, and power. Demand for European goods increased through the 1630s and 1640s, stimulating competition between rival groups for the limited supply of beaver pelts that ensured steady access to trade goods. Such economic competition contributed to new intertribal conflicts in the region. Moreover, imported European diseases had caused a demographic disaster in many communities, placing enormous pressures on traditional social and economic systems. The presence of two competing European imperial powers only added to the potential for conflict. In the 1640s, the Five Nations responded to these challenges with an increasingly aggressive series of attacks on the French and on neighboring Native nations. The Five Nations had a better supply of guns than their enemies because of their trading relationship with the Dutch, who were more willing than the French to trade firearms. The Five Nations successfully exploited this military advantage. They captured beaver furs, hunting territories, and trade routes in order to strengthen their economic and political position in the region. They adopted hundreds of Indian captives to replace population lost to warfare and disease. Paying a steep price in people and resources, the Five Nations preserved their way of life for a time and achieved a supremacy among the region's Native peoples that lasted well into the eighteenth century.[19]

The Haudenosaunee triumph resulted in a major reorganization of peoples throughout the region. The wars shattered the powerful and populous

Wendat confederacy, ending its important trading alliance with the French and destroying the network of Jesuit missions in their country. In 1649, with their population in decline, many of their villages and fields scorched in the attacks, and facing the threat of even more violence, hunger, and suffering, the Wendats dispersed in every direction. Some sought refuge with their neighbors, such as the culturally related Tionontatis. Others traveled north to live among remote lakes and rivers or in the small islands of northern Georgian Bay. Still other Wendat refugees fled to Gahoendoe, or Christian Island, just offshore in Georgian Bay from the Wendat homeland. The Jesuits deserted their most important mission settlement, Sainte Marie, and established a short-lived mission with the same name for the refugees on the island. After a desperate winter of starvation and disease, the Wendats decided to permanently abandon their native lands. Some Wendats, especially those with close ties to the French through Christianity and trade, resettled on the Saint Lawrence around Québec. Others escaped west into and beyond the upper Great Lakes. Even the Five Nations absorbed a large number of the Wendat survivors.[20]

Haudenosaunee attacks and their regional effects soon also forced nearby peoples, such as the Iroquoian-speaking Tionontatis, to search for safer and more stable places to live. During the 1650s, Native peoples paddled west and formed new multitribal villages in an anxious search for safety. The Ottawas remained somewhat insulated from the violence itself but not from its consequences. The Kiskakons on Nottawasaga Bay were most affected. They and many other Algonquian-speaking nations to the west of the Wendat country participated in the regional diaspora. The Ottawas who made their homes in the central Great Lakes offered a familiar refuge for their relatives and allies fleeing the violence. Kiskakon and Sable Ottawas established fortified bases on Green Bay with other Algonquian-speaking nations and with refugee Wendats and Tionontatis. By the late 1650s, some Ottawas had even pushed as far west as Lake Pepin on the Mississippi River, close to the Dakota, or Sioux, country. The Dakotas soon drove them out of this location, and they moved east to Chequamegon and Keweenaw Bays on Lake Superior, where Father Ménard encountered them in 1660.[21]

Several key elements contributed to Ottawa adaptability and survival in this extremely difficult period of disorder and confusion. First, the Ottawas consistently found sites that furnished reasonably reliable subsistence resources. The upper peninsula of Michigan and other places of settlement furnished productive fisheries, access to hunting grounds for meat and furs, and fertile earth for the cultivation of corn and other dietary staples. Second, in rapid fashion, the Ottawas exploited their long experience and extensive regional connections to reconstruct trade networks and political alliances from their new settlements. By the end of the 1650s, the appearance of the Ottawa trading fleet on the Saint Lawrence River became a regular, almost yearly event. Economic connections helped support social and diplomatic ties with the Tionontatis and Wendats and with other Algonquian-speaking groups, allowing the Ottawas to withstand the ongoing conflicts that frequently disturbed the region. Furthermore, while in the past the Ottawas had maintained a largely indirect relationship with the French, in the new era of Ottawa history they established a direct and lasting, though often difficult, relationship with the French that included traders, colonial officials, and missionaries. The basic organizing principles of Ottawa life, kinship and reciprocity, helped the Ottawas adapt to these dramatic social changes.[22]

Finally, although the Kiskakons had left the Nottawasaga Bay region behind, they also restored ancient connections to place that sustained them in their new locations in the upper Great Lakes. Mackinac Island was, in fact, the Native country of Nanabozho, the Great Hare. On that island, he invented nets for fishing by watching a spider weave its web and then taught the Ottawas how to use the nets to fish for themselves. Some Ottawas even traced their origins to the island, declaring that they had been born from the foam of the lake or the eggs of a carp that dried on its shores under the rays of the warm sun. For some of the Ottawas, it was, in this sense, then, a return.[23]

* * *

The Society of Jesus in New France also reorganized and adapted to change in this tumultuous time. In only a few years at the end of the 1640s, disease and Haudenosaunee attacks in the Wendat country destroyed the most promising Jesuit mission in French North America. The Jesuits had placed their highest hopes in the Huron missions, as they knew them, expending great effort and employing some of their most talented men in this work. Swept into the furious regional conflicts, the Jesuits witnessed the martyrdom of missionary priests and the dispersal of their young and growing Christian Huron congregation. Although the severe setback deeply disappointed the Jesuit missionaries, they had no intention of quitting the field. Instead, the Jesuits turned this unhappy history into an inspirational vision in the years that followed. The values expressed by the apostolic workers in the Wendat mission seemed to provide a strong spiritual link to the founding figures of the Society of Jesus who had established the order only a century before.

Ignatius of Loyola, the founder and first general of the society, and his early companions such as Francis Xavier, missionary to Asia, were men of history and myth. It was not as if history belonged to the Jesuits and only the Ottawas relied on myth to understand the world; both missionaries and Indians looked to their pasts, mythic and historical, as a guide. The already legendary saintly men of Jesuit origins, like Nanabozho for the Ottawas, established the most prominent cultural patterns and the important mythic themes that formed the foundation of missionary life in the Jesuit order. The Jesuits of late seventeenth-century New France wove their recent, painful experiences of hope and loss into this growing fabric of Jesuit myth. René Ménard paddled into the Great Lakes to rebuild and extend the Jesuit spiritual empire with this rich past firmly in mind. Ménard and his colleagues measured their experiences against those of the Jesuit martyrs in North America and the towering spiritual figures of Jesuit origins.

The French Jesuit mission in North America opened in 1611, when Fathers Pierre Biard and Énemond Massé arrived at the tiny colonial outpost of Port Royal in Acadia. The two missionaries labored for only two years among the Micmacs and Maliseets before an English warship from Virginia destroyed their mission stations and captured Port Royal. Although they accomplished very little in the way of conversion, Biard and Massé nevertheless developed a missionary program during their brief stay that would be familiar to all the Jesuits who followed them to the French colonies in North America. Biard and Massé were dismayed to discover that some Micmacs who had been baptized by a secular priest showed very little understanding of Christianity. The Jesuits decided to require intensive instruction in Christian beliefs and practices before they would baptize others. They also recognized the power of knowledge and initiated studies of Native culture and language. Massé passed a summer with the Micmacs, studying their language and their way of life. The priests hoped to use this knowledge to explain Christianity more effectively to the Micmacs and to identify the aspects of their culture that would need to be altered or suppressed. Massé and Biard concluded that they would have to introduce some level of French Catholic civilization to the Micmacs. They believed that Micmac seasonal migrations interfered with instruction and greatly reduced their chances of establishing a stable Christian community. The Jesuits waited, however, for more than ten years after the interruption of the Acadian missions to return to North America and continue their apostolic work.[24]

Jesuit missionaries renewed their efforts in 1625 when three missionaries, Massé and two new companions, arrived at the invitation of the viceroy of New France, Henri de Lévis, duc de Ventadour. Although religion had ostensibly been one of the central motivations for French colonization of the Americas from the beginning, a rapidly growing spiritual revival in France had inspired many royal officials, including Ventadour, to take this tenet of colonization more seriously. The fervently Catholic viceroy wanted the Jesuits to join the understaffed and overworked Recollets, missionaries from a reformed branch of Franciscans, in the evangelization of Native peoples in the Saint Lawrence region. The Recollets had been laboring there with only limited success since 1615, working primarily with the Montagnais around the French fur-trade depot at Tadoussac and with the more sedentary Wendats far to the west. Although the Recollets believed the fledgling colony needed more missionaries, they were not altogether pleased to share the work with their powerful, influential, and better-financed Jesuit rivals. The Jesuits immediately targeted the Wendats as the most promising field, but this effort, like the one in Acadia, came to a sudden end thanks to another English invasion. In 1629, English ships sailed up the Saint Lawrence, secured the river, and captured the fort and small settlement at Québec. The Recollets and the Jesuits had to abandon their missions and return to France.

In 1632, when the brief war ended and the French regained control of the Saint Lawrence, the Jesuits returned alone to try once again to implement their ambitious plans for the conversion of Native peoples to Christ. In building their spiritual empire, the Jesuits quickly became a major power in the colony, with an influence that went well beyond religion to affect social, political, and economic life in New France. A 1640 census showed twenty-nine Jesuits in a French Canadian population of only 356 people.[25]

Not long after their return, the Jesuits opened mission stations on the Saint Lawrence to reach the migratory hunting and gathering bands who lived mostly north of the river, the peoples known to the French as the Montagnais and Algonquins. The Montagnais and Algonquins had been important trading partners with the French even before the establishment of Québec. They came down from the interior each spring and summer to trade at Tadoussac and other trading stations, but returned in the fall to their winter hunting grounds as small family groups. Over the winter of 1633–34, missionary Paul

Le Jeune accompanied one such Montagnais band on their winter travels. Le Jeune studied their language and culture and began their religious instruction, but he found the arduous travel and difficult living conditions terribly demanding. The adventures of Le Jeune and his companions started appearing in the *Jesuit Relations*, published in France between 1632 and 1673. The *Relations* shared vivid tales of strange peoples and places and promoted Jesuit work to an eager French reading public fascinated by the exotic and fired by the enthusiasm of a popular religious revival.

Despite Le Jeune's bold experiment in the methodology of mission work, the seasonal movements of Native peoples generally frustrated the Jesuits, who carried with them from Europe the idea that Christianity was most compatible with a settled life. In 1637, the Jesuits initiated a project based on this concept of stability. They obtained a generous donation of land a few miles upriver from Québec to begin a new village for Montagnais and Algonquin neophytes. The missionaries hoped the reduction of Sillery, named for the prominent colonial figure who provided the land, would become a crucible of Christianity and civilization, attracting Native settlers and spreading the holy faith. Sillery soon offered settled living, maize agriculture, a hospital staffed by Ursuline nuns, and a rigorous routine of Catholic ritual. The Jesuits achieved only mixed success at Sillery, however. While some residents displayed the kind of Christian piety the missionaries longed to see in their primitive church, the model community never grew very large. Many of the Montagnais and Algonquin inhabitants did not reside there year round, leaving annually for trading and hunting expeditions into the interior. Haudenosaunee raids during the 1640s and 1650s and occasional outbreaks of smallpox and other deadly diseases posed additional problems. By 1663, only a few Indians remained, and the Jesuits had granted most of the land to French colonists.

Nevertheless, the Jesuits learned a great deal from their experiment at Sillery. They discovered that most Native people, including those who had developed a sincere interest in Christianity for one reason or another, did not find the supposed amenities of the reduction attractive enough to settle there permanently. The Indians preferred to remain in their own country even for religious instruction. The Jesuits responded to this desire by adopting a more flexible plan for missionization that employed multiple models and that incorporated a broader understanding of what constituted authentic Christianity.

They established mission stations in strategic locations, often at important trading sites and larger Native settlements. These stations might be occupied only part of the year, as missionaries frequently spent much of their time away from the post traveling between distant Native villages. This adaptation to Native patterns of settlement and seasonal migration also demanded greater tolerance of Native culture in general. In the future, rather than mount a straightforward attack on Indian cultures, the Jesuits used their ethnographic knowledge in an attempt to graft Christianity onto Native cultural forms, to substitute Christian for indigenous meanings. Jesuit missionaries did not, however, entirely abandon their belief that a sedentary life was more amenable to the practice of Christianity. They continued to operate reductions along the Saint Lawrence and to encourage settlement when they could, but even in these reserves, the missionaries made serious cultural accommodations. Moreover, the Jesuits concluded, in part through their experiment at Sillery, that the French hardly provided the best Christian models for Indian neophytes. In an effort to avoid what they believed were the negative examples of French traders, soldiers, and settlers, the Jesuits fought a generally losing battle to keep their mission communities and Indian reserves segregated from other French institutions and influences.

The Jesuits continued their work with the Montagnais, Algonquins, and other migratory peoples, but they soon devoted more of their energy and many of their resources to the Wendat missions east of Georgian Bay. The Wendat nations were already settled agricultural peoples who had developed strong and profitable trading alliances with the French. From their first brief foray into the country in the late 1620s, the Jesuits had dreamed of creating a network of Christian Wendat communities that could serve as a model for others and as a base for mission work among neighboring peoples. Father Jean de Brébeuf led the Jesuit return to the Wendats in 1634. Brébeuf had become a reasonably competent speaker of the Wendat language during the three years he spent in Wendat country before the last English invasion. He brought two other Jesuits with him to reopen the missions there, and they grew steadily for more than a decade, eventually employing almost twenty Jesuit priests and a few dozen additional lay assistants.

Brébeuf, the Jesuit superior of the missions, wanted the priests to live alongside the Wendats, to lodge and eat in their manner and learn their language and way of life, and he sent them with their servants to settle in the principal villages. The next superior, Jérôme Lalemant, conceived a very different plan. Beginning in 1639, Lalemant reunited many of the missionaries in a centralized residence named Sainte Marie. The compound soon became the Jesuit spiritual capital and the major French cultural center in the

Wendat country. Wendats came to study and pray at Sainte Marie, and the Jesuits traveled from there to visit Wendat villages. When the missionaries again started to remain in Wendat communities, they periodically returned to Sainte Marie for brotherhood and spiritual renewal. The Jesuits also developed broader contacts in the region, opening a mission to the Tionontatis and sending missionaries to visit distant Native nations.

Although the Wendats cautiously welcomed the black-robed priests as representatives of their French alliance partners, Wendat responses to the intensive Jesuit missionary effort varied greatly over time. The Wendat confederacy itself was composed of four distinct and independent nations, further divided into numerous villages, clans, lineages, and households. Natural social and political divisions alone made any sort of united response unlikely, if not actually impossible. The missionaries and their message were controversial from the start. A deadly series of epidemics that struck the nations in the first seven years of the mission provoked anger that many people directed toward the Jesuits. Many Wendats believed the missionaries were responsible for the diseases, and they accused the priests of witchcraft. The Jesuits, in fact, courted these accusations by attempting to supplant Native healers as the primary spiritual practitioners. While the missionaries stoked fears of sorcery in some people, they also convinced others to accept baptism as a ritual that could provide spiritual relief and, possibly, physical healing. Still other Wendats simply accepted baptism and a certain measure of Christian practice as an essential component of their trading relationship with the French. The Jesuits eventually managed to attract a few healthy adults to their nascent church, including several influential figures. Slowly, over the course of a decade, they built a Christian Wendat community of a few hundred souls.

The whole enterprise came crashing down in the late 1640s, however, a victim of the conflicts that engulfed the region. Haudenosaunee raids into the Wendat country intensified after 1640. The Five Nations attacked trading, hunting, and fishing parties and started capturing and destroying outlying Wendat towns. By the end of the decade, they were roaming deep into Wendat territory, threatening every important settlement. The Jesuits continued to stir up controversy as well, exacerbating internal dissension in Wendat communities that struggled to cope with depopulation, rapid social and cultural change, and appalling violence. The church drew more and more converts, most in search of solace and protection as the situation declined, but many Wendats continued to blame the missionaries and the French in general for the disastrous turn in their fortunes. The violence reached the missionaries, too. Eight Jesuits, including six missionary priests, a coadjutor brother (a Jesuit who took vows but was not ordained), and a *donné*, perished in these conflicts and achieved the status of martyrs for the faith. Among the casualties was the veteran missionary Jean de Brébeuf. Finally, in 1650, the Wendat diaspora emptied the country, leaving it to the Five Nations and ending the Jesuit dream. The few remaining missionaries fled with remnants of the Wendat nations down the Saint Lawrence to be nearer Québec.

Ten years later, René Ménard journeyed into the Great Lakes with the returning Ottawa trading fleet to begin the reconstruction and expansion of the Jesuit mission network that had collapsed so spectacularly. In the *Relation* for 1660, the Jesuit superior in Québec, Jérôme Lalemant, noted excitedly that Ménard had started a dangerous new mission among the Ottawas and other Native peoples far to the west. "It is true," he wrote, "the route we are obliged to take is still stained with our blood, but by that blood our courage is increased. . . . The glory, too, enjoyed by those who have died for JESUS CHRIST in making this expedition makes us desirous rather than timid." Lalemant and his Jesuit colleagues believed that sacrifice—physical and mental, including the missionary's life if necessary—was essential to the goals they hoped to accomplish. Of Ménard's mission, Lalemant concluded that "it must be acknowledged that the enterprise is glorious, and promises very abundant returns, in view of the number of Nations dwelling in those countries; but . . . that rich harvest is only secured by watering those lands with sweat and blood. I mean that a Missionary destined for this great work must make up his mind to lead a very strange kind of life, and endure unimaginable destitution of all things."[26]

The opportunity to make this kind of sacrifice was one of the reasons Ménard found this mission attractive. Lalemant reproduced a letter from Ménard in which the fifty-five-year-old priest expressed his intense desire for the difficult assignment. Ménard felt such a powerful call to the work that he thought to avoid it even at his age would cause him to experience eternal regret. "Even if it should be our lot to die of want," he wrote, "it would be a great piece of good fortune for us." A few years later, Lalemant shared one of Ménard's few letters from the mission. In it, Ménard reported that he was pleased with the challenges, with the "Cross which God has prepared for me." He continued, "I can say in truth that I have had more happiness here in one day, in spite of hunger, cold, and other almost indescribable sufferings, than I have felt in all my previous life in whatever part of the world I may have been. I often heard Fathers Daniël and Charles Garnier say, when they were among the Hurons, that the more they saw themselves abandoned and removed from human comforts, the more God took possession of their hearts and made them feel how far superior the favor of heaven was to all conceivable delights which are to be found among finite creatures."[27]

Antoine Daniel and Charles Garnier, two of the Jesuit martyrs from the 1640s, had already become spiritual models for the other missionaries. And these martyrs and the Jesuits who looked to them as examples patterned themselves on the two leading figures of Jesuit spirituality, Ignatius of Loyola and Francis Xavier. These two men, canonized in 1622, developed the core values of the society from its origins and, in the way they conducted their lives, set the standard to which future members of the society would aspire. The ideals expressed through the lives of the two Jesuit saints became the animating principles, the mythic themes, that served as a fundamental source of motivation and as a practical spiritual guide for the missionaries of New France. The French Jesuits constantly compared themselves to Ignatius and Xavier and made their apostolic activities an extension of the already deep history of their religious order.

Ignatius was born Iñigo López de Loyola in 1491 to a noble family in the Basque territory of northern Spain. He participated enthusiastically in the life of the nobility, devoting himself to a military career in a time and in a place that celebrated chivalry. A serious leg injury, suffered in a battle at Pamplona in 1521, dramatically redirected the course of the young man's life. During his lengthy recovery, Ignatius experienced a personal crisis and, inspired by his devotional reading on the lives of Jesus and the saints, renounced his noble life for one dedicated to a newly rediscovered faith in God and Christ. A vision of the Virgin Mary sealed his conversion, and he resolved to make a pilgrimage to Jerusalem. Ignatius put aside his fine clothes for a long tunic of sackcloth and started for Barcelona. On the way, he stopped at Manresa, where he spent ten months living as a hermit, meditating in a cave for hours at a time and begging for alms on the streets. The notes he took on his meditations, readings, visions, and mystical experiences formed the foundation for the *Spiritual Exercises* that every Jesuit would be required to undergo. After a brief visit to the Holy Land, Ignatius returned to Spain and initiated a path of study that would lead years later to the priesthood. His charismatic personality and mystical insights soon attracted a devout following, but his public teaching also got him into trouble with church authorities. Ignatius managed to avoid conviction, but the experience convinced him to leave Spain in 1528 in order to continue his education in Paris.

During his seven years as a student in the French capital, Ignatius recruited a small group of fellow students who committed themselves to his vision of religious asceticism and apostolic service. The young Francis Xavier, like Ignatius a Basque nobleman, was one of these early companions. Ignatius led his followers through the *Spiritual Exercises* and prepared them for lives devoted to the salvation of souls. In 1534, the men made private vows of poverty and chastity, agreed to seek ordination, and determined to go "to Jerusalem, and spend their lives for the good of souls," or, if that plan failed, to "return to Rome and present themselves to the Vicar of Christ, so that he could make use of them . . . for the glory of God and the good of souls." In 1537, Ignatius met his companions in Venice to make plans for their voyage, and he finally received his ordination as a priest. Growing tensions in the Mediterranean prevented a safe journey to Jerusalem, however, so Ignatius traveled to Rome to offer the group's services to Pope Paul III. In 1539, Ignatius gathered his followers in Rome to discuss their future. They decided to form a new religious order obedient to the pope and modeled on the early church apostles who were the first to diffuse the Christian faith in the world. On 27 September 1540, the papal bull *Regimini militantis ecclesiae* formally established the Society of Jesus. The first Jesuits elected Ignatius general of the new order. In the first year, the society counted only about twenty members, but by the time of the leader's death in 1556, the society had an internationally diverse membership of 1,000 Jesuits distributed across Catholic Europe and in missions around the world.[28]

Ignatius, the heroic founder of the Society of Jesus, quickly became the premier Jesuit spiritual model in the order's early years, but after his death, his status as a figure of mythic proportions only increased over time. His own writings, the pious biographies that soon appeared, and his glorious tomb supported a strong cult of Ignatius within the society. Through his life and in his role as founder and spiritual leader of the order, Ignatius placed two themes—conversion and service—at the heart of Jesuit life and practice. In his *Autobiography* and especially in his *Spiritual Exercises*, Ignatius created a model for an intensely personal, ongoing conversion in which the Jesuit struggled to suppress his own will in favor of God's and searched constantly for a true path toward salvation and eternal union with the divine. The corresponding service ideal put these values into motion and carried them to the world at large. As stated in the *General Examen*, an important document that explained the order's aims to potential candidates and their examiners, "The end of this Society is to devote itself with God's grace not only to the salvation and perfection of the members' own souls, but also with that same grace to labor strenuously in giving aid toward the salvation and perfection of the souls of their neighbors." Ignatius institutionalized these basic principles in the larger *Constitutions*, which outlined the society's structure and articulated its fundamental goals, and in the *Spiritual Exercises*, the original spiritual fountain that provided members of the order a constant source of motivation for attaining those goals.[29]

Ignatius's early companion and fellow founder, Francis Xavier, became the missionary hero for the Society of Jesus, the mythic figure who inspired generations of Jesuit missionaries by providing a practical model for the actual implementation and performance of these ideals in mission service. In 1540, even before the society received official recognition from Pope Paul III, Ignatius designated Xavier for the order's first mission to India. Xavier began his journey a year later from Portugal, sponsor of a recently settled colony in India. After the long sea voyage and a winter in Mozambique, he arrived in Goa on the Indian coast in 1542. Xavier organized Jesuit institutions and supervised mission work in India and throughout the East for a decade. He traveled incessantly and widely, from India and Ceylon to the Spice Islands and Japan, seeking converts and founding mission churches.[30]

Xavier's European colleagues and many others enthusiastically shared the missionary's numerous letters and instructions. The regulations set down by Ignatius made regular correspondence with superiors standard Jesuit practice. Xavier's writings, which aimed to edify as much as describe, proved important to Jesuit culture and spirituality from the inception of the order. The Jesuits copied the letters for circulation in Jesuit houses throughout Europe and translated them into several languages for wider distribution. The information and written portraits of exotic peoples and places certainly played a part in their popularity, but they also expressed a missionary spirit that inspired many readers. Xavier's labors to implant Christianity in distant countries offered some consolation to a church suffering severe losses to the Protestants in Europe. His writings served as effective publicity for the Jesuits, highlighting the society's work abroad and attracting many new recruits to the young and rapidly growing order. Within the society, the letters encouraged thousands of Jesuits to volunteer for foreign missions. Roman archives preserve some 15,000 letters from Jesuits who requested foreign missions prior to the suppression of the order in 1773, including those of Father Marquette. Xavier's vivid and reflective letters also furnished an important model for later missionary writings such as the *Jesuit Relations* from New France.[31]

Xavier revealed the animating principles for missionary work and expressed core Jesuit values through striking descriptions of actual mission activity, an inspirational feature that appealed to his many readers. In a brief prayer written about 1548 from Goa, Xavier suggested how critical the Jesuit goal of propelling others to salvation could seem to the Jesuit missionary: "Eternal God, Creator of all things, remember that you alone have created the souls of the infidels, whom you have made to your image and likeness. Behold, Lord, how hell is being filled by them to your dishonor . . . grant that they too may come to know Jesus Christ, whom you have sent, your Son our Lord, who is our salvation, life, and resurrection, through whom we have been saved and freed, to whom be glory for ever and ever. Amen." This understanding of the state of the world and its peoples, coming from a missionary at work on the frontier between salvation and damnation, enlivened and intensified the essential Jesuit aim of saving souls.[32]

Xavier showed the Jesuits how the dual objectives of conversion and service came together in mission work. In a letter written to the society on the eve of his mission to Japan, Xavier reflected on the dangers of the sea voyage and on the potential anxiety of confronting the people of such a well-developed civilization. Xavier told his readers, "I almost always bear before my eyes and mind what I frequently heard from our blessed Father Ignatius, that those who would be of our Society must make great efforts to conquer themselves and to reject all those fears that cause men to lose their faith, hope, and confidence in God, and to take the means to do so." Indeed, Xavier urged them not only to accept the dangers of missionary work but also to seek them actively as a means toward their own more complete conversion. He wrote, "It seems to me that those who are living solely, and without any other intent or purpose, for the service of God in a constant danger of death will soon come to abhor life and desire death, in order to live and reign forever with God in heaven, since this is no life but a continual death and exile from the glory for which we were created." Xavier counseled his colleagues to spend themselves unconditionally in order to fulfill God's will, to serve others, and to find personal salvation. In one of his first letters to his companions in Rome, Xavier reminded them "how peaceful it is to live by dying each day, by going against our own will in seeking *not what is our own but what is of Jesus Christ*."[33]

Finally, Xavier demonstrated his intense love for the Society of Jesus and for his brothers, a powerful emotional attachment to the order and its purposes that helps explain the strong esprit de corps that generated much of the society's vigor and force. In a letter from India, Xavier confessed, "When I begin to speak of this holy Society of Jesus, I am unable to break away from such a delightful topic, and I am unable to stop writing . . . *if I should ever forget the Society of the Name of Jesus, may my right hand be forgotten!* since in so many ways I have come to know the great debt which I owe to all those of the Society." He concluded these thoughts by "asking God our Lord that, since in his holy mercy he brought us together in his holy Society in this most laborious life, he may unite us in his glorious company in heaven, since we are in this life so far separated from each other out of love for him."[34]

Xavier spent two years, from 1549 to 1551, developing the Jesuit mission in Japan before turning his attention to China. After a brief visit to India in 1552, he sailed to the small island of Sancian, off the Chinese coast from the city of Canton. Portuguese traders and Chinese smugglers used Sancian as a base of operations, and Xavier tried to locate someone willing to risk transporting him to the mainland, which was forbidden territory to foreigners. For three months he tried and failed to make arrangements to get into China. Xavier became ill in late November and finally died on 3 December 1552 in a small hut on the Sancian shore. Initially interred on the island, the missionary's remains were carried to Malacca the following spring and, a few years later, to a church in Goa where he had started his mission to the East. Xavier's body reportedly remained incorruptible through the moves, and observers took this as a clear sign of his sanctity. His body and tomb in Goa became a physical center for the cult that quickly developed around his memory.[35]

An unofficial cult for Ignatius also emerged in the years after his death in 1556, and the Jesuits soon mobilized to promote the two founding fathers as holy examples for the larger church. The Jesuit campaign to have Ignatius elevated to sainthood succeeded in convincing Pope Paul V to open the formal process of canonization in 1605. The papacy pronounced Ignatius blessed in 1609, and Xavier was beatified ten years later. Finally, on 12 March 1622, in a magnificent ceremony at St. Peter's Basilica in Rome, the Catholic Church added five new saints to its pantheon in a single day, including three Jesuits: Ignatius, Francis Xavier, and Francisco Borgia, an early Jesuit recruit and third general of the society. With these canonizations, the Jesuits, already successful and powerful, attained an even higher status within the church.[36]

Saint Ignace and Saint François Xavier, as they were known in French, were the exemplary figures that the Jesuits of New France tried to emulate. Inspired by these mythic heroes of the previous century, the Jesuits in the missions of seventeenth-century New France created a corresponding "colonial hagiography" that built on that original memory by celebrating the spiritual accomplishments of their own colleagues. The martyrs from the Huron missions, who ended their lives as Xavier did while laboring to extend God's kingdom on earth, seemed to embody the themes that the two saints emphasized. The martyrs thus provided a sense of attachment to the spirit of Jesuit origins, and they became the first great local heroes for the Jesuits in New France to follow.[37]

Jean de Brébeuf was the most famous of these Jesuit martyrs in North America. Brébeuf, called "the apostle of the Hurons" by his fellow missionaries, first went to the Wendats in 1626, when the Recollets were still there. He led the Jesuit return to the Wendat villages after the French regained Canada from the English, reestablishing his mission in 1634. For most of the next fifteen years, Brébeuf labored among the Wendats and their neighbors. A controversial figure from the beginning, Brébeuf earned both the fear and the respect of the Wendats for his apparent spiritual power. Repeated epidemics and the hundreds of baptisms he performed on dying patients especially alarmed Native observers. In the late 1640s, Haudenosaunee raids intensified, and the escalating violence eventually claimed Brébeuf as one of its numerous victims.

On 15 March 1649, Brébeuf left the Jesuit compound of Sainte Marie with Father Gabriel Lalemant for their regular weekly visit to several Wendat towns. At dawn the next morning, Haudenosaunee warriors stormed the Wendat village the two priests were staying in, taking them captive. The attackers forced their prized prisoners to travel without clothing through the late-winter chill to a nearby village, where they made them run the gauntlet. The Haudenosaunee then tied Brébeuf and Lalemant to posts and tortured them gruesomely for hours, reportedly placing a string of red-hot axes around Brébeuf's neck, wrapping his body in resinous bark and setting it afire, and derisively pouring boiling water over his head in imitation of the ritual of baptism. A hatchet blow to the head finally dispatched Brébeuf on the afternoon of 16 March. Lalemant died the following morning after equally frightful treatment.[38]

The sensational demise of Brébeuf, Lalemant, and the other martyrs of the 1640s represented the dramatic decline and fall of the Wendat missions.

For the Jesuits, however, a larger meaning emerged that made it part of God's mysterious unfolding plan for redemption. Brébeuf had in the Jesuit view lived an exemplary life. He worked hard as a missionary, leaving the familiar comforts of France to found missions in the wilderness. The Jesuits thought that the baptisms Brébeuf performed saved hundreds of people from potential damnation. Brébeuf became a talented linguist who learned the Wendat language and taught it to others. The missionaries believed God had blessed Brébeuf with mystical visions, including foreknowledge and serene acceptance of his approaching death. Brébeuf's reported peaceful tolerance of grim tortures and final martyrdom seemed to recall the passion of Christ. The violence directed against the missionaries, most vividly demonstrated in the mimicry of Christian ritual during Brébeuf's prolonged torture, proved to the Jesuits the depth of their impact and made them vital participants in a momentous spiritual battle that had Native souls hanging in the balance. Indeed, for Brébeuf to be a true martyr according to the canonical standards of the church, it was essential that he actually die for his faith and not simply because he was French and became caught up in the regional conflicts that disturbed the colony's peace.[39]

Charles Garnier, who died later in 1649 in an Iroquois attack on the Tionontatis, wrote to a colleague in France: "I must share with you news of this country that is a great consolation. Our Lord has given the martyr's crown to two of our Fathers, Father Jean de Brébeuf and Father Gabriel Lalemant. They were not put to death by a tyrant who persecutes the Church, as the tyrants of ancient times did, but we call them martyrs because the enemies of our Hurons made them endure the derision of our holy faith." The two missionaries were warned, he said, that the Iroquois would attack, "but they resolved to imitate Jesus Christ, the good shepherd, and to die for their flock." Garnier then described some of the tortures inflicted on the priests. Reflecting on the loss of Father Brébeuf, Garnier finally concluded, "he is the apostle of the Hurons and he always lived piously. We will admire him here. God is blessed by his saints."[40]

Brébeuf's fame spread rapidly. A local cult of veneration appeared to celebrate his memory. The Jesuits treated his remains as holy relics, taking his body to Sainte Marie, and when the Five Nations forced them to abandon the country, they carefully cleaned and preserved his bones and carried them to Québec. People soon started reporting miraculous cures due to the intercession of Brébeuf and the potency of his relics. In New France and Old, the stories of the Canadian martyrs captivated readers and listeners, especially fellow members of the society. With the support and encouragement of the society, the archbishop of Rouen ordered sworn testimony gathered from witnesses who could verify the virtuous lives and saintly deaths of the missionaries. He did so apparently in anticipation of future canonization proceedings, a process not completed until 1930, when Pope Pius XI declared the eight Jesuit martyrs saints of the church.[41]

René Ménard had known these men and remembered their works and words when he embarked on his own dangerous mission to the Great Lakes. He forged the next link in that chain of spiritual meaning that connected the Jesuits of New France to the saintly founders of the order. After his first winter at Notre Dame de Bon Secours on Keweenaw Bay, Ménard became frustrated with his slow progress and decided to visit some refugee Tionontatis and Wendats to the west. In the summer of 1661, Ménard and another Frenchman followed a Native group traveling in that direction after trading with the Ottawas. The two men failed to keep up with the party, however, and the Indians, fearing that they would run out of supplies, left them behind. Ménard and his companion struggled to stay on the canoe route and to follow the portages, but they eventually lost their way. To make matters worse, the two men became separated in the forest and Ménard vanished. Ménard's French companion never found him, and the details of the missionary's disappearance and death remained mysterious. Perrot reported evidence that the Sioux, or Dakotas, were responsible. There were also conflicting reports about whether an Indian man had seen the priest's body or his bag by a lake. Some people claimed that a few of Ménard's personal belongings turned up in an Indian cabin.[42]

Although the Jesuits never learned the complete story, in a very real sense the actual facts of Ménard's demise mattered less than the general pattern to which it adhered. Ménard did not experience the same kind of glorious death as Brébeuf, but the Jesuits immediately compared Ménard to the martyrs who had preceded him. In the *Jesuit Relation* for 1662 and 1663, Father Jérôme Lalemant excitedly told his readers that "this year we have learned of a similar death of one of our old Missionaries, Father René Menard, who had penetrated five hundred leagues into the interior, bearing the name of JESUS CHRIST to lands where he had never been worshiped." Lalemant admitted that the fruits of Ménard's labors seemed insignificant compared to the great hardships he endured, but the superior argued, "In fact, they cannot be called small, and could not, even did they involve the saving of one soul, for which the Son of God spared not his sweat and his blood, which are infinitely precious." There were also comparisons to Saint Francis Xavier, the greatest missionary model for the Jesuits. Lalemant believed that Ménard had suffered greatly "and, in accordance with his own desires, and even in fulfillment of his own prophecy, imitated in his death the forsaken condition of Saint Francis Xavier, whose zeal he has imitated to the letter during his lifetime."

Ménard himself hoped to meet these highest of Jesuit standards in his mission. Lalemant related that before Ménard left for his ill-fated attempt to reach the new country, some Frenchmen who had taken the route tried to talk the missionary out of going. Ménard replied that saving his own life was not worth losing other souls. According to Lalemant, Ménard maintained that "God calls me thither, and I must go, although it should cost me my life. Saint Francis Xavier," he told them, "who seemed so necessary to the world for the conversion of souls, met his death in the act of effecting an entrance into China; and should I, who am good for nothing, refuse, for fear of dying on the way, to obey the voice of my God, who calls me to the relief of poor Christians and Catechumens so long bereft of a Pastor?" To his colleagues, Ménard died a martyr to the reconstruction and expansion of the Jesuit mission that had been destroyed a decade earlier. They believed that Ménard, in the process of missionization, expressed the core spiritual values of the society. He therefore became the next inspirational example for the many missionaries who would follow him to the Great Lakes.[43]

In more practical, earthly terms, Ménard also accomplished several things. He renewed Jesuit contacts with the Wendats and Tionontatis who had escaped the destruction of their villages and the capture of their homelands. He also established a more direct relationship with the Ottawas, including those who had been dislodged by the same violent history. Ménard's travels in the upper Great Lakes marked the entrance of the society into new mission fields. Jesuit missionaries would soon initiate much wider contacts with peoples throughout the region, in the Illinois country, in the Mississippi valley, and far to the north and west of the Great Lakes. The Jesuits and the French traders, colonial officials, and soldiers became a prominent part of the region's cultural, social, and political landscape for the next one hundred years.

Two separate quests for a restoration of order brought the Ottawas and other Native peoples together with the missionaries in the *pays d'en haut*. Visions of a new Christian kingdom, the eternal salvation of Indian souls, and the sanctification of missionary priests inspired the Jesuit outsiders who arrived. For the Indians, it was practical necessity, a need for the basic stuff of life itself, that encouraged them to incorporate the French into a world that both would continue to shape together. The search for spiritual power that could restore a sense of order was an important part of this Native quest. These encounters, the meeting of the tradition of Nanabozho, the Great Hare, with the tradition of Ignatius and Xavier, altered its participants, Indian and Jesuit, in countless ways. The often confusing and contentious meetings produced a significant number of Christian converts and resulted in the genesis of Christianized Indian communities, although the meaning of Christianity was never as fixed as the missionaries would have liked. For the Jesuits, these evolving communities represented the spread of Jesuit and Christian institutions, and they offered a priceless opportunity for the missionaries to put their religious principles into practice and to reach their personal and communal spiritual goals.

Chapter 3

Geographies

Moral Landscapes and Contested Spaces

In the decades after Ménard's mysterious disappearance, many French officials, missionaries, traders, and soldiers traveled the waterways and portages into the *pays d'en haut* to participate in its transformation. On 14 June 1671, Claude Allouez of the Society of Jesus and Simon François Daumont, Sieur de St. Lusson, directed an elaborate ceremony before an audience of Indians, missionaries, and Canadian traders at the Jesuit mission at Sault Sainte Marie. Commissioned by Jean Talon, the intendant of New France, St. Lusson carried a message from Louis XIV to the Indians of the upper Great Lakes. Interpreter Nicolas Perrot translated the message into a Native tongue for the representatives of fourteen Indian nations. He explained that St. Lusson had been ordered to their country "to take possession, in the King's name, of all the country inhabited and uninhabited . . . to produce there the fruits of Christianity, and . . . to confirm his Majesty's authority and the French dominion over it." This message was, furthermore, to be shared with the Illinois, the nations of the north, and still other peoples beyond the basin of the Great Lakes.[1]

Allouez and St. Lusson then conducted a carefully orchestrated pageant to seal the words through action. On a height overlooking the village, they planted a cross in the earth and, near it, a cedar pole on which they affixed the royal arms of France. Three times, voices raised, they claimed all the land between the Northern, Western, and Southern Seas as part of the dominion of Louis XIV, His Most Christian Majesty, "raising at each of the said three times a sod of earth whilst crying *Vive le Roy*, and making the whole of the assembly as well French as Indians repeat the same." The discharge of musketry punctuated the declarations. Père Allouez explained the great powers, spiritual and temporal, that the cross and the cedar post represented. "The whole ceremony was closed with a fine bonfire, which was lighted toward evening, and around which the *Te Deum* was sung to thank God, on behalf of those poor peoples, that they were now the subjects of so great and powerful a Monarch."[2]

The commission given to St. Lusson and the process by which he took possession of the country for the French king brought together the concerns of mercantilist development, religious imperialism, and continental empires. A royal official, translated by a French trader and assisted by a Jesuit priest, gathered in symbolic fashion a vast region and its many peoples into the French colonial system. With their pageant, the French ritually altered the existing landscape to reflect this new colonial vision, planting a cross for the Lord and a post for the French king and raising the earth itself in celebration. They began to reshape lands and reorganize peoples to fulfill their dreams of wealth, religious conversion, prestige, and power.

The dramatic ceremony at Sault Sainte Marie initiated a new contest over the interpretation and manipulation of space, a contest that would transform the cultural and human geography of the Great Lakes region and Illinois country in the century to follow. The process of mutual adaptation between Indians and French was, in part, an attempt to conceptualize, draw, and maintain boundaries and to establish a stable social and moral order in a diverse and swiftly changing social environment. Interaction brought competing geographies—divergent French and Indian visions of geographic order and disorder—*into* encounter, and the prolonged efforts of many parties to enact these visions in space actually altered the region's landscape, producing complex geographies *of* encounter. French attempts to complete the labor of possession and economic and religious transformation, expressed ceremonially at Sault Sainte Marie, tested the power and ability of Native peoples to counter, control, or channel geographic change, to influence the thickness, permeability, and placement of boundaries.

The geographies of this encounter encompassed a series of spatial practices and outcomes that depended on multiple, diverse, often shifting layers of geographical interpretation. Native peoples viewed and interacted with the world around them, discovering layer after layer of meaning in a living landscape. They mapped the locations of spiritually powerful places, important events that occurred in mythic and more recent times, favored travel routes, reliable gathering sites, and much more. They noticed patterns in land and experience and cultivated new cultural landscapes, many not visible to out-siders, others marked into the very land itself. The French carried their own interpretations about the significance of space and the need to transform it as they traveled into the North American interior. St. Lusson and other colonial officials saw potential gain in the natural resources, in the conveniently linked waterways and portages, and in the promise of trade and alliance with Indian partners. Allouez and the Jesuits, from their mission compound at the center of the Great Lakes, looked out on a wild, unchristian land populated by equally wild and unchristian Native peoples. Both land and people, in the Jesuit view, awaited the glorious transformative power of God's healing grace. This specifically Christian mission of spiritual transformation remained the focus of French missionaries, who sought to suppress seemingly savage disor-der and extend the boundaries of the Christian world.[3]

Indians often defended passionately the connection between land and identity that emerged through centuries of living with the land, an associa-tion that contained an essential spiritual element. For others, however, Christi-anity became a vital cultural force for coping with the consequences of change, maintaining recognizable boundaries, and supporting continuing claims to the land that had always sustained them. Encounters between Indians and French forced participants to orient and reorient themselves in an evolving landscape, to interpret and reinterpret the mounting layers of geographical meaning around them.[4]

Geographic metaphors appear naturally and repeatedly in such discus-sions of colonialism and cultural encounters precisely because geography is as essential to the presence and persistence of Native communities as it is to the expansion and contraction of colonial empires. Scholars and observers have for a long time extended geographic ideas to the analysis of a range of social, political, and cultural issues, yet they have largely ignored or treated in only the most general manner the spatial and geographic implications of the very metaphors they employ. Spatial metaphors that describe social differences and cultural encounters—concepts such as frontier, middle ground, center and margin, borders and borderlands—achieve their explanatory power in part from the strong link between colonialism and geography.[5]

All difference is marked in some way by boundaries, at least of perception and often of a more obvious physical nature. Systematic engagement with spatial concerns must include consideration, then, of the complex connec-tions between the perception and the physical manipulation of space and boundaries and of the creation of new geographies through encounter, interaction, and conflict. These issues clearly emerge in colonial circumstances, but they are much more broadly a product of any encounter with difference. Struggles for power and hegemony merely highlight their existence, amplify their effects, and heighten the consequences.

Examination of the geographies of encounter explicitly recognizes the presence of differing perceptions of the land, both as it was and as people thought it should be, and begins to identify the transformations that resulted from attempts to apply these visionary ideals in space. In the Great Lakes and Illinois country of the seventeenth and eighteenth centuries, the confluence of peoples with contrasting perceptions and the contest to implement contending designs produced, in the end, not stability and order but rather diverse and stubbornly inconsistent colonial geographies that left no one entirely satisfied.

*   *   *

The French arrived in the Great Lakes and Illinois country to create connections with Native peoples, to exploit the land and its resources, and, ultimately, to instill a new order. Although many Indians welcomed stronger ties to the French, not all of them appreciated even the symbolic changes the French made in the land. During the elaborate proceedings at Sault Sainte Marie, Native leaders signed an official report of the conference with marks that depicted, according to a French chronicler, "the insignia of their families; some [drawing] a beaver, others an otter, a sturgeon, a deer, or an elk." The French also drew up some documents that they alone signed. They then slipped one of the papers between the iron plate bearing the king's insignia and the post to which it was attached. "Hardly had the crowd separated," the French writer reported, "when they drew out the nails from the plate, flung the document into the fire, and again fastened up the arms of the king— fearing that the written paper was a spell, which would cause the deaths of all those who dwelt in or should visit that district." Of course, the Indians could have become angry because the French did not let them place their marks on the additional documents, but whether it was spiritual or diplomatic concerns or some combination that caused the violent reaction, the Indians obviously recognized the potential power of French objects and actions in their native land. The acceptance of the post itself and the wooden cross, both still standing, became only one of many compromises that sustained French-Indian relationships through the years.[6]

While St. Lusson and other French officials promoted an empire of commerce that would span the continent, linking Indians and French in a powerful and profitable colonial system, French missionaries dreamed of an empire based on a message of Christian salvation. The ceremony of possession at Sault Sainte Marie may have united for a moment French religious and secular concerns in an effort to establish new order and strengthen cross-cultural relationships in the region, but the goal of saving souls remained the paramount Jesuit objective. Although religion was at least initially, and in some cases remained, a major marker of difference between French and Indians, through missionization and engagement with Christianity, religion became a meaningful point of contact as well.[7]

Indians had their own reasons for attending the summit at Sault Sainte Marie and for participating in the regional transformation that followed. Native peoples in general contemplated neither religious perfection nor immense commercial profits. Indian goals were more modest and immediate than French plans, but no less important or visionary in the ways they would transform the country. They simply searched for the stability that would allow them to obtain subsistence from the land and rebuild stressed and fractured communities. They struggled to maintain their hold on ancient tribal territories or, in many cases, to establish new ones to replace those that were lost in the chaos of war, depopulation, and displacement. The Native peoples of the region accepted the French cautiously and not without dissension and debate over the nature and extent of these relationships. They understood all too well, as the reaction to the papers and the pole shows, that their world would be reshaped forever and in ways that no one could yet conceive.

The mission at Sault Sainte Marie became one of many important sites for the contests and compromises that reshaped the region's geography. The Indian village and mission there perched above the rapids of the river between Lakes Superior and Huron, on a peninsula strategically vital to the whole upper country. Transportation routes converged there, and rich fisheries attracted Native peoples from throughout the region, making it a crucial communications, trading, and social center for both Indians and French. Ottawas, Ojibwas, Tionontatis, and Wendats called it home, and numerous other Native groups visited regularly. The peninsula, especially with the growth of Michilimackinac on the straits that connected Lake Michigan with Lake Huron, became the hub of the interior fur trade and the location of important Indian villages and French mission stations and military posts.[8]

At the Sault Sainte Marie ceremony, St. Lusson also claimed the Illinois country beyond the Great Lakes, homeland of the loosely allied bands of Illinois Indians who gave the region its name. Over the next century, this ill-defined area, bounded on the south by the Ohio and Missouri Rivers and on the north by the southern shores of the Great Lakes, became an essential continental link between New France and the emerging colony of Louisiana. In the late seventeenth and eighteenth centuries, it was a major site of Indian settlement and French missionization and economic development. A southern extension of the *pays d'en haut*, the Illinois country connected across a short portage the Saint Lawrence River and Great Lakes to the mighty Mississippi, the Father of Waters.

For the Indians, however, this great expanse of land and water represented more than mere territory. The struggle to adapt to unsettling change took place in a land that was alive with generations of stories and the associations of lived experience, a country populated by manitous, the other-than-human persons who could support or impede human efforts to survive and prosper. Native peoples lived in a landscape of profound, deeply rooted, often spiritual meaning. Not surprisingly, the Jesuits chose a site with a long history of Native settlement for their mission at Sault Sainte Marie. The Algonquian-speaking Ojibwas, who made the place their home, called the Native settlement at the mission Bawating. It was an attractive area for settlement long prized for its abundant subsistence resources. Indeed, some local traditions taught that the native country of fish lay just across the peninsula in the straits at Michilimackinac. The region also had other important connections to myth. An Ojibwa story, for example, related that the trickster hero Michabou created the rapids or falls, *sault* in French, when he crushed a giant beaver dam there as he crossed over the river that flows out of Lake Superior. Such stories explained the origins of the world and its features and grounded people in a living landscape of communal memory and experience.[9]

Claude Allouez first journeyed into this land of diverse peoples and endless stories, meandering rivers and vast lakes, dense woodlands and open prairies in 1665, six years before his appearance with St. Lusson. Until his death in 1689, Allouez traveled ceaselessly to transform what he described as "the sacred horrors of these forests . . . and the thick darkness of this barbarism." Allouez and the Jesuits assumed that the land was an uncivilized, unsacralized wilderness unsettled by the movements of savage peoples and constantly disturbed by the effects of intertribal warfare and imperial and commercial competition. Missionaries applied a new moral geography to the region, a

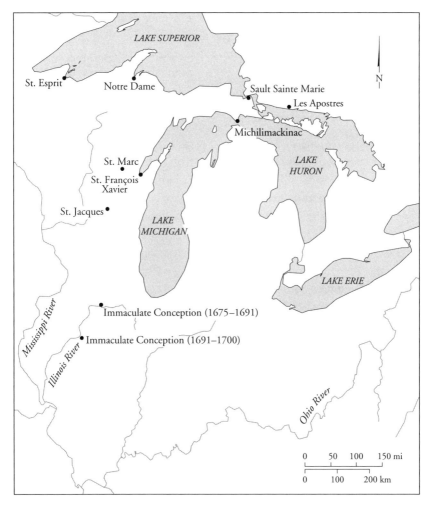

Figure 3. Map of the *pays d'en haut* and Illinois country, 1650 to 1699

Christian interpretation of space and the proper arrangement of people within it. The mission of Sainte Marie du Sault represented for the Jesuits a site of stable settlement, instruction, and sacramental ritual that promised to establish order and improve the moral condition of a seemingly chaotic land devoid of all the essential characteristics of Christian civilization and society. Allouez expressed these dreams of spiritual renewal when he planted the wooden cross at St. Lusson's 1671 pageant. The missionaries also discovered in the wild spaces of the *pays d'en haut* a place where they could easily express the most cherished spiritual values of the Jesuit order.[10]

When Allouez paddled away from the bank at Trois-Rivières and up the Saint Lawrence and Ottawa Rivers past Montréal, powerful imagery and representations prepared him for a journey into another world. Allouez called the Great Lakes a "remote corner of the world, where the Devil has . . . long held sway." According to European moral geography, the Indians and their land were separated from the Word of God in a world of darkness, excluded from the community of man defined properly by the presence of Christian faith. Europeans easily converted these perceived geographical differences into temporal ones as well, for the wilderness and its inhabitants represented to them an earlier stage of cultural and moral development. To travel into this world was also to travel back in time.[11]

The potential moral dangers of travel in this savage land were, for the missionaries, at least as profound as the physical ones. The space beyond the more urban settlements of New France did not yet contain the physical and metaphorical points of reference that sustained a well-developed Christian geography, nor did it supply the regular ritual and instruction that supported the Christian liturgical calendar. The Jesuit Étienne de Carheil wrote to the governor of New France from his mission in the Great Lakes to warn him about the potential consequences of sending young men into the fur trade. He feared that it exposed "those who undertake such journeys to a thousand dangers for both their Bodies and their souls." He argued that travel "takes them away from all the holy places; it separates them from all Ecclesiastical and religious persons; It abandons them to a total deprivation of all Instruction, both public and private, of all devotional Exercises, and, finally, of all the spiritual aids to Christianity. It sends them into savage countries and into Impassable places." This anxious missionary described an abandonment of Christian order and a descent into savagery.[12]

Although the apparently disordered state of this wilderness startled and profoundly frightened the missionaries, the Society of Jesus also trained its members to search for God in all things, even in places and among people that appeared so far from God. On their long journeys by canoe and by foot, they looked for evidence that God's providential plan of salvation was written into the landscape itself, that it was prepared for transformation through the humble efforts of missionaries and, more importantly, the saving grace of God. When Allouez entered Lake Superior on his first mission into the Great Lakes, he noted that its shores provided important seasonal gathering places for many Native bands. Surveying the contours and resources of the lake and its shores, he applied a Christian reading to the region's geography: "These peoples' motive in repairing hither is partly to obtain food by fishing, and partly to transact their petty trading with one another, when they meet. But God's purpose was to facilitate the proclaiming of the Gospel to wandering and vagrant tribes." No part of the world had been left untouched by the creative hand of God, but like so many imperfect souls, this space had not yet reached its full spiritual potential in the Christian providential plan. Inspired by the opportunity to participate in its transformation as a partner of God, Allouez celebrated his first mass since he had left the comforts of Trois-Rivières and thereby "consecrated these forests by this holy ceremony."[13]

Allouez started his first permanent mission, Saint Esprit, or Holy Spirit, at Chequamegon Bay on the southern shore of Lake Superior. He erected a little bark chapel between two large villages composed of several Algonquian-speaking bands and Tionontatis and Wendats who had gathered there for the abundant fish. He tried to capture the attention of the Indians who visited his chapel with frightening images of hell and the last judgment. He baptized many sick children and had the curious recite prayers in an Algonquian language. Early in 1666, the missionary decided it was time to move his small chapel to the middle of the larger Native village, where he hoped to have more direct access to 2,000 souls. Impatient, no longer satisfied with working at the margins of Indian society, Allouez planned to insert himself physically and spiritually into the very center of community life. He noted that "it was just at the time of their great revels; and I can say, in general, that I saw in that Babylon a perfect picture of libertinism."

The Indians hardly welcomed his confrontational style. Many people openly scoffed at the missionary and his teachings. Allouez felt the young people in particular quickly became more insolent. Finally, the cold reception compelled him to withdraw to his previous location outside the village. He was consoled upon leaving, however, "that Jesus Christ had been preached and the Faith proclaimed—not only publicly, but to each Savage in private."

The zealous missionary believed he had planted the seeds of faith in the hard, unbroken soil of a savage Babylon.[14]

Allouez and his brethren received nourishment and guidance in these projects from the *Spiritual Exercises* of Ignatius. The *Exercises* provided a map to the moral geography of the world and suggested a plan that linked its transformation to the personal spiritual quest of each missionary. The meditations in the *Spiritual Exercises* regularly require that the retreatant imagine the spatial dimensions of the sacred, the physical spaces where significant events in the history of salvation took place, and the locations of the great battle between good and evil, Christ and Lucifer. An important segment of the *Exercises* known as the meditation on the Two Standards highlights the sharp division in the world between the holy and unholy. The meditation asks the retreatant to "consider how Christ calls and desires all persons to come under his standard, and how Lucifer in opposition calls them under his." It then contrasts the territory commanded by Christ, centered around the holy city of Jerusalem, with the territory dominated by Lucifer, centered on Babylon. First, "imagine the leader of all the enemy in the great plain of Babylon. He is seated on a throne of fire and smoke, in aspect horrible and terrifying." Continuing, Christ raises his banner "in that great plain near Jerusalem, in an area which is lowly, beautiful, and attractive." Finally, this "composition of place," as Ignatius termed this class of exercises, demands that the retreatant become an active participant in the ongoing battle to enlarge the empire of Christ. "Gaze in imagination on the supreme and true leader, who is Christ our Lord," it instructs, and "consider how the Lord of all the world chooses so many persons, apostles, [and] disciples, and . . . sends them throughout the whole world, to spread his doctrine among people of every state and condition."[15]

The image of Babylon served in this meditation and in missionary accounts from New France as a metaphor of decline, a reminder of the potential consequences of straying too far from God and the holy city of Jerusalem. The apparent savageness of the land in North America revealed the extent of the decline there and the corresponding absence of the civilizing effects of Christianity. The opposing metaphors of Babylon and Jerusalem operated in both human and spatial terms. For the Jesuits, no place in the world was free of the moral implications of the eternal struggle for salvation, and each person, knowingly or not, became part of the spiritual contest, either contributing to the salvation of the world or hindering that ultimate moral goal. The Jesuit missionaries carried these powerful ideas to their work in North America, believing that they followed God's will in joining the battle for souls and the expansion of His kingdom. Allouez noted in discussing one of his wilderness treks that the devil always opposed his endeavors, but the passionate missionary concluded that "[Satan] is hardly pleased, I think, to see me make this latest journey, which is nearly five hundred leagues in length." With every league Allouez paddled or walked, the missionary remapped the continent in a spiritual sense. He moved his Holy Spirit mission to the middle of the Indian village, believing that he would transform a spiritual Babylon into a new Jerusalem.[16]

When Jesuit missionaries established such isolated outposts among the Indians, they reinscribed the land with Christian symbols in an effort to sacralize and instill new meaning in it. They attempted to transform space through the conscious application of a Christian moral geography. Missionaries routinely planted large wooden crosses throughout the region, as in the ceremony at Sault Sainte Marie. Claude Allouez erected another cross in the middle of a Mesquakie, or Fox, village west of Green Bay and, according to a fellow missionary, "thus [took] possession of those infidel lands in the name of Jesus Christ, whose standard he was erecting farther within the realm of the demon than it had ever before been planted." Allouez did so again in 1677, when he traveled to the Illinois country south of Lake Michigan, where Jacques Marquette had opened a mission among the Illinois nations a few years before. Allouez reported that "we planted in the middle of the village a Cross 35 feet in height . . . in the presence of a large number of ilinois of all the nations." "I can say in truth," Allouez continued, "that they assisted at that ceremony with great respect. . . . The children even came devoutly to kiss the Cross, while the grown-up people Earnestly entreated me to plant it there so firmly that it might never be in danger of falling."[17]

Planting these crosses held great significance for both missionaries and Natives. It was more than a mute symbol of Christ's passion. On the simplest level, the act frequently signaled the official establishment or reopening of a mission to a particular Native community. Through the act of planting the crosses, the missionaries also took spiritual possession of land and souls in the name of God and the Society of Jesus. More importantly for their program of conversion, however, the missionaries believed that the crosses brought Christ and his act of atonement through space and time, facilitating a more direct encounter with the holy mystery for people seemingly in need of salvation. One Jesuit recorded that two colleagues assigned to a Great Lakes mission "were delighted at being the first ones chosen to carry Jesus Christ to a Country abounding . . . in darkness and in death." They carried Jesus into the wild country in their canoes, prayer books, and words and in the crosses and chapels they erected.[18]

Finally, and most significantly, when the Jesuits inscribed the land with their symbols of Christian power and authority, they tried to efface other meanings in the process and rewrite the moral geography Indian peoples had developed over the ages. In November 1672, for example, Allouez visited his small mission of Saint Marc among the Mesquakies west of Green Bay. In his journal, he noted that "we found, at a little distance from the Road, opposite a small rapid, a great rock, roughly carved into the figure of a man, The face of which had been painted red. . . . It is an Idol which passers-by invoke for The fortunate result of Their journey." "We rolled It into The water," he stated matter-of-factly. In the next line of his journal, Allouez contrasted this dramatic action with what he did when he arrived at the mission. "When we came near the village," he wrote, "we adored The cross that we had planted in Their village the previous winter."[19]

Although missionaries could not destroy the larger sites as easily as they could a painted rock next to a stream, they nevertheless tried to alter the meaning of even very prominent features of the landscape, activities not limited to the Jesuits. Jean François Buisson de St. Cosme, a missionary affiliated with the Séminaire de Québec and the Séminaire des missions étrangères in Paris, scouted the Illinois country and assessed its potential as a mission in 1698 and 1699. He came to a dramatic rock a hundred feet high, an island that rose above the Mississippi River. St. Cosme reported that the rock "makes the river turn very short and narrows the channel, causing a whirlpool in which it is said canoes are lost during the high waters. On one occasion fourteen Miamis perished there. This has caused the spot to be dreaded by the savages, who are in the habit of offering sacrifices to that rock when they pass there." He ascended the rock and planted a cross at its peak. The missionary prayed: "God grant that the Cross, that has never yet been known in this place, may triumph here, and that our Lord may abundantly spread the merits of His Holy Passion, so that all these savages may know and serve him." Now, when the Indians made an offering at that place, the cross would tower above them. All who passed would see it. This simple act demonstrated that the land was no longer only theirs.[20]

For the Algonquian-speaking peoples of the region, such violent attacks targeted not simply carved stones but the manitous, the other-than-human persons who interacted, communicated, and shared with the human persons of the Mesquakie, Ottawa, Illinois, and other Native communities. Allouez attempted to erase the story that explained the significance of the site and that instructed people in how they should behave there and, perhaps, in other locations as well. The manitous offered essential access to power, the transformative essence in the universe that made life for human persons possible. And beyond these vital, everyday concerns, significant places in the landscape represented the accumulation of communal memory that linked the current generation to the events and ancestors of prior generations, stretching all the way back to the origins of the world.[21]

Ottawa tales remembered that Mackinac Island was the birthplace of Nanabozho, the Great Hare. There, in the midst of waters that flooded the earth in earlier times, Nanabozho created the land on which everyone now lived and depended, from only a little grain of sand brought to the surface by a courageous muskrat. A French official and chronicler explained, "Michilimakinak, according to the old men, is the place where Michapous sojourned longest. There is a mountain on the shore of the lake which has the shape of a hare; they believe that this was the place of his abode, and they call this mountain Michapous. It is there, as they say, that he showed men how to make fishing-nets, and where he placed the most fish." The location provided excellent access to abundant fisheries as well as contact with the spirits that had made such a precious resource possible. These spirits deserved and even demanded respect for their power and their gifts. "There is an island, two leagues from the shore, which is very lofty," the Frenchman continued; "they say that [Michapou] left there some spirits . . . [and] when the savages of those regions make a feast of fish, they invoke those spirits, who they say live under this island—thanking them for their liberality, and entreating them to take care always of their families; and asking them to keep their nets from harm and to preserve their canoes from surging waves."[22]

Another French writer recorded a similar flood tradition among the Illinois, one also commemorated in the shape of the land. In this account, there was a small knoll in northern Illinois, the "great canoe," where the vessel carrying men and animals went aground during the flood. The muskrat dove into the depths and returned with mud, proving that the waters would soon give way to land and reveal a place for each living being. These places and the stories that accompanied them often stressed such themes as the interconnectedness of life, the need for cooperation and reciprocity, and the proper arrangement of social relations. The Illinois called this kind of story *ars8ki8ni*. The French translated the term as "fable," but a better expression would be sacred story. People, places, stories, and gifts together created the social and spiritual connections and formed the moral geography that guided Native peoples through the landscape and through life and that the missionaries sought so zealously to overturn.[23]

Native responses to these aggressive acts of symbolism, both positive and negative, show that they indeed considered them a serious matter. According to Allouez's account, the Illinois bestowed great respect on the cross Allouez planted in their village, earning the missionary's deep admiration, but decades later, a fellow missionary recorded a very different reaction among another Illinois band, which joined the battle over these marks on the land and the meanings they presented. Gabriel Marest related that healers from the Tamaroa band of Illinois celebrated the death of a missionary by dancing before the cross in their village, while invoking their Native spirits and claiming personal credit for the missionary's demise. They ended their triumphant celebration by breaking the cross "into a thousand pieces." The manitous had, at least for a time, vanquished the Christian god.[24]

These crosses became fixed points, metaphorical guideposts in a landscape the missionaries thought was unstable. The missionaries prayed that the markers would promote a new Christian order there. It was not enough, however, simply to erect a wooden representation of the crucifixion. The missionaries also wished to anchor the Indians in space, to keep them near the crosses, chapels, and rituals that sustained a Christian life and culture. Movement, in the missionary view, was disorderly and savage, village life regular and civilized. Priests could carry their portable message across vast distances, but to implant it most successfully they believed they had to cultivate a more stable urban order. If they believed travel in the fur trade debased the moral values of young French *coureur de bois*, the runners of the woods, then Native nomadism threatened the success of the Jesuit mission itself.[25]

Algonquian-speaking nations regularly separated into smaller family and band-based groups and journeyed from their centralized, semipermanent villages to scattered hunting and fishing camps. When they traveled to these vital seasonal subsistence sites, they entered and spent months at a time in the unstable spaces the missionaries feared so much. The Jesuits measured the degree of civilization of different groups in part by assessing their migratory patterns. In this cultural calculation, they judged those peoples who engaged in frequent and extensive travel the least civilized. Allouez concluded with little or no direct experience of one group that "they above all others can be called Savages. They are very numerous, but wandering and scattered in the forests, without any fixed abode." He implied that they wandered aimlessly and that they recognized no true home, although he must have known this was not literally true.[26]

Another missionary, Gabriel Marest, worried about the disorder that continued to plague his mission among the Illinois. He believed they were too independent and full of vice and complained that "if you add to this the wandering life that they lead in the forests in pursuit of wild beasts, you will easily admit that reason must be greatly brutalized in these people; and that it is very little inclined to submit itself to the yoke of the Gospel." Marest made his comments in 1712, almost four decades after the establishment of the Illinois mission. Several major Illinois bands had by then developed strong attachments to Christianity, and they were often praised for their piety. All the Illinois, even those who continued to resist missionary efforts, lived in large, settled agricultural villages for much of the year.[27]

Illinois Christianity and agriculture were not enough to satisfy Marest, however, because the Illinois persisted in their regular hunting expeditions. Marest feared that following game through the forests and across the prairies made the Illinois too much like the wild beasts they pursued. Movement in his view retarded mental development and hindered acceptance of the Gospel. It represented liberty, a lack of restraint deemed incompatible with a life of Christian discipline. The wandering life, "*la vie errante*," as Marest termed it, evoked images of vagabonds, lost souls, and even *le Juif errant*, all people who remained outside or at the margins of ordered Christian society. They were for Merest and his fellow Jesuits truly *les sauvages*, the wild men of the forests.

Moreover, the hunting camps were centers of Indian power and identity. The missionaries worried that Indians left Christian teachings behind in the villages. They fretted because they could not see what the Indians were doing. Marest mused, "Then it is that we wish we could multiply ourselves, so as not to lose sight of them." He asserted that "a Missionary does no great good to the Savages unless he live with them, and continually watch their conduct; without this they very soon forget the instructions that he has given them, and, little by little, they return to their former licentiousness." The missionaries recognized that travel presented regular opportunities to renew connections to important cultural sites, to tell old stories and create new ones, and to refresh vital relationships and satisfy reciprocal obligations with the manitous. The complaining Jesuits assumed that Native Christianity degenerated away from stable mission compounds. However, the Indians could also more easily shape religious practice, including Christianity, to their own needs and desires with the increased independence. Dispersed in hunting camps, the Indians diluted missionary power and augmented their own. They escaped the missionary gaze for a time.[28]

It seems somewhat ironic, then, that the application of this mission ideology to introduce Christian order required that Jesuit priests become peripatetic travelers themselves and confront the perceived disorder of Native villages and the apparent horrors of untamed wilderness. While the dramatic contrast between mission ideals and practical needs produced considerable tension, it also provided significant opportunities for spiritual growth through personal sacrifice. The wandering Jesuits of New France participated in the fundamental Jesuit tradition of spiritually inspired active service in the name of Christ. The Jesuits rejected the stability and solitude of the monastery to pursue the spiritual goals of apostolic service, abnegation of self, and expansion of the kingdom of Christ. These ideals, so clearly expressed in the *Spiritual Exercises*, challenged the missionary to wander in search of God and to seek martyrdom in his service.[29]

Jesuit superior Claude Dablon emphasized these values in his account of Jacques Marquette's death in the Illinois mission in 1675. Marquette died on the shore of Lake Michigan, on his return from the Illinois country, trying to reach the Jesuit mission of Saint Ignace at Michilimackinac. Dablon reported that Marquette prepared for his death by reading and practicing the *Spiritual Exercises* with great devotion and piety, and he described the intensity of Marquette's desire to live up to the ideals of that core spiritual text. "[Marquette] always entreated God that he might end his life in these laborious missions," Dablon wrote, "and that, like his dear st. xavier, he might die in the midst of the woods, bereft of everything. . . . [H]e had, like the apostle of the Indies, the happiness to die in a wretched cabin on the shore of lake [Michigan], forsaken by all the world."[30]

Marquette was not forsaken in death, however. The missionary gave his name to the river where he died. The French missionary, historian, and travel writer François-Xavier de Charlevoix noted in his travel account of the 1720s that both Natives and French associated the river with the Jesuit father. Marquette added a new story to the shifting moral geography of the region. He actually became part of the physical landscape, a point of Christian power in the Great Lakes. Marquette's tomb at Saint Ignace soon emerged as a spiritually potent site in the Great Lakes. Christian Indians repaired to the tomb for prayer, and Marquette, "as the guardian angel of [the] outaouas missions," began to receive credit for alleviating the suffering of the sick. In this sacred space, the relics became a focus for prayers and intercessory power and a symbol of the new colonial geography constructed out of the intersection of peoples and cultures.[31]

*   *   *

The Indians of the *pays d'en haut* variously welcomed, resisted, and repulsed the missionaries and their message, but religion in general and Christianity in particular emerged as a vital point, an anchor, around which individuals and groups positioned themselves in relation to each other. Religion became an instrument of power and persuasion that worked simultaneously at several overlapping levels, from the intensely personal and local to regional and even trans-Atlantic scales. Among the Illinois bands, the Kaskaskias were the most receptive. The Kaskaskias, with the assistance of the Jesuits and the leadership of an influential family, created a Christian Indian community. When the village moved, they brought the missionaries with them. In 1700, the Kaskaskias separated from the Peorias, with whom they had shared a village site, and relocated to the west bank of the Mississippi. They relocated again three years later, moving to the lower portion of what became known as the Kaskaskia River, east of the Mississippi. This village of Kaskaskia developed into the cosmopolitan hub and Christian center of the Illinois country, attracting traders and missionaries, French settlers and other Indians.[32]

The Peorias, on the other hand, chose a decidedly different path. Unlike their fellow Illinois confederates the Kaskaskias, they generally resisted the Jesuit influence for several decades. Father Jacques Gravier translated a speech of a Peoria leader to illustrate the intense resistance he met among the Peorias. According to the missionary, several leaders pleaded with a Peoria convert to abandon Catholicism. One of them pressed, "Let the *Kaskaskia* pray to God if they wish and let them obey [the missionary] who has instructed them. Are we *Kaskaskia*? And why shouldst thou obey him, thou who art a *Peouareoua*? . . . His Fables are good only in his own country; we have ours, which do not make us die as his do."[33] In this argument, there is a clear sense of home and of difference. The speaker perceived a French world and a Peoria world. Identity and cultural tradition were rooted in place and belonged to specific bands. French spiritual figures had no connection to Peoria places, and the invading priests tried to destroy Peoria manitous and erase their presence from the land. The Peoria man also referred to the difference between the French and Indian fables, the *ars8kana* that carried so much meaning from generation to generation. Moreover, Jesuit baptismal ceremonies, often carried out on the gravely ill, appeared to be deadly.

On another occasion, a Peoria leader urged his people to wait at least until after the corn ripened and the harvest was in before they prayed to God in the chapel. The public welfare was simply too important for experiments in religious identity and spiritual power. If the Peorias listened to his entreaties, he perhaps hoped that they would avoid the missionaries altogether, for not long after the harvest, most Peorias would depart the summer village for the long winter hunt.[34]

After the turn of the century, the missionaries remained a divisive influence in the Peoria village, a problem that climaxed with physical violence. After the Kaskaskias resettled in 1703, Father Gravier returned to the Peorias in yet another effort to bring them to Christ. According to Jean Mermet, the missionary who stayed to run the mission at Kaskaskia, a Peoria man who felt slighted by Gravier wounded the priest several times with arrows. Gravier had refused to bury one of the man's relatives in the sacred ground of the church. Mermet justified Gravier's refusal because this was "a favor which the father had granted to no one." Mermet believed also that one of the Peoria leaders encouraged the attack in an effort to gain prestige within the defiant portion of the community.[35]

Many Peorias apparently would not tolerate a man who entered the village demanding changes in custom and identity. Gravier aggravated an already tense situation when he declined to incorporate a Peoria body into the body of the church. One wonders whether the request could have been the beginning of a dialogue rather than a catalyst for violence. Not all Peorias were so opposed to the contending faith. For instance, some Christian women in the village helped nurse the wounded Gravier. Kaskaskias sent by their leader, Chief Rouensa, eventually rescued the embattled and ailing missionary from the village, but he never fully recovered from his wounds. An arrow point remained buried deep in his arm, and he died two years later from complications. The antagonistic faction of Peorias cleansed their territory of the troublesome priests for five years, when they finally invited the Jesuits back. Gabriel Marest, the Jesuit who helped arrange the reestablishment of the Peoria mission, believed an imperfect trade embargo had finally convinced them to reconsider. In the meantime, without a missionary, Christian Peorias had to make the long trek to Kaskaskia to receive instruction and absolution.[36]

Kaskaskia came closest for the Jesuits to a place of genuine bucolic order, an Indian village of abundant harvests, fattening livestock, and, of course, missionaries. In the end, the mission and village of Kaskaskia became a potent symbol of the evolution of the colonial landscape. The area around the mission became a popular settlement for Frenchmen looking for land and economic opportunities, and by 1720 the mission became a parish. This designation indicated a consequential change in status and identity for the community. It had become more French. The settlement first established as a Christian Indian village and mission witnessed increasing French order and development on the general pattern the Jesuits and French officials had outlined, but this transformation forced the Indians to move away to form a separate village. French development may have diminished the savageness of the land from the French perspective, but it posed new challenges for the Illinois.[37]

The first French commandant of Illinois, Pierre Duqué, Sieur de Boisbriant, supervised the division of Kaskaskia and the surrounding area between the Illinois and the French. The officer arrived in 1718 as part of the administrative reorganization of the colony of Louisiana, which had annexed the Illinois country from Canada the previous year. Boisbriant wanted to stimulate the region's development and make it the breadbasket for the settlements and slave-powered commercial plantations planned for lower Louisiana. The Illinois at Kaskaskia, settled on rich bottomland, had to move. Furthermore, Boisbriant believed the separation of French and Illinois settlements would reduce actual and potential intercultural conflicts.[38]

The Jesuits, too, were interested in maintaining distance between the Illinois and French communities. The missionaries wanted to annihilate the boundary between souls—that void which excluded non-Christians from the rewards of heaven—but not necessarily the barriers between people. In their work to prepare individuals to accept God's gift of grace, they believed they talked soul to soul, but they found the outward natures of Indians and French too often incompatible for profitable intercourse. Although missionaries still wished to transform Indian society and culture, they had long ago abandoned as impractical the plan to truly assimilate Indians into French society. But neither they nor the French commandant could stop the association of Indians and French. The people of both villages formed social, marital, sexual, and economic relationships. Some boundaries could be crossed even if they could not be erased. The priests complained about this uncontrollable intercourse and a lack of zeal among their parishioners. They blamed brandy,

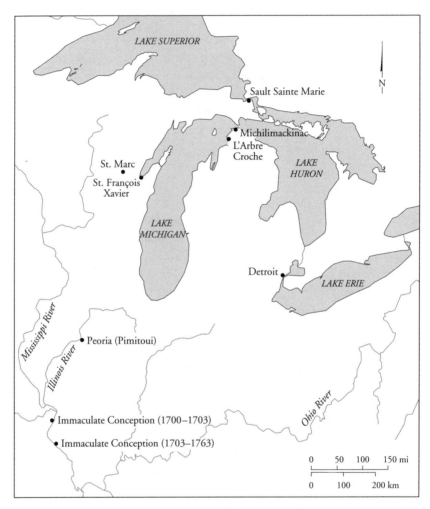

Figure 4. Map of the *pays d'en haut* and Illinois country, 1700 to 1763

the bad example of the French, and the mingling of cultures for their dilemma.[39]

Despite these perceived problems, the missionaries were hardly excited about the Kaskaskias moving away from what was probably the most successful Jesuit mission in the *pays d'en haut*. The relocation certainly disrupted their spiritual work, but it created other significant problems as well. In the two decades since the move to Kaskaskia, the Jesuits had acquired substantial property in land and slaves. Following their flock to a new site was no simple matter, for it required the construction and development of a new Jesuit compound. While the Jesuit property in Kaskaskia supported the missionaries and their labors, it also entangled them more deeply in French colonial politics, tied them more closely to the emerging formal parish structure, and forced them to become intensely involved in the colonial economy. Property diverted their attention from their primary spiritual purpose. When the Jesuits complained about the displacement of the Illinois, they defended not only Indian interests but also their own.

The issues surrounding French settlement were most difficult for the Illinois, however. They wanted and needed the alliance with the French for trade and defense. Furthermore, in the decades since the missionaries arrived, Christianity had become a significant part of many lives. The immigration of French into the country, although it never rose to a flood, nevertheless changed the dynamics of the region economically and socially. The Indians were not always united in values and opinion, but they clearly wanted to maintain a measure of independence. Although displacement disturbed the Illinois, they accepted Boisbriant's plan because they feared the influx of French settlers. The Kaskaskias moved three or four miles up the river that shared their name. The Michigameas, another Illinois band living in the area, moved a mile or two beyond that. The original village of Kaskaskia was left to the French. In return, Boisbriant promised the Illinois that the French would not bother them in their new villages, and the Jesuits made plans to establish new mission facilities.[40]

In typically equivocal fashion, the resettlement both weakened and strengthened the ideals that had guided the Illinois-French partnership. On the one hand, French economic plans and the influx of French *habitants* contradicted the sovereignty the Illinois supposedly enjoyed in the division of land between Indian country and *le domain du roi*. On the other hand, the division represented the application of more rigid concepts of property and possession, drawing starker lines between people. The distance between French imperial claims of general sovereignty and the daily practice of shared sovereignty on the local level created necessary space for negotiation and partnerships, but the ambiguity also generated confusion and strained relationships. This dilemma signified the elaboration of the difficult relationships that seemed to dictate both strong cross-cultural ties and strict divisions. The agreement to divide Kaskaskia hardly dispersed all the tension that flowed in these encounters because circumstances remained ever fluid and dynamic. Continued French settlement and development soon threatened Illinois visions of order again, and representatives of the Illinois traveled long distances to express their views and defend their positions. Colonial boundaries could be crossed in more than one direction.[41]

In 1725, a deputation of Indian leaders from the region, including Chicagou of the Michigamea Illinois, traveled to France to appear before businessmen, royal officials, and the king. Etienne de Véniard de Bourgmont, a politically ambitious *coureur de bois* and official French representative to the Missouri valley Indian nations, organized the trip to impress the Indians with French greatness, to strengthen alliances, and to advance his own career. The Missouris, the Osages, and the Otos each sent one ambassador, while Chicagou represented Illinois interests. The Jesuit missionary and superior of the Illinois missions, Nicolas Ignace de Beaubois, accompanied the delegation, as did a French interpreter and the daughter of a Missouri leader. In the long European tradition of Indian deputations as crafted performances and court spectacles, the party toured Paris and the glittering court at Fontainebleau, but they also had serious business to conduct. The representatives addressed officials of the Company of the Indies, the colonial corporation that controlled the colony of Louisiana, and several members of the ranking nobility. The young Louis XV also granted them an audience. The Indians of the Illinois country held positions of power and influence. France relied on them in conflicts with other Indian nations and in the colonial competition with the expansive British Empire. Before the king and other officials, the Indian leaders used this power to persuade.[42]

Chicagou planted no crosses, although he stressed that he was a man of prayer. He journeyed to France to restore order to his own land, to protect and recapture it. He spoke to officers of the Company of the Indies, which then had jurisdiction over the Illinois country. Chicagou, as a Christian and longtime ally of the French, made the first presentation. He opened by emphasizing his adherence to Christianity and the long alliance of Illinois and French. He asked that the French in turn always love and respect his nation, which had been such a dependable partner. Chicagou proceeded to express his demands and complaints: "We have ceded to [the French] the land we formerly occupied at Kaskaskia. We are pleased, but it is not good that they come mingle with us and put themselves in the middle of our village and our surrounding lands. I believe you who are the great chiefs, you must leave us masters of the land where we have placed our fire."[43]

The king then received Chicagou and the others at Fontainebleau. Chicagou made a formal diplomatic speech urging the French to maintain a strong and healthy alliance with his people, an association that benefited both parties. The delegation presented a letter from Mamantouensa and other notable men of the Illinois country who were unable to make the voyage. Mamantouensa wanted confirmation that the French would not disturb the Illinois in their villages and that his people would not have to move again to make way for the French. He demanded that the French leave him master of his village and request no more changes.[44]

Like the French, the Illinois wanted a certain separation and more visible boundaries. They desired more regular conduct and greater stability in their country. Stability for the Illinois did not mean the end of movement, however, as it did for the Catholic missionaries. Many Illinois continued to follow the buffalo on summer hunts and to pass the long winters in scattered hunting camps, but predictable relationships and protective distance preserved Illinois independence and supported the cultivation and maintenance of distinct identities. It was not a defense of an entirely unchanged identity or a dream of some impossible return to a time before colonial complications. Although the experiences of the past half century—trade, religious change, alliance, intermarriage—had created lasting connections that softened cultural boundaries and altered forever communal and individual identities, even the Kaskaskias, the people most attached to Christian prayer, did not expect to merge with or become subordinate to the French. They moved away from the village they originally settled and built, leaving it to ambitious *habitants* and enthusiastic entrepreneurs attracted by rich soil and commercial opportunities. The Kaskaskias and other Illinois were willing to share the country in exchange for relationships with the French, but they still believed the land that sustained them was theirs. Chicagou and Mamantouensa expressed the fear that the French would displace them as masters of the land, weakening Illinois autonomy and identities.[45]

While deputations, letters, and pleading could not halt change, the Illinois could and did influence the transformation of the country. Beaubois helped them make their case in France, and they returned with assurances from the Company of the Indies that the French would no longer establish themselves *pêle-mêle* among the Indians and that those already with them would leave. Beaubois, looking out for Jesuit interests as well, also obtained rights to land in the new villages to support the missions. The Kaskaskias and Michigameas remained in their separate villages for the duration of the French era.[46]

These contests and conflicts in the history of the *pays d'en haut* show that Indians and French together shaped the colonial geography that emerged in the region. The cultural and social diversity of the upper country challenged inhabitants to confront and manage difference with others. While the French adapted in numerous ways to the needs and desires of the Illinois and other Native peoples, they also demanded conversion and change. Reversing the usual flow of colonial representatives and authority, Chicagou traveled to France in an attempt to regulate these changes, to reemphasize boundaries and limits, and to contain difference. In France, he proclaimed his own ideas for an ordered land, one that would be shared by the Native Illinois and immigrant French as partners and one reshaped by the presence of French and Indian Christianity. The experiences of St. Lusson, Allouez, and Chicagou reveal the presence and the power of sometimes parallel and frequently competing visions for the creation of stability. They all struggled to make the land reflect their diverse notions of the sacred, strengthen or transform personal and communal identities, and support their goals for the present and future arrangement of the *pays d'en haut*.

The acceptance and tolerance of ambiguity were a necessary part of the process of negotiation and adjustment that animated these encounters. The Indians sought both engagement with and distance from the Jesuits and other French, forging relationships while striving to retain their sovereignty and their distinct identities. Through decades of encounter, they tried to balance the forces of cultural and social change with their desire for continuity and control. The missionaries envisioned the total spiritual transformation of the *pays d'en haut* but learned to tolerate intermarriage and the survival of certain indigenous customs. In the Jesuit approach to missionization, the souls of the Indians the missionaries hoped to guide to heaven were ultimately more important than the relationships, boundaries, and patterns of living that existed in the world. The great tension in these encounters arose in part from the need and desire to draw lines and create structure in a dynamic social and cultural environment. The inhabitants of the upper country searched constantly for the space to express cultural ideals and to determine the direction of change and the extent of self-determination. For the Illinois and other Native people of the *pays d'en haut*, relationships between human and other-than-human persons created a geography of deep spiritual and moral significance maintained through the regular conduct of ritual, the exchange of gifts for life-sustaining power, and the sharing of stories. Christianity added additional layers of geographic meaning to an already evolving landscape, threatening the survival of some geographies but also providing new spiritual and political resources for the establishment of social and moral order in space.

Chapter 4

Perceptions

Human (and Other-than-Human) Natures

In April 1670, the Mesquakies welcomed the Jesuit missionary Claude Allouez to their village, Ouestatimong, on the Wolf River near modern-day Lake Winnebago. "This people came in crowds to meet us," Allouez recorded, "in order to see, as they said, the Manitou, who was coming to their country." Allouez arrived at the village to begin a new mission to the Mesquakies, the "people of the red earth," a populous and powerful Algonquian-speaking nation in the contested terrain of multicultural villages west of Lake Michigan. Allouez called the people "Outagamis," an Anishinaabe word meaning "people of the opposite shore" and a name neighboring nations frequently applied to the Mesquakies. The French eventually favored a name of their own, calling them the "Renards," or Foxes. At the time of Allouez's visit, the Mesquakies were recovering from a deadly attack on their village, a raid blamed on the Iroquois, or Haudenosaunees. As much as Jesuit missionaries hoped to increase the territory of the Kingdom of Christ in both real and metaphorical terms, their daily work depended on direct engagement with people in the kind of meetings Allouez described. Despite their long experience in the field by the latter third of the seventeenth century, the itinerant preachers still had much to learn about each new group they encountered. And, in turn, Native peoples such as the Mesquakies expended considerable effort to interpret accurately the nature and significance of these black-robed men.[1]

Allouez first called an assembly of elders to explain his purpose. "When I had, by means of a present which I thought I ought to make them, dried the tears which the remembrance of the massacre perpetrated by the Iroquois caused them to shed, I explained to them the principal Articles of our Faith, and made known the Law and the Commandments of God." The missionary described the heavenly rewards that awaited those who obeyed these new laws and explained the punishments that God would visit on those who ignored the commandments. Allouez had studied Algonquian languages for several years and claimed that the Mesquakies understood his speech without the aid of an interpreter. "But alas," he wrote, "what difficulty they have in apprehending a Law that is so opposed to all their customs!"

The following day, a group of elders came to Allouez's cabin to make their own speech. They laid a gift of skins at his feet and thanked him for the kindness of his visit. According to Allouez, one leader said to him, "Black Gown, who art not dispirited and who takest pity on people, take pity on us as thou shalt deem best. Thou couldst dwell here near us, to protect us from our enemies, and teach us to speak to the great Manitou." Allouez enjoyed this speech, concluding that it had "nothing of the barbarian in it." He left the village pleased with what he had accomplished and looked forward to his return. "There is a glorious and rich harvest for a zealous and patient Missionary," Allouez wrote. "We named this Mission after saint Mark, because on his day the Faith was proclaimed there."[2]

Allouez returned less than a year later, in February 1671, but his reception was not nearly as warm or polite as before. The Mesquakies were angry because they had not been well treated at the French posts during the previous summer, but they may also have resented Allouez's more aggressive approach to evangelization this time around. The missionary "had no sooner entered [the village] than he went from Cabin to Cabin, cheering some with the hope of Paradise, and frightening others with the fear of Hell." Some offended or perhaps amused Mesquakies responded with "jests, repulses and mockery." One Jesuit commentator noted that "several other Nations swell the size of this one [and] make a Babylon of it by the disorder that reigns there."

Allouez believed that his patience, his persistence, and his words soon began to have a great impact on the Mesquakies, "insensibly softening" them, as he put it. "I was preparing myself for death," he remembered, "meeting at first nothing but insolence and repulses from these Barbarians; and lo! they are listening to me with an attention and affection beyond what I could have expected even from the best-disposed peoples." He was especially gratified by a man's response to the crucifix the missionary displayed during public instruction in a cabin. Allouez wrote that the old man "took two or three handfuls [of powdered tobacco], one by one, and, as if offering the censer an equal number of times, scattered it over the Crucifix and over me." He noted with obvious pleasure that the ritual act was "the highest mark of honor that they can show toward those whom they regard as Spirits."[3]

Allouez's descriptions of these two early meetings of the Mesquakies and the French illuminate the ambiguous, fluid, and confusing nature of these encounters. They also reveal some of the methods participants employed to reduce the social and cultural distance between peoples and to begin to fashion some mutually comprehensible meaning as a foundation for further interaction. Indians and Jesuits each perceived the other in simultaneously positive and negative terms. The Mesquakies viewed Allouez as a powerful person and potentially beneficial ally. In their initially cold response to the missionary's second visit, however, the Mesquakies also demonstrated that they would punish Allouez and the other French if they failed to meet Mesquakie standards for ethical behavior. Allouez's perceptions of the Mesquakies balanced his great optimism for the future success of the mission against his concerns about the nature and strength of Native customs, his belief in the universal potential for Christian salvation against his contempt for what he could only label savagery.

In their reactions to each other, as in their perceptions, Allouez and the Mesquakies showed ambivalence. They remained both hopeful and cautious. Together, they started to build on these feelings of hope and worked to counter the consequences of fear by constructing bridges of meaning through diverse modes of communication and rituals of humanization. The effort to establish reliable intercultural communication relied on words, signs, and acts. Allouez adapted to the situation by using the words of an Algonquian language to explain his purpose, create a vision of paradise, and paint a portrait of hell. The Mesquakies used their words to request pity in the aftermath of deadly violence, to complain about relations with the French, and to remind Allouez that he remained an outsider, a visitor from a foreign nation. The crucifix Allouez displayed was for the missionary a spiritually powerful sign of sacrifice and redemption. Although the Mesquakies probably did not read this message in the cross, when the man showered the crucifix with tobacco, he, too, treated it as a powerful object and potent symbol. The gift that Allouez presented to dry Mesquakie tears and the skins the Mesquakies gave to their important guest communicated expectations for mutual respect and reciprocal relations.

Gift exchange and other rituals became a critical part of the larger process of managing perceptions of difference and mediating otherness. Both the missionaries and Native peoples sought to transform and humanize the other. Jesuit dreams focused on the conversion of others. No one, they thought, could reach his or her greatest potential as a human being without Christianity. In their varied responses to the missionaries, the Algonquian-speaking peoples of the Great Lakes and Mississippi valley showed their uncertainty about the status and intentions of these foreigners. When they accepted the missionaries at some level and incorporated them into their communities, as French representatives, as spiritually powerful men, or as teachers of Christianity, they invited the priests to form lasting social bonds through ritual and exchange. When the Indians rejected them as dangerous intruders, it was often because the missionaries failed to conform, intentionally or not, to these standards of sociability.

*   *   *

At the end of April 1670, Allouez left the newly established mission of Saint Marc among the Mesquakies to visit other nearby Algonquian-speaking nations. He traveled south to a multicultural village of Mascoutens, Miamis, and Illinois, where he received another warm welcome. The Indians invited Allouez and his French companions into a cabin, served them refreshments, and rubbed their tired feet and legs with oil. They offered the missionary tobacco and referred to him as a manitou, requesting that he use his power to protect them from famine, disease, and dangerous enemies. Although Allouez stressed his own limited power in his response, he also wanted to be associated with the authority and omnipotence of God. He told the Indians "that wise men nevertheless willingly honored and listened to the black Gown, as being a person who is heard by the great God and is his Interpreter, his Officer, and his Domestic." Allouez was dismayed, however, that "they offered us a veritable sacrifice like that which they make to their false Gods." Later in the evening, Allouez presented several gifts of glass beads and metal knives and axes. He described the basic principles of Christianity and outlined the expectations of God. Allouez acknowledged that "these good people only half understood me," but if the Indians did not comprehend his instructions in literal terms, he felt strongly that the more general spiritual sense of the teachings was already having an impact.[4]

Allouez returned to the village in the autumn to continue his mission, accompanied by the soon-to-be superior of the Jesuit missions in Canada, Claude Dablon. The inhabitants were keenly interested in the potential power they perceived in the French visitors. Dablon reported "that they invited us to many feasts, not so much for the sake of eating as of obtaining, through us, either recovery from their ailments, or good success in their hunting and in war." Allouez and Dablon wanted to credit God for any power that they were able to summon, but they also felt compelled to display such power and thereby meet Native expectations. The priests instructed and publicly baptized a boy of ten or twelve years who had been seriously ill and seemed in danger of dying. The young boy, given the name François in the ceremony, recovered from his illness, according to Dablon. Although the missionaries were more interested in François's spiritual health, the boy's physical recovery must have provided convincing evidence for Native observers that the missionary had access to considerable power.[5]

When the Mascoutens, Miamis, and Illinois received Allouez and, later, Dablon in their village, they had not yet had extensive direct experience with the French, especially compared to the Ottawas, Tionontatis, and Wendats who had come to the western Great Lakes in the previous two decades. This fact alone would have created an atmosphere of both excitement and uncertainty about the growing presence of French missionaries and traders, but conditions in the region were already unstable before the French even arrived. Indian-French encounters in the upper Great Lakes occurred in the context of widespread intertribal conflict, seemingly endless movement and migration, deadly epidemics, and the never-ending challenge of maintaining regular food supplies. The Mascoutens reminded Allouez of these intractable problems and daily challenges when they requested his pity and his assistance. The French strangers brought novel technologies, exotic objects, and unfamiliar spiritual practices to this precarious world, and the Mascoutens wondered whether these foreigners would also help bring new order to the region, or whether they would make an already difficult situation worse. The obvious power and yet ambiguous potential of the French caused the Mascoutens and others to approach them with intense interest as well as a prudent sense of circumspection.

Allouez believed that the Mascoutens and Mesquakies honored him as a powerful god or spirit when they called him "manitou" and offered him tobacco. This interpretation of Native responses was common among the French, as was the idea that manitous were sometimes the equivalent of demons. The French Jesuit scholar Joseph François Lafitau explained that "these spirits are all the subaltern beings; they enjoy, for the most part, an evil character, being more disposed to evil than good; the Indians do not fail to be their slaves and pay them more honour than [they pay] the Great Spirit whose nature is good." The manitou concept was considerably more complex than that, a point that many French observers eventually recognized.[6]

The influential French diplomat, trader, and interpreter Nicolas Perrot had a dramatic and very personal encounter with some Miamis that highlights this complexity. The episode may have unfolded in the same village that Allouez visited. French chronicler Claude Charles Le Roy, Bacqueville de la Potherie, described the incident, probably relying on Perrot's own notes. In late spring of 1671, Perrot traveled to a Miami settlement as part of his efforts to encourage Native peoples in the region to attend the planned French-Indian conference at Sault Sainte Marie in the summer. The Miamis ceremoniously greeted Perrot and his Potawatomi escort outside the town in full martial regalia. They conducted the visitors into the village and tried to make them comfortable. Days later they entertained the guests with an exciting but violent game of lacrosse. After the game, a woman approached Perrot to tell him about her sick son, who suffered from terrible stomach pains. La Potherie recounted that "she asked the Frenchman if, since he was a spirit, he had not the power to heal him." Perrot administered a dose of medicine that he carried, and the man seemed to improve immediately. Three prominent men later woke the Frenchman in the middle of the night and offered a gift of ten beaver skins for some of the powerful remedy. Although Perrot did not really want to share his limited supply of the drug, in order to avoid offending his hosts he accepted the beaver robes and gave them half of the medicine. "It is their custom," La Potherie wrote, "to make presents to those who have spirits (thus they call remedies), which they believed could not produce their effect if one refused their presents."[7]

This account gives a much better idea of the larger meaning of the term *manitou*, which could describe an extraordinary person or spirit as well as the medicine or power that the person or spirit could manipulate. Illinois-language material produced by the Jesuits gives some insight into these meanings and shows that the missionaries eventually developed a more nuanced understanding of the concept. The early eighteenth-century French-Illinois dictionary credited to Father Jean Le Boullenger contains a number of entries for the term. The manuscript translated *manit8* as "genie" and "spirit" and provided possessive constructions like *nimanit8ma* for "my manitou" and *amanit8mari* for "his manitou." The dictionary also included active phrases like *nimanit8cara*, "I make it manitou," and *nimanit8ke*, "I make a manitou of something." Another dictionary translated the first of these phrases, *nimanit8cara*, as "I consider it or respect it as a god."[8]

The idea that Indians welcomed the French as gods overstated the issue in many ways. The French interpreted the Native rituals, conducted to maintain agreeable relationships with manitous, as religious worship in the European sense. This view compelled a missionary to offer a response such as the Illinois phrase *nimaneta8is8*, "I am not a god." The tobacco rituals Allouez witnessed seemed to indicate that he was perceived as a god, but Native concepts of person and power were more inclusive and flexible than European definitions. Indian worldviews recognized both human and other-than-human beings as persons, as agents with the ability to interact with other persons and with the surrounding world. Other-than-human beings included spirits that were rarely seen, manitous that governed human relationships with animals, and some potent physical objects. Power differentiated one person from another, either within a particular category or between the human and other-than-human categories. Some persons had access to more power than others did. If Allouez had uttered such a sentence in one of the Algonquian languages, his listeners likely heard him claim that he was not spiritually powerful. Whether or not they believed his protests or appreciated his intricate explanations of the difference between their manitous and his own is another story.[9]

The Perrot-Miami episode also hints at another important aspect of the manitou concept. Improper or antisocial behavior could interrupt or even nullify the power of medicine. If Perrot had refused the beaver furs offered for a portion of his medicine, the remedy could have been rendered ineffective. Gifts and the rituals through which they were exchanged created reciprocal relationships between persons that provided mutual access to power or, in some cases, helped ensure that power would not be applied against those who continued to nurture the bonds in an appropriate manner. Life could not be successful without the assistance and blessings of both human and other-than-human beings, but power itself remained ethically neutral. Reciprocity, sharing, and mutual obligation formed the guiding moral principles for living in such a world and were central to productive social relations. For many Native people, it was unclear in early contacts with the French and other Europeans what kind of persons these newcomers represented, how much power they possessed, or how they intended to use it. Would they use it, as the elder requested in his speech to Allouez, to bring order and stability to the region, to treat illness during epidemics, and to improve the general welfare of the people? Only experience and the ongoing assessment of French behavior could answer this critical question. Indians therefore frequently greeted the foreigners, at least initially, with the respect that a manitou—an extraordinary or powerful person—deserved.[10]

A missionary like Allouez was a special case. The Jesuits arrived in Native villages as men who explicitly claimed access to spiritual power and who boasted, as Allouez did, that they directly represented the great spirit of creation and the ultimate source of all the power in the universe. Moreover, they assaulted or tried to reconstruct Native spiritual traditions and practices, and they fiercely attacked the ritual specialists and healers who were central to the conduct of Indian religious life. Jesuit attempts to force their way into Native spiritual life and to supersede the most prominent spiritual figures in Native communities created a dangerous situation for missionaries and Indians. The priests, indeed, seemed to be powerful persons, but it was not fully determined whether they would be healers and use their power for positive purposes or whether they would use it for evil, to harm others.[11]

The missionary Louis André illustrated this dilemma. André followed Allouez to the Green Bay region in 1672, where he worked with several nations in the vicinity of the mission of Saint François Xavier. Like many missionaries, André noted the importance of dreams in Native cultures. Dreams and visions were a major medium of communication with other-than-human persons and provided vital information about the world and about a person's status and spiritual health. André complained that the biggest obstacle to conversion among young men was that they refused to give up dreams when it came to warfare, even when he had already persuaded them that they did not need to rely on dreams for successful hunting. André explained that many people believed that he had prophesied correctly the defeat of a group of Sauks, an Algonquian-speaking nation. The missionary tried to convince his listeners that a stone idol carried by the Sauk leader was to blame for the disaster. Some young warriors asked the missionary to help them pray to God, so that they could avoid a similar defeat in their own raids. André refused, however, at least until he could be sure that they had given up their dreams and their prayers to the devils and demons, his labels for the manitous. André's seemingly ambivalent attitude must have been frustrating for the men. He demanded that they change their ways and yet at the same time refused to teach them what they wanted to know. The missionary's true intentions remained hidden for a little longer, as people waited to see whether he would help or hinder, share or hoard his knowledge.[12]

Serious illness often became an opportunity to make such judgments about missionaries. A moment of crisis brought many issues together—baptism and sickness, healing and death—and forced people to act. Natives and missionaries recognized the opportunity as well as the danger. At one of André's mission posts near Green Bay, a young man became sick. Some people suggested the assistance of a Native healer, but the patient refused and sent his brother to André. The young man persuaded the priest to baptize him. André reported that "he was restored to bodily health, shortly after he had obtained that of his soul. The cure of this young man, added to the death of a child, for the recovery of whose health the most celebrated jugglers had spared no pains, gave me an opportunity which I did not miss, for casting discredit upon the enemies of Prayer." While these incidents gave André the chance to distinguish between traditional healing practices and his own spiritual customs, they also provided useful evidence for Native observers about the missionary's intentions and the efficacy of the procedures that he advocated.[13]

These situations went the other way as well, as André himself discovered. A man in one of the villages André visited lost his two children to murder. André had previously baptized one of them. After the incident, the missionary entered the man's cabin and recited some prayers, unaware, he said, that the bones of the children rested nearby. The man became angry and asked André, "Hast thou Sense? . . . I think thou hast none . . . my child was baptized and was killed." The association of baptism with death was common in Native communities. The Jesuit proclivity for baptizing Indians close to death, in a final effort to save their souls, made the connection particularly strong in some quarters. André tried to assuage the bitter, grieving father by shifting the blame from the sacramental rite to the murderer. He also stressed that the rewards of heaven far outweighed anything that could be gained on earth. "I spoke to him," André wrote, "of the happiness of the child who had been baptized." The missionary's words seemed to calm the man, and André believed he was satisfied with the explanation, but the Indians judged the missionaries in part on outcomes, on the results they obtained with their rituals. According to André, the father's deep rage persisted, hidden only for a while, until he finally acted on his deep animosity for the missionary. He burned down André's cabin near the village, leaving the Jesuit temporarily homeless and sending a clear message that not everyone welcomed the missionary and his ceremonies.[14]

The Jesuit missionaries constantly complained about such ill treatment, although they welcomed it at the same time for spiritual reasons. One commentator explained, "It is difficult to imagine the excess of insolence to which their Barbarism carries them. . . . One must make himself, in some sort, a

Savage with these Savages, and lead a Savage's life with them." "And," he suggested, "as God made himself man in order to make men Gods, a Missionary does not fear to make himself a Savage, so to speak, with them, in order to make them Christians." While the missionaries never wavered in their belief that the Indians were fully human and were ultimately capable of achieving all the benefits of salvation, Christianity always remained the standard measurement for judging the status and the supposed progress of Native peoples. Thus, when one missionary tried to convince a group of Natives that he truly believed they were men, the best evidence that he could think to present was that "He recognized [in them] The image of a God who had Created them, who had died for them, and who destined them to The same happiness as the Europeans." Just as the members of a Native community could simultaneously respect and fear missionaries like André and Allouez, the Jesuits found reasons both to love and to loathe the people they sought to convert. French assessments of Indians were as conflicted, contradictory, and filled with tension as Native interpretations of missionaries.[15]

*   *   *

A well-developed intellectual and cultural inheritance colored French Jesuit interactions with the Algonquian-speaking peoples of the Great Lakes and Mississippi valley. These inherited ideas sharply contrasted European conceptions of savagery and civilization. *Les sauvages* was the general French term used throughout the colonial period to refer to Native peoples. Although the reference was generally nonpejorative in tone, probably best translated simply as "Indians," it hardly implied equality. The expression concentrated old French and European ideas of so-called primitive men into a single potent word.

The Latin root for *le sauvage* was *silvaticus*, which referred to a forest dweller or man of the woods. The term retained much of this meaning in sixteenth- and seventeenth-century French usage because of ancient popular traditions that described various wild peoples supposedly residing in dark European forests. The traditions suggested that the forest inhabitants lived without the essential political, social, and religious institutions that provided the foundations for civilization. These "natural men" were beyond the bounds of the human community, separated even from the universal means of grace that God had provided for all people to reach their ultimate spiritual ends. They remained intellectual children, undeveloped by the reason, language, and education that arose naturally in the civilized conditions of European towns and cities. The absence of recognizable European-style institutions in American Indian societies made the extension of these powerful ideas to the New World a fairly simple process for the French and other colonizing peoples. Christianity and European civilization remained the primary perspectives from which the French, including the French missionaries, perceived the Native peoples they encountered in the Americas.[16]

These perceptions of Indians produced dualistic images, which held positive and negative impressions in a constant state of tension. Europeans perceived and admired the physical strength, generosity, gentle disposition, and overall intelligence of Native peoples, but they also believed that Indians were inherently lazy, lascivious, gluttonous, and occasionally vicious. Many French observers recognized the inconsistency of these descriptions of Native character and placed the source of this divergence in the effects of savagery itself on Native peoples. François-Xavier de Charlevoix confronted this issue in his account of a journey through the Great Lakes and down the Mississippi River in the early 1720s. Charlevoix offered an assessment of the generic qualities of Indian character, finding that the absence of civilization was responsible for both Native virtues and vices. He commented, "We perceive in them a mixture of ferocity and gentleness, the passions and appetites of beasts of prey, as well as the virtues and qualities of heart and of spirit which do the greatest honor to humanity." "At first one would imagine them without any form of government, law or subordination," Charlevoix continued, "and that living in an absolute independence, they abandon themselves to the conduct of blind chance, and to the wildest caprice . . . [but they] very rarely deviate from certain maxims and usages founded in good sense alone, which holds the place of law, and supplies in some sort the want of legitimate authority."[17]

For Charlevoix, a passionate love of liberty inspired in Indians an absolute horror of the kind of corruption and despotism that frequently reigned in Europe, but this independence also accounted in large measure for their lack of cultural development. Like many other French commentators, Charlevoix concluded that Native peoples lived eternally in the present, outside history itself, according to only their most immediate sense impressions of the world. While Indians apparently remained uncorrupted by the trappings of civilization, they were also degenerate by nature. Such ideas culminated in the eighteenth century with the slow emergence of the noble/ignoble savage dichotomy. Europeans frequently used the positive dimension of this dualistic vision to comment on the negative aspects of European culture, especially its venality, greed, intolerance, and depravity. Conversely, they used the image of the ignoble savage to condemn Native peoples as culturally and morally deficient compared to ideal European standards and to justify attempts to transform or displace them.[18]

Although the Jesuits believed that the effects of wilderness and the corresponding lack of civilization debased Indians, the Jesuits also assumed that they could reclaim the Indians as men through the process of redemption. For the Jesuits, cultural and not racial differences explained the inferiority of Indians. Culture was learned behavior. It seemed possible to the missionaries that Native communities and individuals could acquire the essential habits of European civilization, given proper guidance and stimulation. Furthermore, and most importantly, Native peoples appeared fully capable of experiencing the spiritual benefits of divine grace.[19]

The sixteenth-century Spanish Jesuit missionary and historian José de Acosta influenced the development of these ideas about Native Americans and proposed methods for correcting perceived cultural deficiencies and leading them to salvation. Acosta was already thoroughly familiar with European intellectual debates about the nature of Indians when he arrived in Peru to begin work as a missionary in 1572. This knowledge and his first-hand observations led him to the conclusion that Indian cultures were human inventions shaped by communal experiences and the physical environment and that they represented an earlier stage of cultural development compared to European civilizations. Education, not human nature, was responsible for this great difference. After all, he noted, there were still pockets of barbarism in Europe, and it had originally taken the strength and influence of Rome and Christianity to promote civilization in Europe. Acosta made education the central component of the missionary program he advocated in Peru and in his writings, which helped shape the Jesuit attitude toward missionization through the eighteenth century. He strongly supported the study of Native languages, both to make instruction more effective and as a way of gaining insights into Native cultures. Acosta also recommended the use of *doctrinas*, or reductions, and boarding schools for Indian children. French Jesuits accepted the core tenets of Acosta's intellectual position and applied many of his methods in their mission work in North America.[20]

While this intellectual inheritance exerted a strong influence on the Jesuits laboring to obtain converts in New France, the missionaries also adapted to direct experience. They never entirely rejected old standards for understanding and judging Native peoples, which were always based firmly on the interpretation of others from the perspective of Christian European civilization. Instead, they constantly incorporated new material into existing paradigms, enlarging and reshaping these ideas to include the diverse peoples and cultures they encountered and to account for new knowledge and for changing circumstances. Soon after the Jesuits started their first Canadian missions in the early seventeenth century, the study of Native religions became an important component in Jesuit ethnographic inquiries. Jesuit analyses of Native religion in particular seem to show this ability to adjust to new information without, at the same time, ever letting go of the fundamental basis for cross-cultural perception.

In the fall of 1670, at the mixed village of Mascoutens, Miamis, and Illinois, Dablon and Allouez encountered an Illinois leader who gave them the opportunity to learn about the religion of the Illinois and to assess the prospects for mission work among them. Dablon recounted that the Illinois chief greeted his Jesuit visitors with the greatest respect and most attentive hospitality. Dablon described the man: "His countenance . . . is as gentle and winning as is possible to see; and, although he is regarded as a great warrior, he has a mildness of expression that delights all beholders. The inner nature does not belie the external appearance, for he is of a tender and affectionate disposition." As evidence of the manifestation of this interior disposition, Dablon cited the man's response to an explanation of the passion and death of Jesus Christ, given by the missionaries to numerous people, with a cross displayed before them. "He showed such tenderness and compassion," Dablon recorded, "which could be read in his eyes and on his whole countenance—that some Frenchmen who accompanied us were greatly charmed and astonished. . . . Therefore we have reason to believe that one who has such fine qualities and suffers himself to be so easily moved by our Mysteries, will not long delay embracing them."[21]

Dablon extended the virtue that he discovered in this leader to the rest of the Illinois, "in whom we have noted the same disposition, together with a docility which has no savor of the Barbarian." Dablon admired the apparently positive attitude of the Illinois toward Christianity and the missionaries, and his first impression of Illinois religious traditions seemed to make them an even more attractive target for evangelization. Dablon argued that "they enjoy a great advantage over other Savages, as far as the Faith is concerned, in that they have hardly any superstitions, and are not wont to offer Sacrifices to various spirits, as do the Outaouacs and others. . . . These people are free from all that, and worship only the Sun." Dablon believed that this feature of Illinois religion could be explained by their subsistence practices. The Illinois relied mostly on agriculture and hunting in an incredibly fertile land, he decided, exposing them less often to the perils faced by more northerly peoples who fished the Great Lakes and lived in a supposedly less productive environment. In any case, Dablon left the Illinois hopeful for their future as Christians, concluding that it would be "impossible to find [a people] better fitted for receiving Christian influences."[22]

In his analysis of the Illinois and their religion, Dablon concentrated on what he thought were the positive aspects of Illinois culture, specifically, the presence of fewer superstitions and an inchoate belief in a supreme being. The inner disposition of the chief and his people and their seeming attraction to Christianity also impressed the Jesuit observer. The fact that the Illinois maintained settled agricultural villages only added to their appeal for the missionaries. Already in these early French-Illinois encounters, Dablon was perceptive enough to recognize crucial cultural differences between the Illinois and surrounding nations, and the Jesuits prepared to exploit them. Whether the Illinois leader whom Dablon described ever embraced Christianity is unknown, but some Illinois bands eventually became the most Christianized Indians in the region and some of the most reliable allies of the French.

Indeed, the Illinois were different. The Illinois language, usually considered a dialect group of a more general Miami-Illinois language, was part of the Algonquian language family that dominated the region, but it differed substantially from the Algonquian tongues the missionaries had previously heard. The first Illinois contacts with the French occurred in the missions and trading posts on the southern shore of Lake Superior. At least as early as the late 1660s, Illinois groups began traveling to these settlements for trade, information, and socializing. In the first decades of their relationship with the French, the Illinois comprised up to a dozen culturally, socially, and politically related tribes and bands. Although the Illinois groups remained independent in many ways, these close ties gave them a more powerful presence in the region than they would have had as entirely separate peoples.

The physical environment the Illinois occupied supported a different subsistence culture. They lived in the river valleys of the Illinois country, primarily along the middle Mississippi and Illinois Rivers, close to both thick forests and the open prairies that stretched to the west. The Illinois took advantage of the ecological diversity that existed in this transition zone, growing large amounts of corn and other crops near their semipermanent summer villages and leaving twice yearly for extended hunting expeditions on the prairies and in the surrounding forests. The communal bison hunt that lasted about six weeks during the summer provided an important food source not easily available to the Native peoples farther north.[23]

Dablon and the other Jesuits became particularly interested in Illinois religion because the Illinois appeared to offer a promising field for sowing the gospel and spreading the seeds of Christianity throughout a vast new territory. Their religious practices paralleled those common in the cultures of other Algonquian speakers. Illinois individuals, for example, also sought the cooperation of manitous in their subsistence efforts, in warfare, and in healing. Ritual specialists, both men and women, practiced healing rites and supervised other important ceremonies. As Dablon suggested, however, the Illinois may have identified more strongly with a supreme being or Master of Life than some other nearby nations, and it was this possibility that most intrigued the Jesuits in the beginning.

Allouez first encountered the Illinois at the mission of Saint Esprit on Chequamegon Bay, and of all the people he met there, he concluded that the Illinois would be the easiest to convert. Allouez found that the Illinois honored one spirit above all others "because he is the maker of all things." The missionary equated this spirit with the Christian God and related that the Illinois kept very long fasts in the hope that they would see the great spirit and thus assure themselves of a long and happy life. Allouez believed that "all the nations of the South have this same wish to see God, which, without doubt, greatly facilitates their conversion; for it only remains to teach them how they must serve him in order to see him and be blessed." A few years later, Allouez's colleague Jacques Marquette drew similar conclusions. He reported that some Illinois had already begun to abandon their "worship" of the Sun and Thunder. "Those whom I have seen," he wrote, "seem to be of a tolerably good disposition . . . they are more moderate in their Sacrifices; and they promise me to embrace Christianity, and observe all that I shall say in the Country."[24]

What excited the Jesuits so much was that certain aspects of Illinois religion and their apparent attraction to Christianity provided important clues to the existence of natural religion among them. In this view, buried underneath layer after layer of false ideas and superstitious practices lay a dormant link to the ultimate truth of God and salvation that was the common heritage of all humankind. The goal of missionization became, then, a process of excavating this natural religion and restoring it to its original purity. It had taken the Jesuits some time to accept these ideas. Many early French observers of Native customs suggested that Indians had no religion at all because they did not find the kind of organized religious institutions they knew in Europe. A non-Jesuit who resided in the Illinois country for many years wrote, "This nation [the Illinois], as well as the Miami, has no religion." He and others easily dismissed the personal relationships with manitous, the ceremonies and healing rituals, and Native concepts of medicine and power as nothing more than superstition.[25]

The Jesuits started to question such interpretations over the course of the seventeenth century. Ongoing ethnographic observation of Indian cultures and personal experiences with Native peoples eventually convinced many Jesuits that Native religions were considerably more complex, organized, and robust than most European commentators had previously believed. Joseph François Lafitau explicitly criticized the former position in his *Moeurs des sauvages américains comparées aux moeurs des premiers temps (Customs of the American Indians Compared with the Customs of Primitive Times)*, published in 1724. Lafitau, a former missionary to the Iroquois, wrote, "I have seen, with extreme distress, in most of the travel narratives, that those who have written of the customs of primitive peoples have depicted them to us as people without any sentiment of religion, knowledge of a divinity or object to which they rendered any cult, as people without law, social control or any form of government; in a word, as people who have scarcely anything except the appearance of men. This is a mistake made even by missionaries and honest men." Lafitau contended that the initial negative impression many observers gained of Indians, which concentrated almost exclusively on what they lacked, was inaccurate. He argued that early visitors saw no temples or regular worship and concluded that Indians were concerned only with what they could understand through their senses, "that they make their god of their stomachs and limit all their happiness to the present life."[26]

A monogenist and diffusionist, Lafitau traced the original revelation to Adam and Eve, arguing that "the author of nature, when he created man in his own image and likeness, at that time imprinted the idea of his existence indelibly on the most ferocious hearts and basest minds." The Native peoples of North America were not irreligious in this view; they had instead suffered from the degenerative effects of original sin. Superstition and idolatry masked the presence of natural religion. As evidence, Lafitau pointed to "the unanimous consent of all peoples in recognizing a Supreme Being and honouring him in some way, a unanimity which shows that people feel his superiority and the need of turning to him." He noted further that "generally all the people of

America, whether nomadic or sedentary, have strong and forceful expressions which can only designate a God. They call him the Great Spirit, sometimes the Master and Author of Life. This is even the case with the Ottawa who, among all these peoples appear the most brutish and least spiritual. Even they, in their invocations and addresses, often call him the Creator of all things."[27]

Charlevoix later incorporated many of Lafitau's ideas and examples into his own synthetic works. He, too, noted the vestigial idea of the supreme being. Charlevoix also contended that Indians were even easier to convert than more civilized peoples, who tended to retain a stronger attachment to their false ideas. Natural virtue was not enough, however, to assure the Indians' proper development as human beings. They needed Christianity and God's gift of grace. "Religion alone is capable of perfecting the good qualities of these people, and of correcting what is wrong in them," Charlevoix argued. "This is common to them with others," he continued, "but what is peculiar to them is, that they bring fewer obstacles to this improvement, after they have once begun to believe, which must ever be the work of a special grace." Charlevoix also felt that Indians had to see Christianity in all its purity because they were especially sensitive to the displays of poor Christians. If the bad example of Europeans posed a significant problem, a still greater obstacle came with the strength of individual liberty in Native American societies. It was difficult to convince even Christians, Charlevoix complained, that subordinating oneself to religious law would help overcome the natural corruption caused by sin and lead toward the original liberty envisioned by God. The tension in these ideas is obvious. Charlevoix may have admired the natural virtue of Native peoples, but, unable to see them as anything other than savages, he could not help wondering how they would deal with the demands of the rigorously organized, institutional, and thus civilized, church.[28]

In practical terms, the perceived survival of innate human virtues meant that the missionaries needed only to clear away the superstitious practices that had accumulated over the centuries, build on the natural theism that already existed, and free Native souls for the more efficient operation of grace. The Jesuits already worked according to this plan well before the texts of Charlevoix and especially Lafitau expressed the ideas so clearly. Jesuit missionaries tended to be optimistic about their chances for success, but they never expected the substitution of Christianity for Native religion to be easy or simple. The persistence of traditional spiritual practices always dismayed them.

In the mid-1670s, Allouez described the process and its challenges at his mission to the Mesquakies, Saint Marc. Allouez complained that the Mesquakies, with few exceptions, continued to believe strongly in the efficacy of fasting, dreaming, and visions. He blamed the problem on the constant fear the Mesquakies faced of being captured and killed by their enemies or of going hungry during a famine. Allouez explained, "They have among them a sort of tradition which makes them Believe that, if they have some vision, or rather some dream, they will be fortunate in Hunting and war. . . . Thence it comes that they cling to dreams and visions of These kinds as they would to life." "In order to establish Christianity on a solid basis," the missionary wrote, "we have baptized only a few, who, as we knew, had given up all these superstitions."

Allouez described one young man at the mission who directly opposed his father by giving up these practices and being baptized. The father argued that his son would be a failure in life without the fasting, dreaming, and proper relations with the powerful manitous, but Allouez reported happily that the young man placed his faith in God and heaven. The convert's brother had more trouble changing his ways and continued to blacken his face to prepare for his fasts. Finally, he appeared before Allouez with his face painted white and asked for baptism. Allouez baptized him in recognition of his altered behavior and his perseverance. The missionary noted that the sisters of these brothers also became fervent Christians, and that together they all attended the chapel regularly for prayer services.

Allouez hesitated to baptize other adults in the community because he feared that the devil might have been at work in their dreams. "I do not know," he wrote, "whether the devil appears to them under the form of their pretended spirits, or whether their brains, weak from their having been so long without food, make them Imagine some spirit." For many of Allouez's Jesuit colleagues at the time, the extent of diabolical influence in Native religion remained an uncomfortably unresolved issue and an occasional worry. A change in attitude had occurred since earlier in the century, when Jesuit missionaries were more likely to blame Satan explicitly for supporting the work of Native ritual specialists and for interfering directly in the work of missionization. By Allouez's time, there was less a fear of the direct intervention of Satan than a belief in some more subtle influence. Either way, Allouez regarded Mesquakie religion as only superstition, believing that the Mesquakies' spiritual practices represented only ill-founded cultural traditions and that their manitous were only "pretended spirits." Jesuits still considered ceremonial leaders and healers to be their greatest foes, but the missionaries increasingly saw them as nothing more than "jugglers," or charlatans, who manipulated others for personal gain.[29]

Some tension certainly remained between this determination that healers were fraudulent performers who preyed on the fears and desires of their communities and the lingering concern that they were somehow linked to a spiritual world of demons and death. The Illinois language dictionary and grammar attributed to Jean Le Boullenger contained a series of religious texts in addition to the linguistic material. One of the texts made explicit comparisons between "juggling" and the passion of Jesus Christ, demonstrating the importance the missionaries attached to the ongoing battle to defeat their spiritual enemies. On the left of two facing pages was a long list of phrases that depicted healers and their ceremonial practices in imaginatively negative terms. On the right was a list that allowed a missionary to explain in detail the sequence of events that occurred in the passion. In the collection on *jonglerie* there were instructions for describing the way in which healers blew on their patients, an important part of many healing rituals, but there was also an entry for "he blows on a person to make him die." Just as disturbing from the missionary perspective were passages such as "a child dedicated to the manitou" or "a child for which he invokes the manitou."[30]

The missionaries also had access to a series of terms that portrayed the physical features of the Native healers. These included items that described "a terrible visage," "eyes full of fire," "hair like serpents," and hands and feet curled into ugly claws. The last entry in the list was *minsaki c8essang8sita a8i8nghigi*, or "a truly terrifying body." Le Boullenger presented a combination of texts that generated contrasting images between the disfigured body of the Native healer and the beautiful yet painful suffering of Christ. The difference between this concentrated example of savagery on the one hand and the apotheosis of man on the other could not have been greater for the missionaries. Later, in the dictionary proper, Le Boullenger declared, "All the jugglers are going to hell."[31]

In the end, the Jesuits developed a practical field scale or applied anthropology for measuring civilization and savagery that was based as much on actual experience and interaction as on abstract intellectual speculation about Native origins, historical development, and natural religion. Docility was on one end of the scale, and overt resistance marked the other extreme. Dissimulation ranged somewhere in between. Docility was passive, peaceful, soft, and virtuous. It revealed common sense. Resistance was active, violent, hard, immoral, and obstinate, characteristics associated most clearly with Native healers. Dissimulation often represented politeness on the part of Native people who wished to avoid confrontation, but to the Jesuits it also showed ignorance and the tenacity of superstition. The French missionaries accepted that all the Indians were savages and held both positive and negative views of their nature simultaneously, but they classified Indians according to how cooperative they tended to be and on how they met French expectations for behavior. The positive views emphasized their human qualities and the absence of the supposedly negative impact of civilization. The negative views stressed the effects of the lack of well-developed social, political, and religious institutions. For the missionaries, these seemingly contradictory views intersected in their ideas of missionization: the Indians were imperfect but capable of receiving the benefits of grace and achieving salvation. As Allouez put it when he embarked on his first journey of missionization into the Great Lakes, "I hope the Holy Ghost, after rendering [the Indians] thus docile, will give them the grace to receive with submissive minds the Gospel seeds which we were bearing to their country."[32]

In this regard, Dablon's encounter with the Illinois in the Mascouten and Miami village seemed promising. Dablon admired the disposition of the leader and the other Illinois, and he thought they might have retained a purer form of natural religion, concentrating much of their worship on the single spiritual figure of the sun. Indeed, the Jesuits discovered that Illinois interest in Christianity continued and, in some cases, even grew as the missionaries extended their reach into the Illinois country beginning in the mid-1670s. The Jesuits waited for two decades to see the first major wave of conversions, however, and they also learned to their dismay that not all Illinois communities and individuals would be as docile as the missionaries had originally hoped. The dissimulation that frustrated them so often and the resistance that they feared became a regular and troubling part of their frequently contentious relationship with the Illinois. And from Illinois perspectives, diverse from the beginning and never static, Christianity and the strange spiritual men who offered access to it seemed to represent both opportunity and danger. Only the exchange of ideas and opinions and the formation and evaluation of social relationships would determine which they truly were.

The narrative of the Marquette-Jolliet encounter with the Illinois is filled with descriptions of the process of communication and exchange that initiated a common quest for mutual understanding. In formal speeches, Marquette explained his purpose in coming into the Illinois country, and the Illinois responded with words of welcome and requests to continue the relationship started there. Marquette did not know the Illinois language well, but he was confident that the speeches conveyed their intended meanings. He noted that Illinois, "on the whole, resembles allegonquin, so that we easily understood each other." If words alone were insufficient, however, gifts could also speak and thus enrich the meaning of each statement. The calumet was a sign of peace and alliance, the food so tenderly placed in the mouths of the French visitors a sign of friendship, abundance, and life itself. The acts of exchange demonstrated respect, but perceptions also set limits to the complete acceptance of the other. As Marquette noted, "When one speaks the word 'Ilinois,' it is as if one said in their language, 'the men.'" Marquette was not a man in this sense. He did not speak properly and had not yet earned a recognizable social role. Marquette naturally believed that the Illinois required religious instruction, but he admitted "that they have an air of humanity which we have not observed in the other nations." At the same time, the missionary found the dog with which they honored him repulsive. It was food only for savages. The small gifts that people presented to the guests as they toured the village were valuable only to the Illinois. These ambiguous exchanges did not negate the constructive engagement that took place in the Illinois village. This meeting represented only one important phase of a much larger and longer attempt to understand, persuade, and transform the other, a long process of "crossing and dwelling."[33]

At the end of his brief stop in the village, Marquette promised to return to the Illinois to begin their initiation into Christianity. The calumet and the exchange of gifts energized the nascent French-Illinois relationship. Marquette did return to the Illinois country, but not to that particular village. Instead, he decided to open a mission at the major Illinois village, dominated by the Kaskaskias, on the upper Illinois River. The Jesuit traveler started out for his new post late in 1674 from Green Bay, but he stopped short of his destination because of a serious illness. Marquette wintered with two French servants in a small cabin not far from Kaskaskia. At one point, a party of three Illinois Indians arrived at the cabin with sacks of corn, dried meat, pumpkins, and beaver skins on behalf of the Illinois elders. The Illinois wanted to ensure that the missionary would not go hungry, and they hoped to obtain a few French goods in return. Marquette reciprocated with metal tools, glass beads, and mirrors. He refused to give them the gunpowder they desired because he feared that they would use it to attack the Miamis, but he also pledged to encourage French traders to bring more goods. The sick missionary told the Illinois that he would attempt to reach their village soon, but only for a few days if his illness continued. "They told me to take courage, and to remain and die in their country; and that they had been informed that I would remain there for a long time," Marquette recorded in his journal.[34]

Finally, in late March 1675, Marquette's health improved enough for him to reach the Illinois village and begin the apostolic work that he had dreamed about for so long. He worked for some time with "the Chiefs of the nation, with all the old men, that he might sow in their minds the first seeds of the gospel," and he gave instruction in cabins crowded with curious Illinois, but Marquette marked the official foundation of the mission with a dramatic theatrical presentation. The ceremony communicated in ways that corresponded to Native sensibilities but that also shared the visual impact of European pageantry.

The Jesuit superior Claude Dablon described the colorful ritual display that took place three days before Easter, on Holy Thursday. Marquette selected a beautiful prairie near the village for a great council in the open air. "[The prairie] was adorned, after the fashion of the country, by Covering it with mats and bearskins. Then the father, having directed them to stretch out upon Lines several pieces of chinese taffeta, attached to these four large Pictures of the blessed Virgin, which were visible on all Sides." Illinois leaders and elders sat in a circle around Marquette, with the young men standing behind them. The men numbered more than 1,500, according to the account. Hundreds of women and children swelled the crowd even more. "The father addressed the whole body of people, and conveyed to them 10 messages, by means of ten presents which he gave them." Marquette explained his purpose in coming to the Illinois country, described the "principle mysteries" of Christianity, and said the Catholic mass. "[On] easter sunday, things being prepared in the same manner as on Thursday, he celebrated the holy mysteries for the 2nd time; And by these two, the only sacrifices ever offered there to God, he took possession of that land in the name of Jesus Christ, and gave to that mission the name of the Immaculate Conception of the blessed virgin."[35]

Marquette's illness prevented him from remaining to continue the Illinois mission beyond its establishment, but he assured the Illinois that other missionaries would follow. The Illinois seemed pleased that the relationship with the French was growing stronger. They expected more French traders to bring valuable goods. The Jesuit mission would provide an opportunity to explore the power of Christianity in a time of bewildering change. For some Illinois, Christianity became a source of comfort and strength that offered a meaningful way of adapting to these changes. For others, Christianity and the intrusive missionaries represented nothing more than a threat to Illinois culture and identity. Marquette departed Kaskaskia, loaded with gifts and escorted for many miles by a number of Illinois.

Almost twenty years later, the Jesuit missionary Jacques Gravier invited all the baptized Illinois to a feast at the mission, which had by then followed the Kaskaskias and others down the Illinois River to the recently established Illinois village on Lake Pimitoui. Gravier's words and actions at the feast communicated a message that certainly resonated with some Illinois, who turned evermore toward Christianity, but that must also have been deeply disturbing in tone and in some of its implications. "On the 10th of June, [1693]," Gravier wrote, "I gave a feast to all the christians, according to custom. On such occasions, one has a right to say whatever one pleases to the guests, without their feeling hurt by it." The missionary reproached some people by name for their general indifference to religion and for neglecting to attend his instructions in the chapel. He explained the proper manner of confessing and reiterated the importance of Christian marriage. Gravier "told them of the blessedness of the faithful, and of the favor that God had done them by placing them among the number of his adopted children. I told them that he looked with horror upon their relatives and countrymen who were so many slaves of the Devil, and would burn with him forever in Hell, unless they became converted." Gravier stressed that the good or evil example set by the neophytes was central to the conversion or the continued resistance of the unconverted.[36]

Gravier committed both social and antisocial acts in this feast, sharing food and conversation yet sharply criticizing individuals and threatening the community with the most divisive possible language of Christian judgment and damnation. The missionary's frank words demonstrated the depth of his feelings for the Illinois. Gravier genuinely wanted to share with the Illinois what he believed were all the joys and benefits of Christianity, but his speech also revealed the limits of his acceptance of the Illinois. In the vision Gravier painted, Christianity ultimately superseded Illinois culture and traditions, and the missionary made the Illinois prime actors in making this vision a reality.

Over the next year, Gravier substantially strengthened Christianity among a significant segment of the population, with considerable assistance from a few enthusiastic Illinois converts, especially young women. The missionary also alienated many people with his aggressive tactics, particularly since his vigorous attacks occurred at the height of a terrible epidemic that struck the community in the fall. Gravier confronted Illinois healers and chastised parents reluctant to let the missionary baptize their dying children. Some Illinois blamed the missionary himself for the spread of the deadly disease. Gravier admitted that in response he baptized several of the sick children in secret, without the knowledge of their parents. These surreptitious baptisms clearly indicated to anyone who may have discovered them that, in the end, Gravier considered the Illinois and all other non-Christians incomplete as human beings without the spiritual "gifts" that he delivered from God.[37]

The participants in these complex encounters attempted to humanize the other through collaborative processes of communication and regular social intercourse, but the results of these efforts to overcome the perception of difference fell somewhere between mutual recognition of the other as a complete subject and simple objectification. For the missionaries, the Indians were "savages," outsiders to the world of Christian civilization. In their view, the greatest obstacles to extending Christianity and incorporating Indians into the Christian world were, on the one hand, the very lack of cultural development itself, and on the other, the deeply engrained cultural traditions that sustained Native societies. The French Jesuits saw a glimmer of hope for the Indians of North America in the apparent survival of the original revelation of God, made available equally to all humankind. This natural religion had been obscured over the centuries by the spiritual traditions and religious practices the missionaries dismissed as superstition, but it was nevertheless to be the basis for the revival of primitive piety and the foundation for the construction of a Christian church in the New World. In the process of trying to implement this plan, Jesuit impressions of Indians did not remain entirely unchanged. Lafitau criticized his predecessors who had failed to appreciate the complexity and richness of Native cultures. At the same time, the missionaries never escaped the tendency to alternate between praise and criticism of the peoples they encountered. The tension arose out of the contrast, in their minds, between civilization and savagery. This conflict could end only through the grace of God and over many generations.

For the Native peoples of the Great Lakes, the missionaries represented powerful beings, manitous in some cases, but they also remained outsiders to Native communities. The motives and intentions of foreigners were undetermined. Power could be used for both the common good and selfishly to do harm. Nevertheless, many Indians made the missionaries an important part of their communities, hoping to see positive benefits from their spiritual power and leadership and from the larger alliance with the French. The primary obstacles to incorporating the missionaries fully into these communities were the social and cultural traditions of the priests, especially their apparently incomplete social development. Despite the intimacy of some relationships between the missionaries and Natives, the priests always remained apart. They lived separately in their own cabins. They were celibate, refused to marry, and lacked critical family and clan connections. They often acted improperly, displaying aggressive and intrusive behavior. Given their uncertain status and spiritual goals, the missionaries were destined to be controversial figures. The difficult and rapidly changing political and economic environment in the Great Lakes region only increased the pressure on these relationships and raised the stakes on their outcome. Natives and newcomers continued to mystify and frustrate each other, but collective experiences contributed to an evolution of perceptions and eventually to the possibility, if not always the reality, of true conversations and reasonably reliable intercultural communication. If the humanization of others remained incomplete from almost anyone's perspective, the interactions of missionaries and Native peoples nevertheless resulted in the reconstruction of human communities and the appearance of new cultural patterns in the Great Lakes region.

Chapter 5

Translations

Linguistic Exchange and Cultural Mediation

The Illinois delegation to New Orleans in 1730, led by Chicagou and Mamantouensa, pleased their French hosts with the presentation of calumets
and other gifts, but they truly amazed the local residents with their performances in prayer. These displays of piety were the result of decades of linguistic exchange and cultural translation. The Jesuits worked diligently and
collaboratively and over many years to understand Native languages and
produce accurate translations of Christian prayers, but the cultural distance
that separated Native and missionary opened spaces for the emergence of
uniquely Illinois linguistic and cultural interpretations of Catholicism. The
Illinois spoke, sang, and chanted Illinois words in a new Christian order and
context, but these words could never be emptied entirely of their indigenous
meaning. In translation, sins became "bad things" that interfered with the
proper conduct of life. A soul touched by the grace of God, illuminated by
the power of the Holy Spirit, became in Illinois a "good heart" cleansed of
those "bad things," a heart steady, peaceful, and secure.[1]

The exceedingly difficult work of reconstructing Native languages and
communicating Christianity to the speakers of these foreign tongues rested
largely on various forms of mediation, on people, processes, and products that
created vital, though frequently unstable, connections between languages and
cultures. Acts of mediation occurred in the lengthy collaborations between
missionaries and Native language instructors, in innumerable acts of translation from one language to another, in the oral dissemination of Christian
teachings by French priests and Indian catechists, and in the reception and

reexpression of translated religious concepts within Native communities, Christian and non-Christian alike.

Meaning became fluid, hard to grasp, and difficult to contain in these open rhetorical spaces. In ideal terms, priests mediated between God and humankind through strict control of the sacraments and places of worship, but daily life in the missions required that they rely on the people among whom they proselytized. Native instructors helped missionaries learn the Illinois language, and Illinois catechists shared responsibility for passing the Christian message on to others. The Jesuits attempted to convert the Illinois language to their apostolic needs, laboring diligently to enhance, suppress, or transform certain Illinois ideas, but in the end they could neither control nor limit meaning itself. The dynamic language environment encouraged linguistic exchange and creativity.[2]

The missionaries produced, with essential assistance from Native people, hybrid religious texts, undeniably Christian in conception and form, yet infused with Illinois cultural concepts and sensibilities. Moreover, the transmission of these texts and their gradual absorption into Illinois Christian practice, on both an individual and a communal level, only reinforced their hybrid nature by encouraging exploration of Christian history and ideals on Illinois terms while simultaneously strengthening attachments to localized versions of Native Christianity. The manuscript religious texts that survive are precious intercultural sources that reveal the many problems of translation, the effects of mediative processes of cultural dialogue and intellectual engagement, and the creation of an Illinois Christian vernacular rich in spiritual meaning.[3]

*   *   *

The Illinois-French linguistic exchange began in the late 1660s, when Illinois representatives started traveling from their villages in the river valleys and prairies south of Lake Michigan to Chequamegon Bay on the southern shore of Lake Superior. There, the Illinois discovered French traders, large multicultural Native communities, and the Jesuit mission of Saint Esprit, founded by Father Claude Allouez in 1665. Although trade goods were a primary attraction for the Illinois travelers, many of them also discussed spiritual matters with Allouez. They seemed especially interested in his explanations of Christianity and in the image of Jesus that he gave them as a gift. Jesuit encounters with the Illinois at Saint Esprit and elsewhere in the upper Great

Lakes over the next few years only increased the desire of the Society of Jesus to open a mission in the Illinois country itself. The Jesuits made learning and adapting to new languages a priority when they expanded their mission network to incorporate additional Native nations.[4]

The Illinois first welcomed the Jesuits into their own villages when Marquette and Jolliet made their celebrated round-trip journey from the Great Lakes to the lower Mississippi valley in 1673. Marquette died in the field in May 1675, however, before the secure establishment of the Immaculate Conception mission. In 1677, Allouez followed Marquette's trail to Kaskaskia, now greatly enlarged by the addition of other Illinois bands, but he too did not stay long, for other Jesuit stations required his attention. The Jesuits made little obvious progress in the Illinois mission with these early faltering efforts or, indeed, for two full decades after Marquette's arrival, but the exchange of information and ideas between the Illinois and the French missionaries that took place during these years formed the foundation for the shared labor that came later with the emergence of an Illinois Christian community at the end of the seventeenth century.[5]

Jesuit linguistic studies of Illinois were both an extension of and a critical foundation for this mission work. The Illinois peoples spoke dialects of Miami-Illinois, one of the many Algonquian languages used by dozens of Native nations over a vast region of northeastern North America. Linguists place Miami-Illinois with its closest relatives, the Ojibwa-Potawatomi and Sauk-Fox-Kickapoo languages in the "Eastern Great Lakes" group of Algonquian. Jesuit missionaries started to untangle some of these connections early in their linguistic labors, well before the establishment of the Illinois mission.[6]

The Jesuits had been studying various Algonquian tongues since the first half of the seventeenth century. As they pushed into the Great Lakes region in the 1660s, they encountered new peoples speaking languages that were noticeably similar to those they had already learned. The missionaries relied on their knowledge of the structure of other Algonquian languages to ease their acquisition of Miami-Illinois. Allouez studied for several years in Jesuit establishments on the Saint Lawrence River before paddling into the Great Lakes. Marquette followed a similar pattern, basically a Jesuit rite of passage, studying Montagnais and other Indian languages upon his arrival in North America. He carried this experience into the field, where his first sustained exposure to the Illinois language came through his work with a young Illinois man given to him as a slave at Saint Esprit. While Marquette explained the requirements of Christianity to Indians at the mission, the young slave "furnished [him] the rudiments of the language." At the Illinois village he visited on the Mississippi in 1673, Marquette noted that the people spoke a language familiar enough that they could communicate with some effectiveness.[7]

Allouez, Marquette, and a number of other Jesuits contributed to a long-term Illinois language project for the ninety years or so the mission lasted. Claude Allouez may have produced the first manuscript in the Miami-Illinois language, a book that contains prayers such as the *Pater Noster*, or Our Father, a mass, and a basic catechism. An inscription at the end of the prayer book indicates that Allouez prepared the translations for Marquette to assist him in the Illinois mission. Jacques Gravier, who accepted the Kaskaskias and other Illinois into the church in the 1690s, conducted the first detailed linguistic analysis of Illinois. A dictionary traditionally attributed to Gravier contains thousands of Illinois words and expressions translated into French. Gravier appears not to have been the scribe for the massive project, an indication of the collective Jesuit effort to create linguistic materials for the missions. Gravier's colleague in the Illinois missions, Gabriel Marest, credited Gravier for the very strength of the missions, remarking in 1712 that it was Gravier "who first made clear the principles of their language, and who reduced them to the rules of Grammar; we have only perfected that which he successfully began." At the end of the seventeenth century, Pierre Deliette, a prominent French trader who spoke Illinois himself, commented that by then "the reverend Jesuit fathers . . . [could] speak their language perfectly."[8]

Marest himself also received recognition for his linguistic talents. A colleague reported that Marest had been able to learn Illinois in only four or five months of assiduous effort and that Marest then helped others with the language, including some who had been in the mission longer than he had. This fellow Jesuit also believed that "Dear Father Marest is somewhat too zealous; he works excessively during the day, and he sits up at night to improve himself in the language; he would like to learn the whole vocabulary in five or six months." "May God preserve so worthy a missionary to us," he added. This missionary and others recognized the importance of such linguistic work, and study of the Illinois language continued through the eighteenth century. Jean Le Boullenger compiled another important document on the Miami-Illinois language sometime after his arrival in the Illinois mission in the early eighteenth century. The surviving manuscript includes a lengthy collection of religious texts, a detailed series of verb paradigms, and a French-to-Illinois dictionary with thousands of translations. Le Petit surveyed a version of Le Boullenger's catechism during the Illinois visit to New Orleans and thought it a superb model of Jesuit linguistic efforts. At least three other Jesuits— Pierre-François Pinet, Louis Vivier, and Louis Meurin—seem to have authored linguistic studies of Illinois in the eighteenth century, and many other Jesuits continued to participate in the language acquisition and translation project.[9]

The Jesuits would never have been able to complete this crucial linguistic work without the assistance of the Illinois themselves, however. Language study constituted a truly collaborative effort, one that sometimes even highlighted the Jesuits' dependency on their hosts. Jesuit linguists like Allouez, Gravier, and Le Boullenger listened carefully to conversations and speeches to gather material for their dictionaries, grammars, and prayer books, but patient Native instructors remained indispensable to accurate and efficient language study. Whenever possible, missionaries utilized written materials to learn Native languages, but becoming truly fluent, or close to it, required immersion in Indian communities and the consistent practice offered in everyday, intimate language encounters. These shared experiences and a common quest for mutual understanding stimulated linguistic exchange and innovation. Missionaries shaped their Christian message to conform to linguistic and cultural demands, and the Illinois received Christian concepts with the freedom to interpret and spread them in their own ways. Translation between languages involved active mediation between cultures and thrust participants in the language encounter into a series of negotiations over meaning. As people struggled to articulate complex ideas in such a volatile environment, diverse definitions and contrasting cultural expressions intersected to produce novel interpretations and new meanings over time.[10]

* * *

In 1673, Claude Allouez traveled to the mission of Saint Marc to continue his work among the Mesquakies. During his stay, the priest prepared a dying woman for baptism with a presumably abbreviated catechism and three core texts of the Catholic Church, the *Pater Noster*, or Our Father, the *Ave Maria*, or Hail Mary, and the *Credo*, or Apostles' Creed. Allouez's colleague in the Great Lakes missions, Louis André, promised a group of Indians that he would baptize them if they learned to recite these same three texts. According to

André's account, the Indians learned them quickly and so well that André was forced to baptize them or be known as a liar. André did as he promised.[11]

The two prayers and the statement of faith employed by Allouez and André were cornerstones of Jesuit teaching in the missions. For many Native people in the region, these three religious texts provided the first systematic introduction to the tenets of Christianity, and every fresh neophyte and firmly established Christian was expected to know them by heart. The missionaries quickly translated them into the various Native languages they encountered and used them as the basis for instruction while they developed and started to work with lengthier and more detailed catechisms. The Illinois prayer book attributed to Father Allouez contains translations of these three essential texts, and they, along with a different version of the *Credo* from Le Boullenger's collection, make ideal subjects for a study of mediation and meaning in the Illinois mission.[12]

In the Illinois versions of the *Credo*, difficult problems of translation appear right away, with the first and most important words of the text, "I believe." The corresponding term in Miami-Illinois, *nitaramita8a*, can also be translated as "I obey," "I give thanks to," or, on occasion, "I pray to" (see Figs. 5 and 6). The Illinois word pushed the concept expressed in the creed beyond purely interior faith or thought and highlighted the disposition of the believer, urging the Illinois Christian toward religious action. In this way, the translation conformed better to Illinois spiritual traditions, based more on proper behavior, precise ritual, and reciprocal spiritual relationships than on any stable set of creedal statements. The Illinois term was in many ways actually richer in meaning than its equivalent in the Christian text. Although admittedly the Apostles' Creed assumes certain obligations on the part of any Christian, the Illinois versions addressed the issue much more directly. The Jesuits could have used other terms to express similar ideas—*nitechitehe*, or "I think," is one obvious possibility—but the conscious decision to employ an Illinois word that stressed active obedience worked well from both a Jesuit and an Illinois perspective.[13]

The Apostles' Creed directs the obedience of the faithful toward the three elements of the Holy Trinity: in the opening section, God the Father; then, Jesus Christ his Son; and finally, in the third part, the Holy Spirit. The earliest significant divergence between the Allouez and the Le Boullenger versions of the *Credo* occurs in the translation of God in line 1. Both Allouez and Le Boullenger emphasized the power of God as creator of the sky (heaven) and the earth in the opening line, but they assigned different

1 *Nitaramita8a Di8 8ak8ississita,*
   I believe in him (obey, give thanks to, pray to) / God / <u>one who invokes
      fear (respect),</u> /
   I believe in God <u>the honored one</u>,
   I believe in God, the Father almighty,

   tcheki kik8 arokahansig8a, kigig8i kechit8ka akiski8i napi.
   / all / things / <u>he does not fail</u>, / sky / he creates it / earth / also.
   all <u>powerful</u>, who creates the sky and the earth also.
   creator of heaven and earth.

2 *Nitaramita8a anitranissari nig8tti8ari Jesus Christ kitakim8minan;*
   I believe in him / his child / the one / Jesus Christ / our chief;
   I believe in his only child, Jesus Christ, our chief.
   I believe in Jesus Christ, his only Son, our Lord.

3 *met8seni8h8a pekisiritchi 8itchimanet8etchiri mit8seni8ihig8ta,*
   he is made human / he is good / he is an accompanying spirit
      (spirit of light) / the one he makes man, /
   He is made man by the good spirit of light,
   He was conceived by the power of the Holy Spirit

   ak8aniss8ari, 8chisik8ri Marieri arechi penarig8ta.
   / his son, / <u>the virgin</u> / Mary / unintentionally / she gives birth to him.
   the <u>virgin</u> Mary unintentionally gave birth.
   and born of the Virgin Mary.

Figure 5. The *Credo*, or Apostles' Creed, from the prayer book attributed to Claude Allouez. Claude Allouez, *Facsimile of Père Marquette's Illinois Prayer Book* (Quebec: Quebec Literary and Historical Society, 1908), 20–22. The translations from Miami-Illinois in figures 5 through 8 are mine, although I have received extensive suggestions and essential advice from Daryl Baldwin and David Costa. Any errors that remain, however, are my responsibility alone. The italicized words are transcriptions from the original manuscript. The symbol *8* represents the phonemes *o*, *oo*, and *w*. The plain text is a literal translation of the Miami-Illinois words and phrases. The bold text represents a smoother and more comprehensible interpretation. Parentheses enclose alternative or expanded meanings. Underlined words and phrases are uncertain in meaning. A standard English version of the Apostles' Creed follows each line in plain text. See *Catechism of the Catholic Church* (Chicago: Loyola University Press, 1994), 49–50.

4   *akimai8ba ponce pirata he mare8itarintchi Jesus, pimitahaganinghi*
    he was chief / Pontius Pilate / <u>as</u> / he is mistreated / Jesus, / on the cross /
    Jesus is mistreated on the cross by captain Pontius Pilate,
    He suffered under Pontius Pilate,

    chinghinig8a-nag8tchinghi: sekah8nta, nepiki, 8rassintchi akiski8nghi,
    / <u>he is stretched out</u>: / he is burned, / he dies, / he is buried / in the earth,
    <u>stretched</u> on the cross, burned, dies, and buried in the earth,
    was crucified, died, and was buried.

5   *aramakinghi pintikitchi, niss8g8ne kikitchi,*
    in the ground / he enters, / three days / he is alive,
    he entered into the earth, and lived for three days,
    He descended into hell. On the third day he rose again.

6   *kigig8nghi aiatchi, 8itapimatchi 88ssari Dieu tcheki kik8 arokahansik8ri,*
    into the sky / he goes, / he sits with him / his father / God / all / things /
       <u>he does not fail</u>,
    he ascends to heaven to sit with his father, God, all <u>powerful</u>,
    He ascended into heaven and is seated at the right hand of the Father.

7   *ab8gi kata pi8a, kata tepihe8a na8i kikitchiki,*
    again / will, / he comes / will / he pleases (satisfies) him / in order that
       they live, /
    again he will come for the purpose of pleasing the living
    He will come again to judge the living

    nepikiki napi.
    / they die / also.
    as well as those who have died.
    and the dead.

8   *Nitaramita8a pekisita 8itchimanet8etchi,*
    I believe in him / he who is beautiful / his accompanying spirit,
    I believe his accompanying spirit is good,
    I believe in the Holy Spirit,

Figure 5. (*continued*)

9   *erigok8akiki tchekirina araminanghiki,*
    <u>all over</u> the earth / <u>all</u> / those who pray,
    all over the earth all will pray,
    the holy catholic Church,

10   *pekaki kek8 8echitatinghi*
    that which is good / thing / one makes it <u>together</u> /
    the good things made <u>together</u>,
    the communion of saints,

    pekaki kek8 echirininghi,
    / that which is good / thing / what one does,
    will be good things done,

11   *kissinana mere8aki echirininghi,*
    it is cleaned / the bad things / what one does,
    what bad things are done will be cleansed,
    the forgiveness of sins,

12   *kiki8aki kata tcheki nepikiki,*
    they live / will / all / they die,
    those who die will all live,
    the resurrection of the body,

13   *Kata mina nip8si8aki.*
    there will be / as well / they do not die.
    and there will be no more death.
    and the life everlasting.

14   *i8nini echiteheiani.*
    this / I feel thus.
    This is how I feel.
    Amen.

Figure 5. (*continued*)

1   *nintaramita8a kichemanet8a kecatetoni 8ssima8a*
I believe in him (obey, give thanks to, pray to) / great spirit / who is / the
father /
I believe in the great spirit who is the father,
I believe in God, the Father almighty,

tchekikic8 arocahansig8a kigig8i tchi akiski8i kechit8ca
/ all / things / <u>he does not fail</u> / the sky / and / the earth / he creates it
all <u>powerful</u>, who creates the sky and the earth.
creator of heaven and earth.

2   *Nintaramita8a anegat8apahaganari kitakim8minanari Jes8s christ irintchiri*
I believe in him / his only son / our chief / Jesus Christ / he is born
(comes into the world)
**I believe in his only son, our chief, Jesus Christ, who comes
into the world.**
I believe in Jesus Christ, his only Son, our Lord.

3   *8assenag8sitchiri manet8ari met8seni8iheg8ta*
he is enlightened / the spirit / he is made man /
The enlightened spirit makes him man;
He was conceived by the power of the Holy Spirit

Marieri ch8ec8ichi ac8essari penarig8ta
/ Mary / truly / nubile girl (virgin) / she gives birth to him
the virgin Mary gives birth to him.
and born of the Virgin Mary.

Figure 6. The *Credo*, or Apostles' Creed, from the Le Boullenger prayer manual.
Jean Baptiste Le Boulanger [Jean Le Boullenger], [French and Miami-Illinois
Dictionary], Codex Ind 28, 2-SIZE, John Carter Brown Library, Providence,
R.I. 10–11. Le Boullenger does not provide translations for lines 10 and 14. The
translations from Miami-Illinois are mine. The symbol *8* represents the phonemes
o, *oo*, and *w*. The plain text is a literal translation of the Miami-Illinois words
and phrases. The bold text represents a smoother and more comprehensible
interpretation. Parentheses enclose alternative or expanded meanings. Underlined
words and phrases are uncertain in meaning. A standard English version of the
Apostles' Creed follows each line in plain text. See *Catechism of the Catholic Church*
(Chicago: Loyola University Press, 1994), 49–50.

4   *akima8ipa Ponce Pilate, niahe acat8cahintchi Pimitahaganenghi*
captain / Pontius Pilate, / there / he is made to suffer / on the cross /
Captain Pontius Pilate makes him suffer there;
He suffered under Pontius Pilate,

chinkiring8ana8nta nepiki metassintchi
/ he is attached (crucified) / he dies (is dead) / he is interred
he is attached to the cross, dies, and is interred.
was crucified, died, and was buried.

5   *Aramakinghigi Mattapi8o niss8namenghi kigig8i apissit8ca*
to hell / he descends / in three days / the sky / he is resuscitated /
He descends to hell and in three days is resuscitated
He descended into hell. On the third day he rose again.

a8i8ssemi
/ the one whom he has as a father
by the one who is like his father in the sky.

6   *kigig8nghigi aiatchi*
to the sky / he goes
He ascends to the sky;
He ascended into heaven and is seated at the right hand of the Father.

7   *Ni8antchi catapi8o teiamatchi[sse]*
later / he will come / he will judge
later he will return to judge.
He will come again to judge the living and the dead.

8   *Nintaramita8a 8assiManet8a*
I believe in him / the spirit of light
I believe in the spirit of light,
I believe in the Holy Spirit,

9   *Erigoc8akiki nig8tin8i araminai8ni*
for all the earth / the one / the prayer

Figure 6. (*continued*)

the one prayer for all the earth,
the holy catholic Church,

10

11   *kissinamaki8ni kiask8enghira*
the cleansing / <u>sins</u>
the cleansing of <u>sins</u>,
the forgiveness of sins,

12   *he a8i8sseminghi apisi8ni*
as / <u>the one who is like a father</u> / the resurrection (second life)
as the one who is like our father resurrects
the resurrection of the body,

13   *Eiascami peraki8ni*
forever / to live (to heal, eternal life)
so that there is eternal life.
and the life everlasting.

14

Figure 6. (*continued*)

names to God here and later in the sixth article, where Le Boullenger neglected any mention of God. Allouez employed the French *Dieu,* while Le Boullenger used *kichemanet8a,* or "great spirit," the term most commonly associated with God in Algonquian languages. The central issue in the decision here appears to be the Illinois concept of *manet8a,* a key word in the Illinois-Jesuit religious encounter.[14]

Gravier's translation of *manet8a* gave a range of meanings for the crucial term: "Spirit, God; of or relating to snow, medicine." His translation reveals both the attempt to graft French ideas onto Native terms, in this case the Christian notion of God, and recognition that Illinois conceptions remained paramount. "Spirit," not "God," was the first definition Gravier provided. Le Boullenger not only listed the term under his entry for *Esprit,* "spirit" in French; he also included a second, separate entry for *manet8a* among the otherwise French words translated in his dictionary. He defined the term there as "genie" or "spirit." It was the constant need for medicine or power and for positive reciprocal relationships with the *manet8aki* that made action rather than belief the defining feature of Illinois religion.[15]

Clearly, Le Boullenger acknowledged the importance of the concept, and, like most other missionaries at the time, tried to build on it by adding the modifier *kiche*, meaning "great." Le Boullenger accepted and attempted to enlarge the association between God and traditional Illinois ideas about *manet8aki*. In this view, the Illinois would redirect their prayers, rituals, and requests for aid toward the Christian God, or great spirit. Allouez, on the other hand, seemed intent on avoiding associations with traditional Illinois spiritual concepts. In the first and sixth lines of the Apostles' Creed, he did not employ a variation of *manet8a* to describe God. His use of the French *Dieu* suggests an attempt to introduce and maintain the purity of a new concept for the divine being responsible for the creation of the universe, the God who looked down on the world and its peoples from his glorious throne in heaven. Allouez did not want the Illinois to mistake God for an everyday *manet8a*.[16]

Maintaining the purity of Christian concepts in translation was a frequent concern of the French missionaries, who complained often about the absence of indispensable concepts in Native languages and about the challenges posed by the major structural differences between French and indigenous languages. The eighteenth-century Jesuit missionary and historian François-Xavier de Charlevoix believed that Indian languages were difficult for Europeans to learn because they were so different, but he noted as well that "the poverty and barrenness into which [the languages] have fallen cause an equal confusion." Charlevoix referred in his statement to the supposed degeneration of languages in the aftermath of God's destruction of the Tower of Babel and the dispersal of humanity. Charlevoix described the severe consequences of this event and the subsequent degeneration: "Having no regular form of worship, and forming confused ideas of the deity and of everything relating to religion, . . . and being never accustomed to discourse of virtues, passions, and many other matters which are the common subjects of conversation with us, . . . there was found a prodigious void in their language." Recognizing the need for careful mediation, Charlevoix explained "that after learning their language, we were under a necessity to teach them a new one partly composed of their own terms, and partly of ours."[17]

The perceived poverty of these languages became a common complaint of missionaries and a regular observation of European scholars. The missionaries worried that abstract concepts such as god, trinity, grace, and salvation had no equivalents and that innumerable biblical references were completely foreign to Native experiences. In reality, the disconnection between French and Native languages was a natural result of the French-Indian cultural encounter. Indian languages were fully capable of expressing complex thoughts and abstract ideas and of incorporating new experiences, concepts, and terms. Charlevoix, for example, commented on the two great language families of northeastern North America, Algonquian and Iroquoian: "Both have a richness of expression, a variety of turns and phrases, a propriety of diction, and a regularity, which are perfectly astonishing."[18]

The problem, then, was not the Illinois language itself, but rather translating across the cultural divide, constructing a bridge of understanding between cultures. As Charlevoix noted, missionaries and Natives had to create new expressions that combined features and terms of both languages. Allouez introduced *Dieu* to the Illinois and used Illinois words to explain his conception of God. Le Boullenger chose instead to rely on Illinois words in his version of the Apostles' Creed, trying to give them new meaning. He called God *kichemanet8a*, "the great spirit," a term that Gravier translated as "the spirit of creation." Although there is little specific evidence about Illinois explanations of creation, Allouez and his Jesuit colleagues found that the Illinois honored one spirit above all others "because he is the maker of all things." Allouez equated this spirit with the Christian God and gave him a new name. Le Boullenger simply incorporated the Illinois concept into a Christian account of creation.[19]

Making such fine distinctions about the supreme being was not easy, but explaining God's only son presented, at least on the surface, an even more difficult set of problems. To begin, Miami-Illinois obviously contained no term for "Lord," a word that defines a hierarchical relationship between Jesus Christ and Christians who accept him as their savior. Allouez and Le Boullenger both described Jesus Christ as "our chief," utilizing the Illinois term *akima8a* in the second article of the *Credo*.[20]

Their decision created some potential problems of interpretation, however, for a vast conceptual distance separated the kind of relationship prescribed for a lord and his subjects on the one hand and an Illinois chief and the members of his community on the other. The difference between a relationship based on submission and one based on the assent and input of the governed made for a sharp contrast in definitions. Illinois chiefs had limited authority in a variety of reciprocal relationships that defined both the rights and the obligations of leadership. As one Jesuit missionary put it, "The Chiefs have no authority; if they should use threats, far from making themselves feared, they would see themselves abandoned by the very men who had chosen them for Chiefs." Effective leadership among the Illinois required careful maintenance of political and social ties, demonstrated ability to solve problems and make good decisions, and a well-cultivated talent for persuasion. Missionaries tried continually to emphasize the total submission to God's will that came with true acceptance of Christ, but the actual meaning of *akima8a* would likely have lingered indefinitely, inviting Illinois Christians to view Jesus as a potentially powerful leader in both spiritual and human terms and to develop a relationship in which both the leader and his followers could introduce their own very personal expectations. In addition, Allouez and Le Boullenger also applied *akima8a* to Pontius Pilate (line 4), the Roman leader who condemned Jesus to crucifixion, making questions about the difference between the merely human figure and the man-god all but inevitable.[21]

Even more difficult than establishing Jesus as the paramount spiritual leader of the Christian Illinois was finding a way to explain clearly his miraculous conception, incarnation, and birth. The Allouez translation of the *Credo* in particular struggles to describe the circumstances of his birth and the larger concept of the Holy Trinity. While the Apostles' Creed states simply that "[Jesus] was conceived by the power of the Holy Spirit and born of the Virgin Mary," a word-by-word gloss of the same article (line 3) in the Allouez prayer book reads: "he is made human / he is good / he is an accompanying spirit (spirit of light) / the one he makes man, / his son, / the virgin / Mary / unintentionally / she gives birth to him." The Illinois version is strikingly convoluted and very hard to untangle. That the "accompanying spirit" or "spirit of light"—the Holy Spirit—conceives Jesus and makes him man is relatively clear, but the Virgin Mary giving birth to the son of the Holy Spirit "without intention" is at best rather vague. Le Boullenger offered a less convoluted translation that contributed to a generally more streamlined version of the *Credo*, which overall contains fewer words, phrases, and lines.[22]

Le Boullenger and Allouez used variations of the same term for the Holy Spirit, who conceived Jesus in Mary. Le Boullenger's "*8assenag8sitchiri mane-t8ari*" and Allouez's "*8itchimanet8etchiri*" both rely on the Illinois word for spirit, *manet8a*, to describe the Holy Spirit. Both translators also added modifiers that would stress the extraordinary power and unique position of the Christian spirit, thereby distinguishing the Holy Spirit from traditional Illinois *manet8aki*. The modifiers *8asse-* and *8itchi-*, which appear to be different transcriptions of the same Illinois root, associate the Holy Spirit with light and with the power to touch a person's heart, infuse the soul with grace, and inspire interior enlightenment. Allouez inserts another Illinois word, *pekisirit-chi* in the first occurrence and *pekisita* in line 8, to further emphasize the point that the Holy Spirit is special. The Illinois means "good" or "beautiful." The Jesuits adopted this term as an equivalent for the French *saint*, or "holy," attempting to stretch its meaning to encompass French and Christian concepts of holiness, purity, and the sacred.[23]

Altogether, the two Illinois versions of the *Credo* explained that Jesus has two fathers and a mother. Jesus is the only son of the great spirit of creation, who lives in the sky and who commands fear and respect in those who obey him. The beautiful spirit of light comes down to earth and makes Jesus man through Mary, the pure nubile girl, who gives birth to him so that he can come into the world, where he suffers, dies, returns to life and his father in the sky, and becomes chief of all Christians. A curious feature of this description is that, unlike the standard Christian text of the Apostles' Creed, the Illinois translations related most of the events, including the story of Christ's passion, death, and resurrection, in the present tense. The translators must have made a deliberate decision to rewrite the text in this manner because Miami-Illinois has a past tense that they could have used. The choice suggests an attempt to instill a sense of immediacy about the existence of the Trinity, the life of Christ, and Christ's mother, Mary. This stylistic device likely conformed to traditional methods of Illinois storytelling. Indeed, the grammatical construction for the past tense indicates that an action "used to" take place, that it "is no longer true or relevant" in the present. Native storytellers often employ the present tense in their oral narratives. Storytelling is a creative event that invokes not only the memory but also sometimes the actual presence of the story's actors. Retelling a tale nurtures an ongoing dialogue between its subject and its listeners, the past and the present. These were sacred stories, *ars8kana*.[24]

In the transition to its third and final section, the *Credo* turns to the future with the reminder that Christ will come again from the sky "for the purpose of pleasing the living as well as those who have died," as the Allouez version promises. The Le Boullenger text adheres more closely to the original, warning that judgment is coming. The Apostles' Creed then lists the last few articles of faith required for the Christian to pass Christ's judgment successfully and participate in the rewards of eternal life. After stressing the necessity for acceptance of the spirit of light, or Holy Spirit, the Illinois creeds affirmed the primacy of the church and its sacraments as the only path to salvation. The Allouez and Le Boullenger translations differ slightly, yet they both emphasize the act of prayer over place or doctrine. For Allouez, "the holy catholic Church" of the *Credo* became "all over the earth all will pray," while Le Boullenger translated the same phrase as "the one prayer for all the earth." The act of praying was indeed central to Illinois understandings of Christianity.[25]

The *Credo* also demands that those who pray in the church believe in "the forgiveness of sins" that will prepare them for resurrection and "the life everlasting." As translated in the Allouez text, sins became merely "bad things," a much more general meaning than sin, defined as an offense against God and his moral commandments. Missionaries constantly struggled to explain this central Christian doctrine to Native people. The missionaries recognized that the Christian concept of sin and forgiveness did not translate easily into other cultures. For the Illinois, social or spiritual transgressions could have immediate or long-term consequences, breaking the bonds of reciprocity or initiating a series of reprisals and reactions. Nevertheless, such negative actions did not mark the soul for eternity. Le Boullenger introduced a word, *kiask8enghira*, of uncertain etymology, but this change likely reflected an attempt to refine Illinois understandings of sin and forgiveness. *Kiask8enghira* may relate to the Illinois root *isc8-*, which marked a fault or defect in something. Le Boullenger also recognized a term for sin based on the same root, *mare8-*, meaning "bad," that Allouez employed.[26]

In any case, prayer and proper behavior demonstrated the internalization of values, no doubt a blend of Illinois and Christian ideals, which led to right action in the world, to the combination of belief and obedience expressed in the opening line and repeated twice more in the *Credo*. The Illinois Christian using the Allouez translation ended the recitation with the exclamation "That is what I think." The Miami-Illinois *echiteheiani* ("I think") contains the root for "heart," *tehi*, providing an expanded translation that reads, "That is what I have in my heart." The *Credo* translated into Illinois asked Illinois Christians to attach themselves to the statements of faith—to take them inside their hearts—and demanded that they express them in the present through the everyday actions of their lives.[27]

If the *Credo* provides the foundational structure for Christian faith, the *Pater Noster*, also known as the Our Father or Lord's Prayer, defines in greater intimacy the Christian relationship with God while also supplying an essential model for an active Christian piety based on prayer and forgiveness.

1   *88ssemiranghi kigig8nghi epiani,*
    We have you as (like) a father / in the sky / you sit (are located),
    We have you, who is like our father and sits in the sky,
    Our Father who art in heaven,

2   *kitiramat8tche ki8ins8rimi.*
    let it be <u>esteemed</u> (sanctified, important) / your name.
    your name is <u>honored</u>.
    hallowed be thy name.

3   *he nag8siani 8anantaki apianghi kati;*
    <u>as</u> / you appear / peace (tranquility, happiness) / we will sit;
    when you appear we will live in peace;
    Thy kingdom come.

4   *kitaramitag8a arig8ntchi kigig8nghi,*
    he obeys (believes in, gives thanks to, prays to) you / from there /
        in the sky, /
    he obeys you from beyond in the sky,
    Thy will be done on earth,

    aramit8ringhi kati 8ahi akiski8nghi;
    / you are obeyed (believed in, thanked, prayed to) / will / here /
        on the earth;
    you will be obeyed here on earth;
    as it is in heaven.

5   *n8nghi miriname nimitchi8aneminani, mamitchimi miriname
        nimitchi8aneminani.*

Figure 7. The *Pater Noster*, or Our Father, from the prayer book attributed to Claude Allouez. Claude Allouez, *Facsimile of Père Marquette's Illinois Prayer Book* (Quebec: Quebec Literary and Historical Society, 1908), 19. The translations from Miami-Illinois are mine. The symbol *8* represents the phonemes *o*, *oo*, and *w*. The plain text is a literal translation of the Miami-Illinois words and phrases. The bold text represents a smoother and more comprehensible interpretation. Parentheses enclose alternative or expanded meanings. Underlined words and phrases are uncertain in meaning. A standard English version of the Our Father follows each line in plain text. See *Catechism of the Catholic Church* (Chicago: Loyola University Press, 1994), 661.

now / give us / our food, / often (always) / you give us / our food.
give us our food now and often.
Give us this day our daily bread,

6   *Kik8 nitirerindans8mina a8ia 8echakitehiaminthe,*
Something / we do not think of it / someone / <u>he who angers us</u>, /
We do not think of the things or people <u>who anger us</u>,
and forgive us our trespasses,

echitehes8kane kik8 he 8ichakitehiranghi.
/ you must not think so / something / <u>as</u> / he makes us angry.
and you must not think things of those <u>who make us angry</u>.
as we forgive those who trespass against us,

7   *Kirahama8iname arima8e kata, mere8iteheianghi.*
Prevent (defend) us / bound to / will, / we have a bad (sick)
    heart (stomach).
Please prevent us from having a bad heart.
and lead us not into temptation,

8   *Tcheki mare8aki kirahama8iname.*
All / the bad things / prevent (defend) us.
Defend us from all bad things.
but deliver us from evil.

Figure 7. (*continued*)

The opening lines of the *Pater Noster* invoke the reality of God, attempting to make him a less mysterious and more comprehensible figure connected by an intensely personal bond to the petitioner (see Fig. 7). The fatherly relationship described tempers somewhat the transcendence of God without upsetting the hierarchical nature of the affiliation. There is tension in this distinction. The Lord's Prayer cannot reduce entirely the vast distance between father and child, God and petitioner. The Illinois version of the Our Father stressed the existence of this gap, even widening it in a certain sense, while simultaneously demonstrating God's willingness to reach across it. Like the original on which it is based, the Illinois text placed God almost out of human reach, in the sky or heaven, but the Illinois prayer deviated slightly in its description of

God as father. God was only "*like* our father and sits in the sky," suggesting in the first place that the relationship was a fictive rather than a literal one.

The Illinois version seems to add an additional degree of separation from God in its spiritual genealogy. However, the Illinois term *88ssemiranghi* also implied that the petitioner had accepted God as an adopted father, which reflected well the experiences of Illinois converts who had decided to associate themselves with the imported faith. The entry for *adopter*, "to adopt," in the Le Boullenger dictionary includes a translation for "God adopted me." In this way, the Illinois *Pater Noster* stressed the significance of a deliberate choice in the creation of the father-child relationship. The introduction of the Illinois term *epiani*, apparently meaning "you sit," showed further that God would come down from his seat in the sky to provide for those who reached up to him and who called also for the establishment of his vision of peace for the earth and its peoples.[28]

Illinois Christians reciting the Lord's Prayer, probably for the most committed of them on a daily basis, awaited a time when people would remain at peace, *8anantaki* in Miami-Illinois, their world finally free from conflict (line 3). The Native peoples of the Illinois country and Great Lakes region had many reasons to dream of such a future. A series of devastating conflicts disturbed northeastern North America for much of the late seventeenth and the eighteenth centuries, leaving few communities untouched by violence and its consequences. Attacks and reprisals, the loss of population to warfare and disease, and a stream of refugees from eastern conflicts created a sense of crisis for many peoples, which made trading, military, and religious alliances with the French seem attractive, even essential at times. The bewildering transformations initiated by these problems and the political, social, and economic dilemmas they posed encouraged many Illinois and other Native peoples to explore the spiritual teachings of the Jesuit missionaries. The Illinois concept of peace relied on the understanding and acceptance of alliances and kinship relations. The term united these meanings. The peaceful future imagined in the Illinois version of the *Pater Noster* likely seemed a wonderful alternative to those who suffered the effects of such terrifying violence and dizzying change. The absence of an Illinois term for "kingdom" required that Jesuit translators identify a more immediate, specific, and earthly vision of the future than that embodied in the Christian idea of God's millennial kingdom. Peace served this purpose well.[29]

The following line of the prayer only reinforced the earthly nature of this tranquil dream, placing responsibility for its inception on obedience to God not only "beyond in the sky," but "here on earth" in daily life as well (line 4). Again, as in the Illinois *Credo*, faith alone was not enough to alter the spiritual course of a person or the world. Only right action, following closely the will of God, ensured the strength of the divine connection to the supreme being on which the petition for peace was based. Together, lines 3 and 4 demanded recognition of God's simultaneous transcendence and omnipresence, both in the world as a whole and in the lives of individuals. Gravier supplied a beautiful image in his dictionary that vividly illustrated the promise of peaceful repose for those who obeyed the will of God. According to Gravier, *8anantakisk8aki*, which contains the root for "peace," described a bird that flies without moving its wings. As a metaphor, this image suggested that living with God freed one to soar without effort high above the vexing problems of the mundane world.[30]

The petition for food that followed extended these thoughts, explicitly recognizing the precariousness of common, everyday existence and acknowledging God's role in meeting even the most basic needs of life (line 5). Coming right after the lines acknowledging the primacy of God's will, this point provided yet another example of the reciprocal relationship formed between Christians and God. The concept must have seemed quite natural to the Illinois, who had always relied on such productive relationships with *mane-t8aki* in their constant quest for dependable food sources. The more general Illinois term *nimitchi8aneminani*, meaning food, employed in place of the standard "bread" did, however, miss the important connection between bread and spiritual nourishment made so clear in the ritual of communion, in which the communion wafer represented the very body of Christ.[31]

The next petition of the *Pater Noster* emphasizes yet again the responsibilities of good Christians, in this instance pardon and reconciliation as modeled by Jesus in the gospels (line 6). Illinois culture in this period provided an important parallel to this merciful exchange. Illinois families, bands, and individuals regularly offered gifts in a number of situations to restore order within or between communities. The ritual of covering the dead represented the most sensitive and delicate of these acts of reconciliation. The French trader Pierre Deliette noted in his memoir that the relatives of an Illinois or Miami man killed in a dispute sought revenge against the killer or his kin, unless the aggrieved party was willing to accept presents as appeasement. Deliette explained, "Ordinarily blankets, kettles, guns, and slaves are given for this purpose." Covering the dead in this way encouraged an end to the cycle of violence by stressing a complex process of exchange and pardon over outright revenge.

1   *8iaghitehero Maria,*
    Be joyful / Mary,
    Rejoice in Mary,
    Hail Mary,

2   *tcheki kitintare pekitehei8na,*
    all / you are the master / good hearts, /
    you are the master of all good hearts,
    full of grace,

    nenetta8i ki8intchit8nig8a kitchiakimamanet8a,
    / always / he takes care of you / the great chief spirit,
    the great chief spirit always takes care of you,
    the Lord is with thee.

3   *tcheki mitem8ssaki tchirerimig8tchiki kichemanit8ari,*
    all / the women / he loves them / the great spirit, /
    the great spirit loves all women,
    Blessed art thou among women

    kira tchitchi kitari8apaharig8a.
    / you / more (better) / he loves you the most of all his children.
    but he loves you the most of all his children.

4   *kit8assi8a kik8ississa Jesus.*
    <u>he is great</u> / your son / Jesus.
    Your son, Jesus, <u>is great</u>.
    and blessed is the fruit of thy womb, Jesus.

Figure 8. The *Ave Maria*, or Hail Mary, from the prayer book attributed to Claude Allouez. Claude Allouez, *Facsimile of Père Marquette's Illinois Prayer Book* (Quebec: Quebec Literary and Historical Society, 1908), 19–20. The translations from Miami-Illinois are mine. The symbol *8* represents the phonemes *o*, *oo*, and *w*. The plain text is a literal translation of the Miami-Illinois words and phrases. The bold text represents a smoother and more comprehensible interpretation. Parentheses enclose alternative or expanded meanings. Underlined words and phrases are uncertain in meaning. A standard English version of the Hail Mary follows each line in plain text. See *Catechism of the Catholic Church* (Chicago: Loyola University Press, 1994), 643–44.

5   *pekisita Maria Di8 anitranissiani gar8tama8iname.*
   who is good (beautiful) / Mary / God / you have children / speak (pray)
     for us. /
   Beautiful Mary pray to God for us, your children.
   Holy Mary, Mother of God, pray for us sinners,

nirep8as8mina, n8nghi, katkinte nipeianghi techi gar8tama8i8kanghe.
/ we are not wise (do not know), / now, / will / soon / we die / only /
   you must speak (pray) for us.
we do not know how soon we will die, only that you must pray for us.
now and at the hour of our death.

Figure 8. *(continued)*

Deliette also observed that war chiefs who lost men during raids provoked lasting hatred in the relatives of the dead, "unless by dint of presents he finds means
(to use their language) to mend their hearts." These Illinois cultural practices
reinforced the Christian ideal of forgiveness expressed in the *Pater Noster*, even
relying on similar language of hearts and healing.[32]
   Such rhetoric of the heart continued to the final lines of the Illinois version of the prayer, where the Our Father balances the assurance of forgiveness
with a request for God's assistance and support in avoiding disorder and living well. Instead of "Lead us not into temptation, but deliver us from evil,"
the Illinois version reads, "Please prevent us from having a bad heart. Defend
us from all bad things." The Illinois translation altered slightly the image of
purity and strength presented in the prayer, changing significantly the meaning of the verse. In Illinois, a good heart that is not sick—a strong, pure heart
filled with light—supported spiritual health and a moral equilibrium. In this
prayer, the one who is like a father in the sky ultimately defended the Illinois
Christian not simply against the temptation to sin and the evil to which it
inevitably led, but rather "from all bad things" that caused people to suffer.
For those who honored and obeyed God, according to the Illinois *Pater Noster*,
he would bring peace, provide physical and spiritual nourishment, and, importantly, cultivate and care for a good heart.[33]
   The *Ave Maria*, as translated into Illinois, also employed the theme of
the good heart in its supplication to Mary, referring to the mother of Jesus as
"the master of all good hearts" (see Fig. 8). This creative interpretation underscored two serious problems of translation. The first involved the concept of
grace, a complex Christian idea the missionaries struggled to explain. The

Illinois text exchanged this Christian concept of grace for the Illinois idea of a good heart, seeking an illuminating intersection between cultures. Gravier defined grace as *8asseteheï8ni*, adding the additional related meanings "interior light, consolation, . . . beauty of the heart." In Illinois, Mary, rather than being "full of grace," was "the master of all good hearts." Le Boullenger explained in his dictionary that a good heart was one embellished by grace. Mary modeled the internal and external balance, the communion with God and the moral purity that maintained a strong, stable, and healthy heart. In the translation, the effects of a strong heart transformed Mary, and she acquired the power, through the Lord, to touch others, to heal their hearts and make them good.[34]

Translating the term "Lord," for the spiritual figure who stayed with Mary and always cared for her, provided a second major challenge in this section of the prayer. The translator here used a different strategy than he did in the Apostles' Creed that appeared alongside the Hail Mary in the Allouez prayer book. In the *Credo*, the missionary avoided the Illinois root *manet8a* when describing God. In the *Ave Maria*, the translator incorporated the Illinois spirit concept into the prayer, calling the Lord God *kitchi-akima-manet8a*, or great-chief-spirit. Two possible explanations for this change in approach seem logical, neither one necessarily negating the other. First, the missionary needed to make a distinction in this case between God the Father and the Lord Jesus Christ of the *Credo*. In the biblical text on which the *Ave Maria* is based, the archangel Gabriel is God's messenger to Mary, revealing her unique destiny as the mother of God. Mary would be united with God, "the great chief spirit," through the action of the Holy Spirit so that she could give birth to Jesus Christ, the man-god, the lord or chief who created the link between heaven and earth. The missionary needed to make absolutely clear that it was God the Father who "always takes care of [Mary]" and that the fruit of her union with God, "[their] son, Jesus, is great" as well (lines 2 and 4).

Second, the translator of the Allouez texts may have wanted to introduce a variety of terms to explain the distinctions and the connections between the three dimensions of the Holy Trinity, another intransigent concept. In the Apostles' Creed, the foundation of faith, the translator called Jesus "our chief" and the Holy Spirit "the beautiful accompanying spirit." For God, he used the French word *Dieu* and named him "the honored one, all powerful, who creates the sky and the earth." He purposefully avoided the term *manet8a* in these references. The *Pater Noster* described God as one "who is like our father and sits in the sky," adding another dimension to the emerging description. In the *Ave Maria*, however, God became "the great chief spirit," or simply "the great spirit," as in the third line of the prayer. *Kitchiakimama-net8a* acted as a unifying term that brought together many of the ideas about God and his role in the world and gave the Illinois an opportunity to understand the Christian God in an Illinois cultural context, as a particular kind of *manet8a*. This translation linked God to the other two facets of the Trinity and seems particularly appropriate in a prayer based on a request that Mary ask for God's favor. The Lord God appeared as Gravier's "spirit of creation," the chief spirit of the world who chose Mary from among all women as the sacred vessel for his incarnation in human form, impregnated her through the power of the spirit of light, and gave the world a new spiritual chief for all time. By giving God a variety of names, a precedent set in the Bible itself, the missionary created a complex portrait of God and the Trinity for his Illinois listeners. Of course, the range of translations also provides evidence that the priests discovered no simple method of defining the deity, recognition of the problems of mediation and the potential for misunderstanding. Together, the texts they produced portray God as the beginning and the end, the first and the last spirit, the all-powerful father and chief.

Mary, as God's favorite child, held a special, elevated position in the spiritual hierarchy the Jesuits described. She maintained an intimate association with her father, the chief spirit, and the closeness of this bond emerged as the basis for the petition that closed the *Ave Maria* (line 5). The Jesuit translator called her "beautiful Mary," again utilizing the term *pekisita*, to which the Jesuits tried to attach the new meaning "holy." The missionaries described Mary as a saint, or beautiful and powerful woman, who offered relief, counsel, and inspiration. The Illinois version of the petition presented Mary not as the Mother of God, but rather as the mother of all the children of the earth, the very ones who requested her aid. The connection of kinship expressed in the prayer encouraged Mary's children, faced with the many uncertainties and unavoidable setbacks of life, to look to their spiritual mother for help in acquiring and retaining a good heart.

Enormously important, too, was the translator's choice to have children and not sinners ask for Mary's prayers. The translator must have considered the implications of his decision to avoid another opportunity to explain the indispensable Christian concept of sin. In ideal terms at least, children possessed a certain purity and innocence despite the stain of original sin, and the Jesuit missionaries placed great hope in the children they worked with in the Illinois missions. Perhaps, in making the petitioner a child of Mary, the missionary hoped to create a positive connection to her that might have been marred by the more negative idea of sinners plagued by the *mere8aki*, or bad things, that tainted the heart and made it sick. The Allouez versions of the *Credo* and the *Pater Noster* emphasized the presence of these bad things in all people and the universal need for cleansing and spiritual enlightenment. The Illinois *Ave Maria* stressed Mary's ability, as "the master of all good hearts," the champion of grace, to intercede on behalf of her children and heal the human heart through the power of prayer and the compassion of her beneficent father, the great spirit.

One of the Illinois words for conversion, *antchitehe*, again linked Christianity to notions of the heart, describing the process as a "change of heart." An important Illinois convert, Marie Rouensa, inspired by her own spiritual transformation, or change of heart, turned both inward and outward to explore and express her new attachment to Christianity. She followed a rigorous daily order of spiritual exercises designed by Jacques Gravier. Her Jesuit mentor reported that she felt a special bond to her namesake Mary, yet she also feared that she did not live up to the example of her Holy Mother. Asked about her love for Mary, she responded, according to the missionary, "I pray to her with every endearing term, to be pleased to adopt me as her daughter. . . . I am still but a child, and know not yet how to pray. I beg her to teach me what I should say to her, that she may protect me against the Demon—who assails me on all sides, and would cause me to fall . . . [if she did] not receive me in her arms, as a good mother receives her frightened child." Reciting the rosary, which combined repetitions of the *Pater Noster* and *Ave Maria* with meditations on central Christian mysteries, reminded Rouensa to concentrate as well on the spiritual assistance and model life of Mary's son, Jesus.[35]

Marie Rouensa also moved out into the surrounding community to search for others who might find rebirth in a Christian life. Rouensa assisted Gravier with catechism classes and added to his explanations of the Bible, often using copper plate engravings to illustrate biblical tales. Gravier praised her, writing, "This young woman . . . has so well remembered what I have said about each picture of the Old and of the New Testament that she explains each one singly, without trouble and without confusion, as well as I could do—and even more intelligibly, in their manner."[36]

These last words, "even more intelligibly, in their manner," underscore a number of important points about the dissemination and incorporation of Christian texts and concepts in the Illinois community. The admission that Marie Rouensa's explanations were superior to those of the missionary himself revealed the continuing need for the cooperation of Native people to translate Christianity in an effective manner, to act as mediators. Gravier also recognized in his statement that despite his efforts, brilliant for the time, to learn the Illinois language and understand Illinois culture, significant cultural barriers remained that he could not cross. Translated into Illinois, the mediated religious texts carefully constructed through intercultural dialogue became the possession of the Illinois Christians who interpreted them, used them in ritual and prayer, and instilled them with meaning. The Illinois acquired the prayers, hymns, and biblical stories, the questions and responses of the catechism, and all the Christian ideals shared by the Jesuits and placed them as they wished into Illinois contexts.

The Kaskaskias and some other Illinois, especially women, rapidly incorporated texts like the *Credo*, the *Pater Noster*, and the *Ave Maria* into their Christian ritual practices. Two decades after the first great wave of conversions, the Jesuit Gabriel Marest described, most likely in ideal terms, the daily routine at Kaskaskia. Early in the morning, people preparing for baptism met at the church to practice their prayers, listen to instructions, and sing hymns. A mass followed for the already baptized Christians of the community. The whole community, "Christians and Catechumens, adults and children, young people and old people," gathered in the afternoon for catechism. People returned to the church in the evening to hear instructions, say their prayers, and sing hymns. "They generally end the day with private meetings, which they hold in their own houses, the men apart from the women," Marest recorded. These gender-based groups recited the rosary and sang hymns. According to Marest, the hymns were actually instructions set to music so they could be more easily memorized.[37]

Oral expression of these religious texts formed the foundation for Christian ritual among the Illinois. Kinship bonds, economic relations, and political ties also shaped the Illinois encounter with Christianity, but ritual life revolved around prayer, singing, storytelling, and the constant recitation of catechisms and instructions. Belief, faith, and knowledge may have been important, but ritual action and performance assumed the paramount position in the practice of Illinois Christianity. Native worldviews often stress the generative power of language. In these views, speaking actually alters the world. Prayer is an act of creation and re-creation. Storytelling brings the past into the present. Ritual renews spiritual connections. The words used to describe Illinois Christians and the places where they worshiped reflect such an emphasis on prayer. Illinois Christians were *araminatchiki*, "those who pray."

And while Gravier originally translated "church" as *mant8egane,* a word that recalled the *manet8aki* of Illinois tradition, Le Boullenger, working several years later, employed the terms *aramina8ikiami* and *araminagane,* which stressed the act of prayer itself rather than the spiritual figures to which the prayers were addressed. In Le Boullenger's translation, the house of spirits became the place of prayer.[38]

Despite the emergence through time of a strong, prayerful Illinois community, the Jesuit missionaries never stopped worrying about the nature of Illinois Christianity. The Jesuits and other observers agreed that the Illinois, and the Kaskaskias in particular, were the most Christianized of the Native peoples in the region. Marest commented in 1699 that, "in fact, we may say that this is one of our finest missions." Thirteen years later, he reported that almost all the Kaskaskia villagers were Christians and that French settlers had been drawn to the thriving community. Yet, Marest and his colleagues also expressed anxiety and frustration about the progress of the mission and the state of Illinois Christianity. Marest worried, for example, that Illinois Christian life degenerated when the Illinois left the missionaries, chapels, and services behind on their long winter and summer hunting expeditions. "All that we can do," Marest explained, "is to go in succession through the various camps in which they are, in order to keep piety alive in them, and administer to them the Sacraments."[39]

These anxieties highlight the effects of cultural mediation on the meaning and practice of Illinois Christianity. The missionaries recognized the simple fact that they lost control of the concepts they presented from the moment they left their mouths. When the Kaskaskias divided at the end of the day into separate groups of women and men for private meetings of prayer and song, the priests could not always be certain their instructions were strictly followed. Such mysteries troubled the Jesuits, who feared the potential for degeneration, disorder, and the appearance of unorthodox ideas and practices.

The missionaries worried that their words would lose meaning in translation, but they also acquired new meanings that could enhance their Christian content or make them more comprehensible in Illinois terms. Translation allowed the Illinois to make Christianity their own, to shape the Christian faith and traditions to their evolving experiences, distinctive cultural requirements, and specific spiritual needs. Historian Vicente Rafael notes in his study of the Spanish colonial Philippines, "Translation . . . resulted in the ineluctable separation between the original message of Christianity . . . and its rhetorical formulation in the vernacular." The Illinois-language prayers offered new sources of inspiration in the ongoing personal and communal struggle to find a way to live well in this world and in the next, a combination of Illinois and Christian concepts for understanding and avoiding the many bad things that disturbed a good, peaceful, and healthy heart. Marie Rouensa recited the rosary in her private apartment, seeking spiritual guidance from the master of all good hearts. Children repeating the catechism for Jesuit missionaries and Illinois men and women singing hymns late into a winter night professed their faith in God but also heard reminders of manitous that populated the Illinois spiritual landscape. The Illinois delegation at New Orleans shared a Gregorian chant with Ursuline nuns, and yet they presented a calumet to the French governor that had as much to do with traditional notions of Illinois reciprocity as it did with Catholicism. Mamantouensa said to the governor, according to Le Petit, "All that I ask of you is your heart and your protection. I am much more desirous of that than of all the merchandise of the world, and when I ask this of you, it is solely for the Prayer."[40]

Chapter 6

Turnings

Spiritual Transformations and the Search for Order

"I will find in New France the will of God . . . my own perfection, and the salvation of souls with much suffering." Jesuit missionary Claude Allouez left these words in some personal writings that expressed his feelings about his work in Canada. The superior of the Jesuit missions in New France, Claude Dablon, included the papers in a letter of 29 August 1690 informing his colleagues in France of Allouez's recent death after more than three decades of dedicated service, primarily among the Algonquian-speaking peoples of the upper Great Lakes. The superior believed that Allouez's "Sentiments" would be inspirational reading for those contemplating service in the difficult mission fields of New France.

In one of the pieces Dablon forwarded, apparently written in 1657 soon after Allouez received permission to go to the colony, Allouez reflected on his good fortune in being called to what he labeled "the most sublime of all the vocations." The young missionary recorded his views on the ideals and central goals of mission work and on his own expectations for spiritual growth in New France. First, he explained that he had requested this position "because it is for the greater glory of God that I can become most like Jesus Christ, . . . who to secure the salvation of mankind preferred the cross to joy." Second, recognizing that he would leave behind, probably forever, the familiar pleasures of France, Allouez happily anticipated "the separation of [his] soul from [his] body" that would occur as he spent his physical self in the project of enlightening the Native nations of New France. Finally, he expected "to find in New France the will of God" as he labored to convert others and to purify his own needy soul.[1]

Allouez's statements reveal his strong desire to further his own personal spiritual advancement and even to attain spiritual perfection through his work on the French-Indian religious frontier. Although the apostolic enterprise emphasized the conversion of Native peoples, the missionary experience provided an arena for the practice of intense spiritual discipline. This process of self-discovery demanded that the missionary consciously turn to engage the world in an effort to stimulate a spiritual transformation. The missionary impulse combined in potent form individual enthusiasm with the universalistic ideology and ardor of the Catholic Church. The Jesuits described their work in reflexive spiritual texts that highlight the vital parallels and connections between the exterior experience of struggling to obtain converts and the interior experience of the missionary's own spiritual growth. A thorough understanding of the Jesuit beliefs embedded in these texts illuminates more vividly the goals and expectations of missionaries regarding conversion, the nature of French-Indian encounters, and the impact of missionization on Native peoples.

Allouez and his brethren brought their message of conversion and eternal salvation into a world already undergoing rapid change. Indian communities in the Great Lakes and Illinois country struggled to cope with the problems and to take advantage of the opportunities presented by the expanding fur trade, imperial competition, and intertribal warfare. Flexible spiritual traditions, indigenous and Christian, furnished a rich resource for adaptation and creative change in the quest for order. Religious conversion in this unsettled land constituted a multidimensional process of encounter and engagement, interaction and dialogue, that encompassed a variety of personal and communal experiences and that transformed Native peoples and Christian missionaries alike.[2]

*   *   *

Claude Allouez arrived in Canada to begin his mission work in July 1658, at the age of thirty-six. He had been trained for his new role by almost twenty years of well-structured education and teaching in the Society of Jesus. Allouez entered the Jesuit novitiate at Toulouse in 1639, when he was seventeen. After two years of preliminary preparation, he studied rhetoric and philosophy for four years at the Collège in Billom. After teaching in Billom from 1645 to 1651, Allouez returned to Toulouse for four years of training in theology. He then took his third probationary year, or tertianship, at Rodez and served as a preacher there until his departure for New France. On 18 October 1657, not long before Allouez left and about the time he probably wrote his "Sentiments," the new missionary priest made his fourth vow, committing himself to a lifetime of apostolic service "for the greater glory of God and the good of souls."[3]

In his "Sentiments," when Allouez made the explicit connection between his own spiritual destiny and his work for the salvation of others, he maintained a core Jesuit tradition that had its roots in the foundation and early development of the order. Ignatius of Loyola and his sixteenth-century followers had given the Society of Jesus two interrelated goals: the sanctification and salvation of its own members and the sanctification and salvation of others. Ignatian spirituality idealized service in the name of Christ, coupling imaginative interior spiritual contemplation with inspired action in the world. In contrast to the quiet monastic life of solitude, prayer, and stability, the Jesuit placed limits on the time spent in individual prayer and ascetical effort and ordered his life toward sanctification through apostolic service.[4]

Allouez and his brethren received nourishment for this project from the *Spiritual Exercises* of Ignatius, which formed the foundation for Jesuit spiritual life. Ignatius originally designed the *Exercises* as a guide for directors of intensive spiritual retreats that lasted up to a month, both for members of the order and for the spiritually inclined public. The retreats included careful examination of one's conscience, a series of detailed guided meditations on the life of Christ, and a search for God's will through discernment of the spirits that moved one's soul. The explicit aim was to assist retreatants to overcome their disordered affections and create room for an infusion of God's grace so they could make meaningful and appropriate life decisions—the "election," as Ignatius termed it—within a Christian context. The Jesuits, however, quickly adapted these concepts to a range of situations and activities for guiding people to an interior conversion followed by a commitment to an ordered life of Christian service. The higher aim of the practice, then, was to promote union with God in everyday life.[5]

Entrants into the society made the complete thirty-day exercises two times during their training and preparation and repeated them each year thereafter during a retreat of eight days. The missionaries of New France returned again and again to the spiritual themes and processes inspired by the Ignatian model of discernment. Father Louis André, for example, noted in March 1673 after a long winter in the mission of Saint François Xavier near

Green Bay, that Father Allouez arrived from his own station among the Mesquakie, or Fox, Indians, allowing André to perform the exercises. Thirty years later, Gabriel Marest, then working in the Illinois missions, went into retreat as part of his preparation for a move to a more distant and isolated mission in the northwest.[6]

Even at the end of his life, the Jesuit missionary frequently found inspiration and solace in the *Spiritual Exercises*. Claude Dablon reported that Jacques Marquette prepared for his death in 1675 "by the retreat of st. ignatius, which he performed with every feeling of devotion, and many Celestial Consolations." According to Dablon, in his final days, the suffering Marquette prayed and communed with Christ, the Holy Mother, and all paradise and had his companions read the *Spiritual Exercises* to him every day. Dablon's hagiographic descriptions of the missionary's death reveal his belief that Marquette, through long and difficult service in the missions and rigorous spiritual contemplation and practice, had attained one of the higher levels of prayer, thus achieving the elusive spiritual goal of "uninterrupted union with God." He made Marquette a prime example of someone who had lived the core Jesuit values expressed in the *Exercises* of Ignatius.[7]

Two brief segments of those *Exercises*, the Foundation and the Kingdom, provide essential insight into the central ideas of this spiritual program and the manner in which the concepts could be applied in the everyday life of the missionary. The Foundation, which establishes the basic orientation of the rest of the *Exercises*, declares, "Human beings are created to praise, reverence, and serve God our Lord, and by means of this to save their souls." It directs the retreatant "to desire and elect only the thing which is more conducive to the end for which [one is] created." The Foundation, therefore, forges a connection between the individual and the drama of salvation and prepares the exercitant for the contemplations that serve during the rest of the *Exercises* to confirm the individual's role in that drama as a servant of Christ.

The ideas of the Foundation, by themselves, could easily support an individualistic, interiorized quest for personal spiritual perfection. Ignatius countered this possibility with the reflections contained in the Kingdom, which urges the retreatant to put the ideas of the Foundation into practice, to work toward their fulfillment in the world. The Kingdom asks that the exercitant heed Christ's call "'to conquer the whole world'" and demands that "those who desire to show greater devotion and to distinguish themselves in total service to their eternal King and universal Lord will not only offer their persons for the labor, but . . . will work against their human sensitivities and against their carnal and worldly love." The *Exercises* showed the missionary a path toward eternal union with God that led through unending, disciplined, and rigorous toil in service to Christ's kingdom.[8]

The life of apostolic service celebrated in Jesuit spirituality made the complete abnegation of self the somewhat paradoxical central aim in the construction of a mature missionary identity. Jesuit spiritual ideals called the missionary to detach himself gradually from his own individual concerns and to identify increasingly with Christ and his message of salvation for the world. Ignatius reminded the exercitant "that in all spiritual matters, the more one divests oneself of self-love, self-will, and self-interests, the more progress one will make." In an ongoing process of self-reformation, ascetic struggle, and personal conversion, the Jesuit missionary worked to suppress disordered passions within himself and to thus free his soul for better service to God.[9]

Trends in seventeenth-century French spirituality only reinforced the Jesuit emphasis on the abnegation of self as the key to eventual union with God. Louis Lallemant, who trained a generation of French Jesuits in the seventeenth century, taught that the very quality that defined a human being was a spiritual emptiness, a void that could not be filled by any means other than the grace of God. He argued that only by recognizing this fact and working to move beyond the petty distractions and enticements of the world and toward the disciplined suppression of sin could one find fulfillment in the infinite plenitude of God. In a similar fashion, Pierre de Bérulle, the great reformer of the French secular clergy and a major influence on religious and political life in France, argued in his works that annihilation of self and separation from the world stimulated the conversion that bound one permanently to Christ. Bérulle's own experiences making the *Spiritual Exercises* in 1602, in fact, helped inspire and shape these views on spirituality and salvation.[10]

Allouez's "Sentiments" and Dablon's memorials in the *Jesuit Relations* were representative writings of this French spiritual tradition and the strong missionary fervor it inspired. Allouez tried to apply these guiding principles of Jesuit spirituality—apostolic service and abnegation of self—to his life as a missionary in North America. He wrote that "Old France is good for conceiving fervent desires, New France for executing them" and concluded that missionaries "must be men dead to the world and to themselves, apostolic and saintly men who search only for God and the salvation of souls." Three thoughts consoled him as he contemplated his difficult task: "the first is that I am where God wants me, . . . the second is that the more I suffer, the more

I will be consoled . . . , [and] the third is that one never finds a cross, nails, and thorns where one does not also find Jesus."[11]

It was not enough simply to suffer, however. The ultimate validation of missionary identity came with the conversion of others. The Native peoples among whom Allouez labored became vital participants in the spiritual encounter through which he hoped to find holiness. In a letter written after a painful winter of constant traveling between isolated mission outposts, Allouez praised God, "who gives us all these opportunities and richly recompenses, besides, all these hardships by the consolation that he makes us find, amid the greatest afflictions, in the quest of so many poor Savages' souls." He found joy in the physical and mental hardship he endured, relished the conflicts he initiated with Indian healers, and actively shared in the human suffering he witnessed because each conversion justified his very existence. Allouez explained that the pleasure he experienced from each baptism "surpasses all the joys that one can imagine in this world" and that "one no longer remembers the labors of the past, but would suffer one thousand times more if it was necessary to obtain the salvation of even one more soul."[12]

The conversion of Joseph Nikalokita, an elder of a Mesquakie band living in a village west of Lake Michigan, represented a model of spiritual transformation to Allouez. It is, therefore, a useful example with which to explore the many connections between the process of spiritual transformation he expected to unfold in the missions and Jesuit spirituality in general. Allouez established the mission of Saint Marc among the Mesquakies in April 1670 and traveled there periodically as he made his rounds between the mission stations he served in the Green Bay region. When he arrived for his visit in the late autumn of 1675 to continue his work, the Mesquakies had already left for their winter hunting camps, so he decided to follow them.[13]

Allouez found Joseph Nikalokita, blind and gravely ill, in one of the Mesquakie camps. The missionary explained that he had instructed Nikalokita during previous visits to Saint Marc and revealed that he "admired in him the operations of grace, and was surprised to see the way in which the holy ghost had prepared him for baptism." When Allouez entered the cabin, Nikalokita first made the sign of the cross and demonstrated his knowledge of the Christian mysteries by explaining them to the other Mesquakies present. The missionary gave him further instructions on the incarnation and passion of Christ and then offered the sick man a crucifix. Allouez described Nikalokita's reaction: "He pressed it upon his eyes, and, with a voice Broken by sobs, he cried out many times: 'Son of God, have pity on me; I am dying.

Make me live with you in Heaven!'" Following this emotional plea, Allouez baptized him, and Nikalokita began to speak out against the divinities he had formerly worshipped, declaring that "there is only He who made Heaven, and earth, and all Things; he alone can cure me if he will. I do not Fear death, for I shall live Forever in Heaven with him."

According to Allouez, Nikalokita did not die. "God was pleased to re-store him to health," Allouez said, "[and] to make him the herald of his great-ness." The missionary saw Nikalokita in his village later during the winter and admired his fervor for the Christian faith. Allouez reported that Nikalokita continued to deride the traditional Mesquakie deities. He prayed passionately, especially in using his rosary beads, which he always carried about his neck. When Nikalokita's wife, children, and nephews became ill, many people in the village blamed his beads, but even his family could not separate him from his new religion. Nikalokita responded that he alone re-mained in good health, and he gave credit for his good fortune to the success of his prayers with those beads.[14]

Allouez considered Joseph Nikalokita's spiritual transformation to be a model conversion because it so closely followed the pattern he anticipated as a product and representative of the Jesuit spiritual tradition. Nikalokita's transformation began with a phase of encounter and instruction, followed by an infusion of grace and the action of the Holy Spirit, and was confirmed with baptism, expressions of piety, and public testimony in favor of Christianity. The process of transformation marked out in the *Spiritual Exercises* envisions a similar course of intensive guidance and instruction, the discernment of spir-its and the discovery of God's will, and commitment through a wise election and Christian service. It is imperative that such connections be part of the analysis of conversion narratives in French sources. Although Joseph Nikalok-ita's perspective on his spiritual transformation likely differed from Allouez's, careful analysis of the assumptions contained in Allouez's text opens the way to a better understanding of that perspective.[15]

The first encounter between the missionary and the nonbeliever initiated the process of conversion. Allouez and other Jesuits recognized that the mis-sionary's own living example could be a crucial factor in his influence on others. He listed the qualities he believed the missionary must possess to en-sure any chance of success: "graciousness and affability, humility and abne-gation of self, force and patience, and a charity and magnanimity of heroic dimensions." It is no coincidence that these were the same qualities that advanced the Jesuit's own personal quest for salvation. Allouez's superior in

1683 described a winter of hunger and hard travel that Allouez spent among the Miamis and explained that "these fatigues, which showed them How much the father loved them, were a powerful inducement to make them Believe." Allouez made force the counterpoint to the virtue of patience in his list because he also found that dramatic actions, such as interfering with a healing ceremony or destroying a Native holy site, could have a particularly strong impact. The successful missionary could not often display weakness.[16]

Once he had earned a certain amount of respect from his patient, deliberate, and frequently provocative actions, Allouez counted on words to move the souls of the people who agreed to hear him. Discourse—in public preaching, in teaching catechism, and in devout conversation—had been a major aspect of the Jesuit ministry from the inception of the order. Allouez, of course, accepted every opportunity to speak publicly in Native villages, but he found that private conversations were particularly effective, even necessary, for a successful conversion. The ability to translate not just words and concepts but also emotions became a critical instrument for inducing the change of heart that constituted for the Jesuits an authentic conversion. It was through such private conversation, for example, that Allouez confirmed Joseph Nikalokita's sincerity and made final preparations for his acceptance of the sacrament of baptism.[17]

Although Allouez placed great value on conversation in conducting his missions, he also believed that all conversions required clear evidence of grace. His words prepared the potential convert's soul for the effective presence of the Holy Spirit. Joseph Nikalokita's conversion certainly demonstrates this concept, as does the story of another Mesquakie convert. According to Allouez, a Mesquakie captain, also named Joseph, was in imminent danger of death but could not confront his mortality and would only pray for his present life. Allouez consoled him through conversation for two hours before convincing him to accept the will of God. "Nothing touched Him so much as The example of Our lord, when I told Him of His agony," Allouez wrote. "He yielded then, and, in spite of The Suffering of a Long illness, I saw a marked Change effected by grace in his soul." As if he were directing a much compressed version of the *Spiritual Exercises*, Allouez asked the man to meditate on Christ's passion, to feel the movement of spirits within his soul, and to accept the consolation of the Holy Spirit and submit to the will of God. Only when satisfied that such a transformation had occurred would Allouez consent to baptize an adult, unless he was certain the person would die without the rite. The prayer book attributed to Father Allouez in fact contained a condensed set of instructions to be shared with dying Indians prior to baptism.[18]

Although the sacrament of baptism signified the new Christian status of the convert, it did not end the process of conversion. Jesuit spirituality insisted that converts seal their commitment through self-reformation. The battle over behavior was less a project to make the Indians French than a plan for making all action conform to God's will. Allouez believed that indigenous ceremonialism and polygamy should cease, yet he searched for ways to harmonize other Native customs with Christian standards. He tried to replace traditional Native fasts with Christian ones, for example, calling "it a duty to sanctify their very superstitions, and to make of a Guilty fast a meritorious one."[19]

Spiritual concerns, as well as the inability of missionaries to enforce major changes, formed the context for such Jesuit relativism. The civilizing mission proved secondary to the much more significant spiritual project of achieving salvation. For Allouez and the other Jesuits, disordered lives perpetuated suffering and exposed the individual to diabolical influences. Reformation of self confirmed the conversion, reduced disorder in individuals and communities, and encouraged the disciplined avoidance of sin. Pious behavior opened the individual to the action of the Holy Spirit and, in turn, inspired further expressions of piety. In the process of conversion, interior renewal and exterior action reinforced each other. Jesuit plans for reform generally looked only to remove serious obstacles to grace, and not to entirely transform Native communities and individuals.

An emphasis by many scholars on Jesuit programs of social reconstruction reflects a focus on the missions and methods of the first half of the seventeenth century and, sometimes, a refusal to take seriously the spiritual work the missionaries hoped to perform. The Jesuits learned many lessons from their labors in the 1640s at the Sillery reduction and in their Wendat missions, and these experiences induced them to modify their conversion strategy. The Jesuits replaced a plan that required an almost total transformation of Native peoples with a more flexible model that utilized both reductions and missions in Indian villages and that was significantly more tolerant of indigenous traditions. What did not change in this transition, however, was the overriding importance of the reconstruction of the soul in the quest for eternal salvation: transform the soul, transform the person.[20]

Allouez pushed his neophytes to strive for the highest ideals in their projects of self-reformation, to seek spiritual perfection within the context of an accessible Native Christianity. When Joseph Nikalokita spoke publicly in favor of Christianity, prayed fervently with his rosary beads, and rejected the complaints of his own family, Allouez believed the convert was making spiritual progress. A good Christian death offered the ultimate example of these higher ideals, for it implied the abnegation of self through total acceptance of God's will. Nikalokita recovered from his terrible illness to live, at least for a while, according to Allouez, a life of Christian service. Joseph, the other Mesquakie convert, did not. He impressed Allouez, however, with the depth of his apparent spiritual transformation. "He took The Crucifix," Allouez wrote, "and Himself said his prayer, like that of our lord, with perfect submission and Christian indifference to life and death."[21]

In overseeing such a death, Allouez fulfilled his own spiritual goal to spend himself utterly in service to Christ. In his "Sentiments," he reflected, "They say that the founders of churches are ordinarily saints. This thought truly touches my heart and, although I am good for nothing, I want to consume myself more and more for the salvation of souls." When he died in 1689 in the mission to the Miamis, Claude Dablon, at least, believed he had done so, writing that "from his arrival in Canada until his death, he was intrepid in the face of danger and indefatigable in his work for the conversion of souls." Dablon generously credited Allouez with the evangelization of twenty-three Native nations, the instruction of more than 100,000 individuals, and the baptism of over 10,000 people, most of whom died soon after the rite. Although Dablon's account was surely an exaggeration, Allouez, Marquette, Dablon, and other Jesuit missionaries nonetheless thought they had discovered in the French-Indian religious frontier an ideal place for the pursuit of their own salvation.[22]

*   *   *

In his long and difficult years of labor with the Native nations of the Great Lakes, Allouez searched constantly for ways to connect with the people he encountered. His use of words and gifts, his performance of Catholic rituals and demonstrations of moral judgment, and his attempts to translate abstract theological concepts into a culturally relevant form forged those links, even while generating persistently ambiguous results and many opportunities for Native self-expression in the complex process of conversion. Allouez passed his first winter in the upper Great Lakes, from 1665 to 1666, at the large international community at Chequamegon Bay on the southern shore of Lake

Superior. He dedicated his mission to the Holy Spirit, naming it Saint Esprit, and spent the cold winter days and nights visiting the villages of various nations to proclaim the gospel. There, Allouez met some members of the Illinois confederacy who had traveled from their country in the river valleys and prairies south of Lake Michigan. The enthusiastic missionary reported "that this Mission is the one where I have labored the least and accomplished the most. They honor our Lord among themselves in their own way, putting his Image, which I have given them, in the most honored place on the occasion of any important feast, while the Master of the banquet addresses it as follows: 'In thy honor, O Man-God, do we hold this feast; to thee do we offer these viands.'" Allouez thought the Illinois were potentially "the fairest field for the Gospel," and he wished that he had the time to visit their villages. In the meantime, eighty Illinois returned home with news of their brief encounter with the black-robed priest and his teachings.[23]

The inclusion of an image of Jesus Christ in Illinois feasts during these initial contacts represented a crucial convergence of two very different worldviews and spiritual traditions, a point of exchange that produced opportunities for dynamic cross-cultural dialogue and negotiation much like the development of the language material. The imagery and ritual of the feasts were flexible cultural symbols open to a variety of interpretations. Allouez understood at least in a general way the nature of Illinois spirituality and, more broadly, the spiritual practices of other Algonquian-speaking peoples. The Illinois maintained reciprocal relationships with the spirits or manitous who populated their country, offering them gifts in return for power, protection, and the necessities of life. Allouez knew very well that the Illinois could not fully comprehend the significance of their inclusiveness from his Christian perspective. He admitted that they paid tribute to Jesus "in their own way." Nonetheless, he welcomed the opportunity to establish the cultural connections and personal bonds that might eventually grow into something more traditionally Christian. Allouez prayed that the Illinois interest in the simple image of Jesus suggested the initial operation of grace in their souls that would, over time, lead to their definitive conversion to the faith. As he put it, "The seeds of the faith which I have sown in their souls will bear fruit when it pleases the master of the vine to gather it."[24]

For their part, the Illinois respectfully greeted a man who possibly possessed great spiritual power. They explored the potential of Jesus Christ to bring abundance and success to a people troubled by violent conflicts with the Iroquois to the east and several Indian nations living west of the Mississippi.

If their experiments went well, then perhaps they would invite the priests to their country. If they treated the French with warm hospitality, they might attract French traders with useful and powerful goods. Not surprisingly, even while the Illinois and other Native peoples recognized the missionaries and their teachings as something new, they also initially interpreted them from within a familiar cultural context.[25]

This intersection of Christian symbolism and Native spiritual practice marked only the starting point for a complex process of encounter, engagement, and transformation that resulted in the conversion of many Native individuals and the establishment of numerous Christian Indian communities throughout the region. Although joyful missionaries and Native converts recognized significant events and dramatic turning points in personal lives and communal histories, they also viewed conversion and change as a part of a much longer series of interactions that played out over years, decades, and generations and that affected different people in different ways. The variable process of conversion rarely concluded with a stable synthesis or clear endpoint. Religious encounters created enough space for people to shape Christianity to fulfill their own needs and desires, spiritual and otherwise.

Many Native communities tested the power of Jesus Christ in this period. Around 1673, near the Jesuit mission of Saint François Xavier on Green Bay, a prominent Sauk man frankly explained to Jesuit missionary Louis André this openness to experimentation. "We care very little," he said, "whether it be the devil or God who gives us food. We dream sometimes of one Thing, sometimes of another; and, whatever may appear to us in our sleep, we believe that it is The manitou in whose honor the feast must be given, for he gives us food; he makes us successful in fishing, Hunting, and all our undertakings." The Sauks and others waited to see how Jesus would provide.

André related that the nearby Menominees were waiting for the sturgeon to run and had placed a picture of the sun at the top of a pole as an offering to the master of life. The fish failed to appear, however, and the Menominees became fearful. André asked if he could replace the sun with a crucifix, and they consented. The missionary reported happily that the fish arrived the next day, which prompted one person to say to André that "now we see very well that the Spirit who has made all is the one who feeds us. Take courage; teach us to pray, so that we may never feel hunger." The Menominees, especially women, soon became more interested in Christian instruction. Some people stopped conducting fasts and other rituals, or at least they kept them out of the missionary's sight. Despite these encouraging signs, André only baptized a few children and two sick adults because he wanted to see further evidence of Menominee resolve and sincerity.[26]

Another missionary, Jean de Lamberville, observed that "all these tribes, who are chiefly guided by The senses, needed that God should instruct Them in a sensible manner,—not only by The preaching of the missionaries, but also by The sight of some effect beyond the usual course of nature. The truths of The Gospel would have been too weak had they rested solely . . . on reason and common sense." He noted "that all Their reasoning does not go beyond what relates to The health of Their bodies, The success of Their Hunting and fishing, and good fortune in trade and in war." Despite Lamberville's negative characterization of Native abstract reasoning abilities, his statements contained two important insights. First, the missionaries believed that their instructions alone were insufficient for conversion. God had to intervene and touch the potential neophytes in some way. Second, he correctly identified the crucial connection between Native religious practice and the concerns of daily life. Lamberville recounted in detail several instances at the mission of Sainte Marie du Sault in which God seemed to shield warriors from harm, heal the hopelessly sick, provide food for the hungry, and protect Christians from the disease and general misfortune that affected others. He reported that these holy signs contributed to more than one hundred baptisms at the mission during 1673, many of them adults who had to meet the most stringent requirements before undergoing the ritual.[27]

The quest for power and grace yielded the cultural intersection linking the experiences of Indians and missionaries in these episodes. The Christian concept of grace and Native notions of power overlapped. For the missionaries, grace was the unmerited supernatural gift of God graciously granted for the purpose of achieving the eternal salvation of the recipient. In this "economy of love," the Holy Trinity mercifully favored mankind and called for the free response of the recipient through faith, hope, and charity. In the worldviews of Algonquian-speaking peoples, power was the transformative essence in the universe, manifest in the land, in persons, and in certain cycles and connections.

Closely related to this idea of power was the concept of person. The category of person included both human and other-than-human beings who collected, manipulated, shared, and lost power through their actions. Algonquian-speaking peoples stressed personal causation through the application of varying degrees of power over the influence of impersonal natural forces. Thus, maintaining positive reciprocal relations with human and especially with

potent other-than-human persons was a major concern of daily life, influencing success or failure in everything from subsistence and healing to trade,
warfare, and social life. The concepts of power and person overlapped in the
term *manitou*. Native people could perceive the Christian God and holy beings as manitous with strong wills, potentially beneficial powers, and specific
demands for reciprocal relationships that promised success and good fortune
in this life and the next.[28]

The Jesuits carefully documented Native spiritual beliefs and practices so
they could effectively exploit these connections while suppressing those aspects that seemed incompatible with Christianity. Missionaries like Allouez
and Claude Dablon described the spirits of the animals who provided and
withheld game according to the actions of hunters, and they explained the
process of fasting, dreaming, and reflection through which Native individuals
established a relationship with a manitou and accumulated personal power.
Jesuit ethnographers delineated the links between these concepts and Native
healing practices, and they chronicled the feasts and rituals that helped maintain the reciprocal balance between human and other-than-human persons.

The missionaries experienced some tension between two opposing perspectives on the Indian spirituality they observed. On the one hand, they
complained that the belief in personal divinities typified, as Dablon put it,
"the most detestable of all the customs existing among the Savages." While
the Jesuits frequently dismissed Native religion as merely superstitious, they
also sometimes suspected diabolical influences. On the other hand, missionaries recognized how difficult it would be to undermine religious practices so
deeply embedded in everyday life and experience. Rather than mount a comprehensive direct assault on Indian religious customs, they instead worked to
replace the indigenous idea of power with the Christian concept of grace. The
Jesuits saw evangelical opportunity in the "false Gods and . . . superstitious
customs" they detested.[29]

Marquette described this approach while working at Saint Esprit in 1669
and 1670. He accepted the Native practice of offering sacrifices at each feast,
but he reported that "the Christians have now changed their methods of
procedure; and in order to effect this change the more easily, I keep a little of
their usage, and take from it all that is bad." When Christians made speeches
at the beginning of feasts and requested good health and prosperity, Marquette had them address themselves to God instead of to traditional manitous. Marquette believed that God responded to this simple but important
shift, for all but two of the Christians had maintained their health over the

winter. The two exceptions, Marquette lamented, were children hidden away from him and taken to a local healer. He finally discovered them and administered the sacrament of baptism shortly before they died.[30]

At the conceptual intersection of power and grace, illness became a prominent path to conversion. Illness and healing revealed the efficacy of Christian grace in terms Indians could easily comprehend and assimilate without entirely rejecting Native understandings of power and its operation in the world. Joseph Nikalokita, Allouez's model convert, and numerous others first turned toward Christianity in their search for relief from disease and suffering. Allouez and his companions were pleased and prepared when people called for their services during illness, and the graver they found the situation, the greater they felt the opportunities for successfully saving the patient's soul.

At his mission of Saint Jacques to the Mascoutens and Miamis southwest of Green Bay, Allouez urged a woman with horrible facial abscesses to pray and make the sign of the cross. The next day, she arrived at the chapel healed and with a gift of corn. Allouez also worked with a Mascouten man who refused to eat because he claimed to be already among the dead. The man was indeed quite ill, so Allouez seized the chance to instruct him. Allouez believed that God had moved the man to reflect on the end of his life in order to prepare him for the grace of baptism. Throughout his instruction, the man asked Allouez to baptize him, even accusing the missionary of not loving him when the rite was delayed. Finally, after several days of instruction, Allouez granted the man's wish. In the days after the ceremony, Allouez "recommended that He should make various acts of faith, hope, and Charity." He reported that the man stroked Allouez's crucifix, saying, "Jesus, God-man, I love you; if you restore me to life, I shall love you as long as I shall live on earth; and if I die I shall love you forever in Heaven. Have pity on me." According to Allouez, the man died in the same sentiment some weeks later, representing in the missionary's view another fortunate conversion and good death.[31]

Even such failure in the healing enterprise and the resulting death of the patient could fit the pattern that made the spiritual encounter work. First, there was no contradiction in Christian thought between death and the receipt of God's unmerited gift of grace. The Jesuits taught that God's will was mysterious and must be accepted with holy indifference and resignation. And in the Native economy of power, great variability existed in access to power and in the ability to manipulate it successfully. Furthermore, Indians recognized a need for scrupulous behavior in daily life and for precise action in ritual to maintain balanced spiritual relationships and potent personal power. The Jesuits similarly emphasized the importance of pious and disciplined conduct in preparing oneself to respond to God's gift of grace. Death could suggest many things, but it did not necessarily weaken either spiritual system, nor did it preclude effective exchange between them.

The mutual concern with the potential link between behavioral transgressions and death or other more mundane personal and communal setbacks created yet another possibility for cultural conversation between missionaries and Indians. Observers have for a long time argued that ornate Catholic rituals played an important role in attracting American Indians to Christianity, especially when compared to the plainer style of Protestant rites. However, for the Algonquian-speaking peoples of the Great Lakes region, and perhaps for many other Native peoples of North America, Catholic ritual created an affinity for Christianity not because it dazzled them or because they had some natural appreciation for pageantry. Catholic ritual worked, at least initially, because it made sense in Native terms.

Catholic missionaries understood the potential appeal of the sacraments as performances and believed that ritual could lead the participant toward the faith in God and Christ that was essential for salvation. Ritual, prayer, and contemplation in the Jesuit spiritual tradition promoted union with God and prepared one for holy action in the world, which in turn strengthened the believer's faith. An inner state of spiritual order became the primary goal. Native religious traditions, in contrast, stressed performance and behavior over thought and belief, the exterior social order over interior disposition. In traditional spiritual practice, ritual expression itself was the vital action that released the transformative power contained in ritual knowledge and in relationships with the manitous. Ritual action helped maintain balance and order in the world.

The ideal of reciprocity was central to this Native religious culture and, more broadly, to overall social organization. Powerful persons, human and other-than-human, displayed generosity and hospitality by using their abilities to benefit others. Sharing and gift giving activated the bonds of kinship between persons and ensured access to the power that made life possible. Morality in Algonquian-speaking communities was, therefore, situational and preeminently social, defining personal responsibility toward others and encouraging community integration. Ritual expressed these moral values of cooperation, exchange, and good conduct.

For Christian missionaries, on the other hand, morality involved a more individualistic perspective that made fundamental distinctions between good and evil. Immoral or sinful thoughts and behavior weakened the personal spiritual connection to God and threatened one's place in the transcendent spiritual community of the church. The conceptual challenge for missionaries was not in defining sin as a transgression of standards, but rather in promoting an asocial, nonreciprocal notion of sin and evil. The Jesuits handled this problem by attempting to redirect ritual relationships in Native religious practices to a relationship with the Christian God and a pious disposition toward others in the community. They wanted Christian Indians who acted immorally to fear not only social ostracism and the loss of personal power but also the punishment of the Lord and the pain of eternal damnation.[32]

When Allouez described the seemingly positive reactions of the Illinois at Saint Esprit to his initial instructions, he concluded, "All the nations of the South have this same wish to see God, which, without doubt, greatly facilitates their conversion; for it only remains to teach them how they must serve him in order to see him and be blessed." Allouez and the other Jesuits, indeed, recognized that the ideal of service, of a reciprocal relationship with God, would be a critical component of successful conversions. The holy relationship offered access to what the missionaries claimed was the unlimited spiritual power of saving grace in return for personal prayer, pious behavior, and participation in the sacraments.[33]

Overlapping cultural concepts in part explain the course of Joseph Nikalokita's conversion. In this case, God healed the gravely ill Nikalokita, establishing the foundation for a reciprocal relationship. Nikalokita responded thankfully to this expression of God's power by continued Christian practice, in particular through ritual reliance on his rosary beads. His behavior, pious in Allouez's view but perhaps somewhat more practical from Nikalokita's own perspective, allowed him to see God and receive his blessing. There is evidence, however, of a deeper transformation in Nikalokita's experience. His willingness to defy family and community when others became sick and blamed his Christian objects suggests a stronger and more profound cultural and social reorientation that represented the emergence of a new self-definition rooted at least in part in his practice of Christianity.

Many Indians who accepted some form of Christianity, either as individuals or as groups, subsequently displayed dramatic cultural nonconformity and social separation. This common behavior for converts strongly suggests that Christianity became an important element in the development of new forms of identity. In the unpublished *Jesuit Relation* for 1672–73, Jean de Lamberville reported that a woman who had previously resided at the Ursuline convent in Québec refused to attend traditional feasts and dances and had finally withdrawn from her village to live in solitude in the woods with only a six-year-old girl for a companion. In her cabin near the Jesuit mission of Les Apostres on the north shore of Lake Huron, she welcomed other women and girls for instruction and prayer. Lamberville observed that "she knows so well how to regulate her conduct that The Most slanderous Tongues, far from finding fault with what she does, render her the homage that she does honor to prayer. She receives more visits from all, in her retreat, than if she were in The village; and it seems to have been God's will to reward Her, even in this world, by abundantly requiting Her for what she has abandoned for love of him." He gave as an example of her disciplined piety an episode in which the woman refused to make an exchange with another woman because she feared that traditional dreaming practices had inspired the proposed trade.[34]

A few years later, a woman, possibly the same one, still lived near the chapel and continued to introduce women and girls to Christianity. One Jesuit missionary reported that she ordered her life so well that even non-Christian Indians respected her. This anonymous Christian woman appears to have been socially isolated but also potentially powerful. Her Ursuline education in Québec and time away from her people may have left her outside existing social networks, between contrasting cultures. Her uncertain social status and association with Christianity caused people in the surrounding community to be cautiously respectful and possibly even to fear her. The women and girls she led to the chapel perhaps hoped to determine this woman's true status and power and discover whether Christianity and the missionaries offered anything for them. In any case, the woman made a significant decision to attach herself to the Jesuits and the Christian Indian community in the region. Her physical separation from her Native community, avoidance of traditional social obligations, and proselytization of others imply the emergence of a new identity, stimulated at least in part through engagement with Christianity.[35]

Many others also experimented with Christianity, often during illnesses and other crises, although not always with the same apparent intensity as the woman at Les Apostres. These encounters frequently turned Jesuit missionaries into ritual healers and purveyors of power in Native terms. The missionaries believed they were preparing souls for the operation of God's saving grace as they advanced in their own personal spiritual journeys, but Indians discovered additional or alternative sources of power to address the challenges of living in a dangerous and quickly changing world. These corresponding concepts of grace and power, sufficiently flexible to contain a range of meanings, made this cultural exchange possible. The potent concepts became the starting point for cultural innovation and social change. Assimilating Jesus as a powerful manitou did not necessarily represent the end of the process of engagement and conversion. For some Native people, investigation of Christian spirituality and experimentation with the rituals that supported a relationship with Jesus Christ formed the foundation for further exploration and became the basis for personal and communal transformations. In their struggles to find solutions to many kinds of problems, some Indian people in the Great Lakes and Illinois country used Christianity to reinterpret the world and their position in it.

*   *   *

The Ottawas, the Kiskakons in particular, were a prime example of a people who experimented with Christianity in a conscious effort at cultural revitalization. In the early seventeenth century, when they first encountered the French, the major Ottawa bands resided on the Bruce Peninsula south of Georgian Bay and on Manitoulin Island in Lake Huron. The Kiskakons left their homeland in the east in the 1650s to escape the savage warfare that plagued the lower Great Lakes and Saint Lawrence valley. The Kiskakon Ottawas moved several times over subsequent decades in a search for order that never really came to an end. Throughout these migrations, they maintained regular contact with the French, enhancing their reputation as astute diplomats and traders in the Great Lakes and demonstrating their influence across the region. Jesuit missionaries followed the Kiskakons through many of the moves, hoping that they might finally discover a way to bring the influential Ottawa nation into the church. In 1660, as the Society of Jesus started to rebuild and expand its mission empire, the Jesuit missionary René Ménard found a group of Kiskakons at Keweenaw Bay. A few years later, Claude Allouez worked with Ottawas at the mixed Indian community at Saint Esprit.[36]

Nevertheless, although missionaries secured occasional isolated Ottawa converts, most Ottawas remained reluctant to accept Christianity and seemed much more interested in finding safe and stable places to live and in retaining a central position in regional alliances and trade networks. The Ottawas tolerated the Jesuits, even occasionally allowing them to travel in their trading fleets between the Great Lakes and the Saint Lawrence valley, but they resisted missionary teachings, finding them largely irrelevant to their situation. A frustrated Allouez complained that only a few women and children practiced Christianity in any form. In the summer of 1668, however, in a dramatic turnaround that surprised even the most optimistic missionaries, the most populous and prominent Ottawa band, the Kiskakons, made a communal decision to embrace Christianity. This extraordinary action demonstrated cultural creativity in the continuing process of Ottawa adaptation to the new worlds of encounter and change in the seventeenth century. After many years of rejecting Christianity, or at least of viewing it from a distance, the Kiskakons opted for active engagement with new religious practices and ideas. In their search for order, the Kiskakon Ottawas made Christianity a force for community renewal.[37]

Several years before the Kiskakon conversion, a few Ottawa pioneers initiated the process of cultural exploration that familiarized the Ottawas with Christianity and demonstrated its potential spiritual and social power. The actions and experiences of these forerunners show evidence of deep personal engagement with Christianity as well as the emergence of new interpretations of the world. Witnesses reported that René Ménard gathered some of the earliest significant converts during his first winter with the Ottawas, but not without considerable difficulty. The Ottawas did not welcome Ménard, and the first converts often faced the contempt of their families and peers. Ménard had to baptize dying children by stealth because the Ottawas hid their sick children, fearing like the Hurons that it killed them. He managed eventually to convince two old men to convert, both just before they died, but the Ottawas mocked one of the men when he publicly professed his new faith. Like many of his colleagues who followed him into the region, Ménard discovered that women sometimes developed a keen interest in Christianity. A widow christened Anne at her baptism became one of his prized converts when she decided not to remarry and to remain chaste for the rest of her life. One Jesuit recorded joyfully that "alone and on her knees, while all the family are indulging in filthy conversation, she says her prayers, continuing this

Holy exercise of devotion to the admiration of our Frenchmen, who have found her in later years as fervent as on the first day."[38]

Ménard's most prominent convert was a young man about thirty years old who took the name Louis at his baptism. Reportedly from an important family, Louis refused to meet his traditional social obligations and instead made Christianity a central focus of his life. Several times Louis had approached Ménard about baptism, but the missionary feared that his unmarried status made him too unsettled to be a devout Christian. After several conversations, Louis convinced Ménard of his sincerity, promising never to marry unless he found a chaste woman who could live the kind of Christian life he planned for himself. The conversion of a prominent community member created disruptions and conflicts. In one case, according to Ménard, Louis did not participate in a healing ceremony for a very sick man despite the pleas of his own relatives. Louis's family scolded him for his defiance, and others laughed when he tried to pray. "As he is alone in this kind of life," Ménard wrote, "he is obliged to endure a thousand insults on all sides."

Louis did not remain alone in his convictions for long. His elder sister, a widow with five children, soon joined the small church. Her oldest child had suffered for months from an illness that "hindered her in speaking, and choked her voice." Louis's sister carried her daughter to Ménard to see what the missionary could do for her. Ménard taught the girl to pray and had her bled. Surprisingly, she seemed to get some relief from the procedure, and she regained her voice. The thankful mother then brought her entire family to the chapel for prayer. After the requisite instruction and a sufficient trial of their piety, Ménard baptized the family members, naming the mother Plathéhaha-mie. The woman rewarded Ménard by contributing toward his subsistence.[39]

A decade later, in November 1671, another missionary encountered Louis with some Ottawas on Manitoulin Island. Henri Nouvel called Louis "the miracle of this part of Christendom; for it is no small wonder to see a barbarian who for several years has stood firm in his resolve to spend the remainder of his days in Celibacy,—his sole object being to render himself more acceptable to God by this mode of life, which is unheard-of among the Savages." Nouvel gave Louis holy communion, noting that he had received the sacrament of confirmation from the bishop, François de Laval.[40]

In the ten years since Ménard had supervised the first conversions, much had changed for both the missionaries and the Ottawas. Louis, Anne, and a few others introduced Christianity to their families and communities, and many people started to perceive Christianity as a potentially powerful set of spiritual concepts and practices. By then, Christian Ottawas also did not always have to fear shame and ridicule, and they sometimes even earned respect. Nouvel observed, for example, that the young Ottawas on Manitoulin Island respected Louis, perhaps for his Christianity or perhaps for his spiritually potent celibacy. The Jesuits continued to meet resistance in some quarters, but they also found a greater number of people receptive to their teachings. In the 1660s, they managed to build a small corps of devoted Christians among the Ottawas and other neighboring nations. This slow and laborious process of mutual discovery climaxed with the spectacular conversion of the Kiskakon Ottawas in the summer and fall of 1668. It was a turning point for the Ottawas and the Jesuits.[41]

Allouez proudly described the remarkable episode in the *Jesuit Relation* for 1668–69. Ménard worked with the Ottawas in the early 1660s and Allouez had been with them since 1665, but as a group the Ottawas continued to avoid making any definitive commitments to the missionaries. Determined to provoke a confrontation, Allouez finally spoke at a Kiskakon council and threatened to leave Saint Esprit because the Ottawas had shown so little interest in Christianity. To dramatize his seriousness, he claimed that he even slipped his shoes off to shake away the dust, for he planned to take nothing but himself when he left the Kiskakons behind. With this action, Allouez recalled the instructions of Jesus to his apostles to shake the dust from their shoes as a testament against communities that refused to receive them and hear his teachings of salvation.[42]

Allouez believed his argument had a strong effect. He wrote, "During all this address I read, on their faces, the fear that I had inspired in their hearts; leaving them then to deliberate, I immediately withdrew, with the intention of going away to the Sault." "But an accident having detained me," he continued, "by a special providence of God, I was soon a witness to a change on their part that can only be attributed to an extraordinary stroke of grace." Some elders stood to speak in favor of Christianity and the continued presence of the Jesuits. "By common consent," Allouez recorded triumphantly, "they abolished Polygamy entirely; they did away with the sacrifices that they had been accustomed to offer to their genii; they refused to be present at any of the superstitious ceremonies observed by the other nations in the vicinity; in a word, they showed a fervor like that of the Christians of the primitive Church, and a very great assiduity in all the duties of true Believers." "They all took up their abode near the Chapel," he recorded, "in order to facilitate for their wives and children, during the Winter, the instruction that is given them, and in order not to let slip a single day without coming to pray to God in the Church."[43]

In his narrative of the communal conversion, Allouez emphasized his own influence, although he gave ultimate credit for the transformation to the grace of God. The Kiskakons, however, had their own reasons for deciding to align themselves with the Jesuits and to begin a more intensive exploration of Christianity. Ottawa actions and statements recorded in the accounts of Allouez and other Jesuits show that a variety of perspectives contributed to the decision to Christianize the community. Individual experiences and group responses varied greatly, revealing different levels of cultural engagement and different degrees of personal transformation. The goal that held the community together despite these divergent experiences was the communal quest for stability, strength, and order.

The surprising decision compelled Allouez to remain at Saint Esprit through a fourth autumn and winter to instruct the Kiskakons and prepare them for baptism. He baptized about one hundred people, including at least some of the principal Kiskakon men and other adults. Allouez then moved on to Green Bay to extend his mission to other, more distant nations. Jacques Marquette arrived during the autumn corn harvest in September 1669 to replace him and to continue the work of conversion at Saint Esprit. Marquette felt that the community welcomed him, and he was quite pleased with the situation, finding that many people displayed a great fondness for learning and prayer. He baptized the newborn children and visited with elders to learn about the community and to share his plans. The Kiskakons demonstrated in several ways their intention to listen to the Jesuit. They moved to be near the chapel as Marquette requested, and a prominent man pulled down a dog sacrifice when Marquette said it was not proper behavior for Christians.[44]

Marquette told the Kiskakons that because of their faith "they should never be forsaken, but cherished more warmly than all the other nations; and that they had only one common interest with the French." He believed the Kiskakons had already gained a more prominent position in the evolving political landscape than other Ottawa bands and nearby Indian nations. The Kiskakons responded well to such talk of strong alliances with the French. Close connections strengthened their military position during times of conflict and encouraged preferential treatment in trading relationships. The Jesuits provided guidance and acted as brokers between the Kiskakons and the French. Around 1672, just after Marquette opened the mission of Saint Ignace at Michilimackinac, the Kiskakons moved to the mission of Sainte

Marie du Sault. In 1676, they relocated again, settling near the Saint Ignace mission and the Michilimackinac post that quickly became the nexus of the vast French-Indian trade network linking the Saint Lawrence valley to the upper Great Lakes and regions beyond. Even non-Christians among the Ottawas recognized the importance of Christianity in this relationship. According to a Jesuit observer, one person wondered aloud why the community bothered to erect a cross in the middle of the village. An Ottawa leader who had still not formally converted replied, "One might as well ask . . . of what use is prayer to us? of what use are the black gowns to us? of what use are the french, and all the comforts and advantages that we have received with prayer?"[45]

Kiskakon leaders also believed that Christianity could contribute to the maintenance of good order in the community. Frequent relocation, the increasing French presence in the western Great Lakes, and the intermingling of peoples in the multitribal villages of the region created a host of disruptions. While the examples of early Native converts like Anne and Louis showed that Christianity could disrupt families and communities, the converts also demonstrated the role that the new religion could play in regulating personal conduct in the difficult social environment. Marquette explained that "the elders told me that the young people had not yet any sense, and that I must check them in their dissolute conduct." Marquette himself was particularly concerned about the social challenges girls faced, and he spoke often to men about the behavior of their daughters. He believed that Christian women possessed the discipline necessary to maintain a modest character. By the late 1670s, the Jesuits had baptized most of the Kiskakon leaders and older people. These leaders often exhorted the young people to practice Christianity and self-restraint. The influential Joseph Chikabiskisi assembled the older Christians after having confessed in preparation for his first communion at Easter. He provided gifts of French tobacco and told everyone to confess and to urge others to do so because "it was the best method of establishing good order among them."[46]

The spiritual dimension of Christianity also offered reasons to convert. Several men appeared to view their conversions as an expansion or enlargement of Ottawa religious practices. Dreams, visions, and traditional notions of spiritual power and reciprocity continued to be an important way for people to approach Christianity. Allouez, for example, reported that one old man had a vision after his baptism in which he saw two roads, one very narrow and difficult leading upward and one very wide and easy leading downward. The man explained to Allouez that he had chosen the former, more challenging but potentially rewarding road. Another man, about sixty years old and named Joseph at his baptism, claimed that he had always worshipped a supreme being. He recommitted himself to this worship with his formal conversion to Christianity. Allouez related the story of still another Ottawa man, who believed that God had saved him when he was trapped on an ice floe on Lake Huron for thirty days. When he heard Allouez speak, he recognized that God was the powerful spirit who had sustained him during the trial.[47]

Other Ottawas made the connection to Christianity through myth. Marquette was instructing Kiskakon elders about the creation and other Old Testament narratives when he discovered that they had a tradition of something resembling the Tower of Babel. The Kiskakons told Marquette that their old men related a story about a large house that was built and then thrown down by a strong wind. Marquette noted that such associations made his own tales seem more credible to them.[48]

Through the 1670s, the Kiskakons developed a strong identity as Christian Ottawas, coming to call themselves "those who pray." By 1677, the Jesuits had opened a separate chapel for them, dedicated to Saint François de Borgia, not far from the mission of Saint Ignace and the settlement of Michilimackinac. The small mission was hardly large enough for the 1,300 Ottawas congregated in the village, and it received constant use, especially from young boys and girls. "This fervor was not equal in every case," missionary Jean Enjalran admitted, "and did not proceed, perhaps, in all from a will disposed to embrace our holy faith, but the example of some attracted others; and God will know how to draw from it in his own time, the good which he intends therein." Baptism of children became common, and several adults chose to undergo the rite each year. The Kiskakons continued to explore the power of other Catholic rituals as well. The Jesuits made the celebration of mass the ritual highpoint of each week. In Ottawa terms, according to Enjalran, the mass became "an Instrument for doing honor to the great spirit." The Kiskakons also regularly participated in processions and exchanged feasts on important Catholic festivals with the Christian Tionontatis and Wendats who worshipped at Saint Ignace. Eventually, the growing political, trade, fishing, and religious center at the Straits of Mackinac attracted other Ottawa bands from Manitoulin Island, who then joined the cultural and economic exchanges occurring there.[49]

A supreme example of the expression of this evolving Christian identity was the respect the Ottawas showed for their former missionary Jacques

Marquette after his death on the eastern shore of Lake Michigan in 1675. Some of the Kiskakons spent the winter of 1676–77 hunting in the vicinity of Lake Michigan. On their return to Michilimackinac, they stopped at the place where Marquette had died and uncovered his body. In an act that recalled the mortuary customs of the Wendat and Algonquian Feasts of the Dead, the Kiskakons "cleansed the bones and exposed them to the sun to dry; then, carefully laying them in a box of birch-bark, they set out to bring them to [the] mission of st. ignace." The Indians and the French of Michilimackinac greeted the funeral procession of thirty canoes as it approached the post. The Kiskakons and some Tionontatis carried the box into the church at Saint Ignace, where the remains lay exposed for a day before being lowered into a small vault in the middle of the church.

The Algonquian Feast of the Dead, in which different bands placed the carefully washed and wrapped bones of their deceased relatives into a communal grave, functioned in large measure to forge or strengthen social bonds between disparate bands and nations. In this case, the treatment of Marquette's bones seems to have demonstrated the creation of a cultural and social bond between the Christian Ottawas and the French. This significant episode reveals the extent of the Kiskakon transformation. The Kiskakons employed Christianity in a thoughtful effort to revitalize their community and to reposition themselves for the future. In the process, they became both Ottawa and Christian and helped complete Marquette's own transformation. The Christian Ottawas raised the missionary to a special spiritually powerful position after his death, a status that transcended cultural boundaries.[50]

In one sense, the legitimate assertion that the Ottawas and other Algonquian speakers simply assimilated Jesus as a particularly powerful manitou seems an appropriate recognition of cultural continuity and flexibility in Indian spiritual life. True continuity did appear in the ongoing personal quest for spiritual power or grace, in the continued emphasis on ritual, practice, and proper behavior, and in the reexpression of cultural ideals and traditions in modified forms. But, in a larger sense, this innovation represented a remarkable metamorphosis not yet adequately recognized, a radical reorientation of spiritual concepts and practices obscured by such a simple explanation.

The adoption of Christianity in almost any form involved several crucial conceptual shifts, a reorientation on a continuum of change from the local toward the universal, from the horizontal toward the vertical, and from the communal toward the individual. Christianity altered the scale of spiritual life in the Great Lakes. The intimately local concerns and practices that dominated Native spirituality became entangled with the more hierarchical, universal ideas and concepts of Christianity. Christian tales of human sin, the merits of Christ, and the struggle for eternal salvation emphasized a spirituality of transcendence over one of immanence. Moreover, there had always been a very strong connection between myth and place in the cultures of Algonquian speakers. Spirituality was rooted in specific places in a living cultural landscape. Even certain manitous who generally remained distant from everyday human life had powerful associations with significant places, with the horizontal landscape that enveloped people and communities. The foreign spiritual beings of Christianity, in contrast, remained largely apart from and above this known landscape. They did not have these connections to local places. Only direct experience with Christianity could create such associations.

The process of conversion also transformed personal and communal identities, altering notions of self, personhood, and community. Kinship ties and reciprocal obligations in Algonquian-speaking communities formed a strong web of social relations that moderated the strength of individual self-identities. Christian conversions often severed these bonds, dividing families and communities. The intensely personal nature of the quest for Christian salvation encouraged a more individuated self as well as the formation of new relationships and communities. Many converts, in their defiance of family, community, and tradition, seemed to embrace this process of self-reconstruction. Others incorporated their families with them, maintaining important social bonds through the transformation. On a very basic level as well, Christianity also enlarged the universe of persons, introducing new spiritually powerful beings to Native worlds.

Conversion was, then, a process of engagement and transformation, a particular form of cultural, personal, and social change that stressed religious practice. For the Ottawas and other Algonquian-speaking peoples of the Great Lakes region, Christianity appeared as both a promising opportunity and a potentially disruptive threat. Furthermore, as Allouez's "Sentiments" and Marquette's death demonstrate so clearly, missionization transformed missionaries, too. It encouraged the reorientation of the Jesuit self. Allouez marveled in his statement that "one would never believe without experiencing it, how abundant are the graces and how powerful the assurances that God bestows on his servants in the midst of even the most terrible trials. The heart grows in proportion to one's labors for Jesus Christ." This spiritual growth prompted an inward turn toward rigorous self-examination and the constant effort to cast out sin, to purify the soul, and to suppress those natural desires that interfered with apostolic work. The outward impulse balanced this emphasis on interior reflection. Finding God required engagement with the world. The spiritual process took place out there, with the ultimate goal of finally turning oneself inside out, emptying the self completely, filling the void entirely with God, and sharing the intense passion and joy of this union with others. Jesuits and Natives traveled very different spiritual paths, but the trails crossed in the rivers, lakes, and forests of the *pays d'en haut* and in the many experiences of conversion.[51]

Chapter 7

Generations

Gender and Power

In the summer of 1725, the Illinois woman Marie Rouensa lay in her bed, ill and prepared to die. She called to her side the local French notary and the Jesuit Jean Le Boullenger and at least two other prominent men so she could dictate her last will and testament. This moment was an important one for her and for the community of Kaskaskia. Rouensa had been one of the most important leaders among Illinois, and especially Kaskaskia, Christians since the 1690s. In the three decades since, her influence had only grown. Rouensa became a catechist and successfully encouraged others, including her parents and husband, to join the church. She served as godmother to a number of children in the maturing French-Indian community at Kaskaskia. Rouensa also became quite wealthy. Her rare fortune comprised land, houses, barns, livestock, agricultural products, tools, household items, and five slaves—four of African descent and the other a young Indian boy. One of her lots, with two houses and a cabin on it, faced the Immaculate Conception church that she attended in the village of Kaskaskia, a central location that reflected her high status in the community. Legal custom directed one half of the large estate to Michel Philippe, whom she married after her first husband, Michel Accault, died in the early 1700s. Her eight children would divide the rest— that is, all but one of them.[1]

The will read: "As for my children, my property will be divided according to custom except for the share of Michel Ako [Accault], whom I have disinherited for his disobedience and the bad behavior that he has exhibited toward me and his entire family." The younger Michel Accault, baptized in 1702, had grown into a rebellious young man by the 1720s. Marie Rouensa had no intention of rewarding his bad behavior with a large inheritance. A week later, however, her position softened a bit and she recorded a codicil to the original will. "I take pity on my son Michel Aco," she stated, "who has given me grief with his foolishness, and I no longer believe that he should absolutely and forever be deprived of his claims on my estate. If he should repent, he may be returned to my will and may enjoy once again his rights to my estate. If he is so unfortunate as to persist in his foolishness and fails to repent and also remains among the savage nations," she warned, "I transfer his share of the estate to his brothers and sisters and he will never again have any claim to it." What was this foolishness that had caused so much grief for the family and its matriarch? It appears that Michel had left the combined French-Indian community of Kaskaskia for a nearby Native village—to live "among the savage nations"—where Catholicism had significantly less influence.[2]

This conduct was unacceptable to a woman so clearly dedicated to the church and to Christian practice. In her will, Rouensa "offers her soul to God, to the Holy Virgin, and to all the saints when her body is laid to rest." She also, the document states, "asks her husband to pray to God for the repose of her soul in the church where she will be interred and in the mission of the village where she was raised." Rouensa received the honor she requested. The burial record indicates that she was interred in the church, under the pew where she had worshipped, on 25 June 1725. As she had hoped, her son finally did return, and he reconciled with the family. Three years later, Michel Accault and his stepfather, Michel Philippe, left their marks on a document that provided for the son's share of the inheritance.[3]

This family drama illuminates some of the dynamics at work in the establishment of the larger Christian Illinois community. Gender and generational divisions influenced the community's formation from the beginning. For the Illinois and others who incorporated Christianity at some level, the attraction, experience, and meaning of the innovative practices frequently differed for men and for women and for people of different generations. Marie Rouensa quickly emerged in the 1690s as a leader of what was in many ways a women's movement. The "gender frontier" sharpened contrasts between French and Indian cultures, provoking internal reflection and stimulating accommodation and exchange. Native women seemed to discover in Christianity new avenues for the acquisition and expression of social and spiritual power. Prominent men, on the other hand, appeared to find in Catholicism a useful addition to their system of trade and diplomatic alliances as well as a source of social order in unstable communities. With the exception of the ceremonial leaders and healers, there were no greater opponents for the missionaries, however, than the young men competing for limited positions of leadership in the next generation. The young Michel Accault's rebelliousness and his mother's deep disappointment fit a pattern that many people noted as they observed and participated in the transformation of these communities. When men and women decided whether to accept Christianity to become *araminatchiki*—those who pray—they seemed to express divergent hopes and dreams for the effects of their choices.[4]

*   *   *

In his long journal covering the events of 1693 at the mission of the Immaculate Conception, Gravier recorded many other details about his methods of proselytization and described diverse Illinois responses to Christianity during this critical period. Gender and generation figured prominently in these descriptions. Gravier started 1693 with the culturally related Miamis, having passed the winter with them, but returned to the Illinois by March or April. Some of the Illinois, he said, "had met every day during my absence to pray to God in the Chapel, night and morning, as regularly as if I had been present,—after which an old man, who had for a long time been infirm, went through all the streets of the Village calling out that the women and children also were to go to adore God, and to say their prayers to him." The chapel was new. In 1691, the large village of Kaskaskia where Marquette had founded the Illinois mission moved from its location opposite La Roche, or Starved Rock, to a site down the Illinois River on Lake Pimitoui, near modern-day Peoria. The Kaskaskias and the Peorias were the dominant and most populous Illinois nations in the new village. At the end of April 1693, Gravier blessed the new chapel and its three-story cross, built just outside Fort Pimitoui. The chapel became an important community center for the growing Christian Illinois community and a focal point for the dramatic events during the rest of the year.[5]

It was the proposed marriage of Marie Rouensa to the French trader Michel Accault that set off the bitter dispute that permanently changed the community. Accault, a Frenchman who had been in the country for many years, and Marie Rouensa's father, a notable Illinois leader of the Kaskaskia band, agreed that Accault would have the hand of the seventeen-year-old Marie. Neither Accault nor Chief Rouensa had any interest in Christianity, probably agreeing to the marriage in order to seal a social and trading alliance. Marie Rouensa refused to wed the reputedly dissolute Accault. The chief expelled his assertive daughter from his home and demanded that no one in the village attend chapel services. Gravier arranged to have the young woman sheltered in the cabin of a Christian Indian family. Some people, mostly women and children, continued to go to services despite attempts to intimidate them.

Marie Rouensa eventually resolved the tense situation when she agreed to marry Accault. She believed she would be able to influence her husband and family and lead them into the Christian fold. Her vision largely came true. She convinced Accault to become a practicing Catholic and her parents to convert to Christianity. Many Kaskaskias followed the prominent family. According to Gravier, once the affair was settled, Chief Rouensa requested in public that people should return to the chapel. Gravier closed the church for several days, however, to demonstrate that he controlled access to sacred Christian knowledge, services, and space. Marie Rouensa, under Gravier's tutelage, became a successful catechist. In a small oratory she constructed for her daily sessions of prayer and meditation, she instructed the young children of the village. Gravier reported proudly that she even physically afflicted herself to strengthen further her Christian devotion. When Chief Rouensa and his wife declared their intention to become Christians, they celebrated with two feasts in the village, one for men and one for women. Finally, the missionary baptized the leader and his wife in public ceremonies, marking the close of the conflict.[6]

The divisive episode collapsed a multitude of issues into a concentrated series of defining events. Religion became a visible marker of the reorganization of society. At the level of community, of local encounters, the construction of a Christian society initially produced dissension among the Kaskaskias and divided the French. Marie Rouensa became the key to an alliance important to imperial relations and to the local situation. French colonial officials wanted the alliance to strengthen their position in the Illinois country. The Kaskaskias probably expected improved trading relationships, closer cooperation with the French in regional conflicts, and preferential treatment in general. Accepting Christianity, they also added a potent new dimension to local and personal identities. Among the Illinois, the Kaskaskias became the most enthusiastic and committed explorers of Christian practice. The Jesuits were ecstatic with the triumphant conversion of a leading family and much of the village.

Interpersonal encounters in the confrontation also reveal the creation of a new social landscape. Christianity, a very sharp social knife, severed families and village networks, at least temporarily. Rouensa forced his independent daughter to leave his cabin when she refused the proposed union. Marie Rouensa found succor in the Christian home of a fellow neophyte. Furthermore, the adoption of Christianity stimulated a major reordering of gender relations in Kaskaskia society. Numerous French observers commented that the Christian message attracted women far more than men among the Illinois. Women had always had their own responsibilities, privileges, and spaces. Now they claimed access to a special higher power outside the previous cultural experience of the Kaskaskias. Dozens of women and children perilously ignored Rouensa's directive that no one enter the Jesuit chapel during the controversy. Encouraged by the Jesuits to attend, they made the house of worship a woman's place for a time. Even when men later joined them at worship as the Kaskaskias turned generally toward Catholicism, the women continued to sit and worship separately from the men. In subsequent generations, Kaskaskia and other Illinois women, like Marie Rouensa, discovered in Christianity a comforting source of spiritual renewal and a viable outlet for their social energy. Men, on the other hand, tended to emphasize the contribution their Christian faith made to the larger relationship with the French and to the maintenance of social order within their communities.[7]

Finally, Marie Rouensa illustrates the potential intensity of personal encounters, the meeting with difference in the interior spaces of the mind and soul. The young woman defied her parents and much of her village in cleaving to her Christian faith and refusing a man she regarded as dissolute. She isolated herself in a small private space to contemplate, reflect, and pray and to afflict herself with the pain of penance. Yet, there, she also shared her faith and her knowledge of Christianity with others. This dramatic social repositioning and spatial reorganization confirmed her conversion and emphasized the formation of a different identity and an altered status. The time she spent in her oratory and the fasting, prayer, and self-affliction were all reminiscent of Illinois ritual practices surrounding puberty rites, menstrual separation, and the quest for spiritual guidance. Rouensa's conversion represented a major shift in the meaning of these practices, dictated by the addition of new cultural content.[8]

In the end, Marie Rouensa persuaded many of the Kaskaskias to follow a new cultural path. Her position—as the daughter of a Kaskaskia leader, as the object of desire for a French trader, as a woman with a culturally recognized independence, and as a fervent Christian—presented a unique constellation of powers that she wielded to great effect. She received high recognition for her labors on behalf of Christianity when the Jesuits granted her request for burial under the floor of the parish church in Kaskaskia. She was the only woman so honored. Like Marquette fifty years before her, Marie Rouensa in death became part of a new colonial geography created through the fusion of peoples and cultures.[9]

In the aftermath of the events that originally divided the community, Marie Rouensa went regularly to the chapel for instruction and prayer. Gravier admired her persistence and piety. Rouensa's fervor, he wrote, "has nothing of the savage in it, so thoroughly is she imbued with the spirit of God." The missionary placed his faith in her continuing transformation and the effect that it might have among the Illinois, a people he regarded with equal measures of hope and disdain. "She tells me the thoughts and the elevated sentiments that she has regarding God,—with such ingenuousness," he acknowledged, "that I cannot sufficiently thank God for revealing himself so intimately to a young savage in the midst of an infidel and corrupt nation." Rouensa took three months to prepare for her first communion. On the feast of the Assumption, she participated for the first time in the sacramental rite. Gravier concluded, "We may believe that Jesus Christ enriched her with many graces on the occasion of his first visit, and I observed in this girl the manifest effects of a good communion."[10]

Rouensa turned inward for signs that these good effects would become permanent, and she strained to orient her thoughts toward God and to regulate her behavior in the world. She maintained a strong attachment to Jesus and Mary, frequently worrying that her love for Jesus was insufficient and wondering whether she lived up to the name she acquired in baptism. Gravier reported that in the room where she repaired for prayer and meditation, Rouensa wept while she gazed at a picture of Jesus crowned with thorns. The pain she felt over her own guilt for the crucifixion compelled her to afflict her body with a girdle of thorns. Gravier had to warn her about the immoderate use of such implements and practices after she wore the girdle for two days straight. Later, the missionary gave his prized neophyte "a daily order to regulate her prayers and occupations, from the hour of rising until night." Gravier wrote that "her most frequent prayer consists in saying: 'My God, I am still but a child; I am weak. If you cease to sustain me, the Devil will deceive me and make me fall into sin.'" Although Gravier tried to encourage positive thoughts in his anxious convert, that she had apparently become so humble as a Christian obviously pleased him. Like most of his fellow missionaries, he more often associated Native people with the intransigent qualities of arrogance and independence.

For Gravier, Marie Rouensa appeared to be undergoing the transformation from savage to Christian, her soul touched by grace, but many of the people around her refused to open their hearts to the gospel. Rouensa's prominent role in changing this situation gave Gravier even more reasons to appreciate his passionate and persuasive young supporter. Rouensa started with her husband and parents. Michel Accault was a trader more concerned with business relationships and profits than with religion when Rouensa finally consented to marry him, but his bride hoped to bring him back to the church of his birth. Gravier instructed Rouensa in the obligations of Christian marriage, relating that she took "for her special patronesses the christian Ladies who have sanctified themselves in the state of matrimony,—namely, St. Paula, St. Frances, St. Margaret, St. Elizabeth, and St. Bridget, whom she invokes many times during the day." Rouensa's pleading and encouragement convinced her husband to reconnect with the Catholic faith. According to Gravier, Accault acknowledged "that he no longer recognizes himself, and can attribute his conversion solely to his wife's prayers and exhortations, and to the example that she gives him."

She also urged her parents to maintain their attachment to Christianity after their public conversion and baptisms. The first tests of their new commitment did not take long to arrive. At one point, Rouensa stopped her mother from seeking revenge against a brother who allegedly killed one of the mother's slaves. Her mother refused to attend church services until she obtained satisfaction, as tradition demanded, or until God himself struck down the guilty party. Chief Rouensa, Marie's father, also had doubts because some of his friendships and personal alliances cooled after his conversion. Marie pressured her parents until they again returned to the confessional and resumed regular Catholic observance. "Their daughter was so pleased at this," Gravier recorded, that "she went to her father and mother separately to rejoice with both of them, and to encourage them to maintain themselves in God's grace."

After attending to the spiritual state of herself and her family, Marie Rouensa applied much of her remaining energy and enthusiasm to strengthening the nascent Illinois Christian community. Gravier described her labors for the mission: "This good girl displays admirable care in getting the children and young girls of her village baptized, and it gives her great pleasure to be chosen as Godmother. The grown girls and the young women who have been baptized she induces . . . to come to her home, that she may instruct them; and she tries to inspire them with horror for dances, for night assemblies, and for evil of all kinds, and to instruct them regarding confession." Rouensa held prayer sessions in her cabin, helped children with the catechism, and shared stories from the Bible using Gravier's engravings as illustrations, even at times addressing the old and the young men of the village. "Her discretion and virtue give her marvelous authority, especially over those to whom she speaks of prayer without even any aged women finding fault with her," Gravier explained, "reproving them sometimes more energetically than I myself would do."

Gravier reported 206 baptisms between 30 March and 29 November 1693. Some of these were for sick children who later died, and despite the obvious and growing interest in Christianity, Gravier feared that this initial enthusiasm would fade. "So great are the inconstancy and levity of the savages that we cannot yet rely upon the first steps that they take; but, judging from the assiduity that they continue to display, there is reason to hope that . . . God will not allow the enemies of their conversion and of the mission to ruin these good beginnings. . . . Pray to God," he asked, "to preserve the neophyte chief, his wife, his family, and his son-in-law in their 1st fervor." As he hoped, many Kaskaskias and some members of the other Illinois nations rapidly incorporated Christianity into their communal identity, and the descendants of Marie Rouensa and her family remained prominent in the region's Christian community for generations to come.[11]

Marie Rouensa was not the only Illinois woman to display a deep interest in Christianity and an attraction to new forms of social behavior. Gravier discovered a young woman who had been unhappy in her marriage. According to the missionary, she had not wanted to be married in the first place but had not had the courage to resist her parents or her husband. When her husband was close to death, he begged his unmarried brother to marry her. This time the unnamed woman refused to give her consent, resisting her parents' solicitations for three years. Gravier reported that she attended services in the chapel daily for four years yet never told him directly that she wanted to become a Christian. Finally, she let him know through some of her companions, and Gravier baptized her in the spring, presumably in the new chapel. The widow explained to Gravier that she did not want to marry because she disliked what she witnessed in the marriages of others. Gravier's account did not specify what the disturbing behavior was, although he did relate that "she did not think that [her aversion to marriage] was because God specially loves Virgins, and she had not been taught to have that idea; but [she] said that, in [the] future, she would always tell God that he alone fully possessed all her affections—that her heart was too small, and he too great, to divide it." Gravier worked with the woman to strengthen this resolution and to place her on guard against the tendency of even the best-intentioned Christian to sin.[12]

Gravier also targeted children in his ministry. He dreamed of cultivating a new generation of Christian Illinois. Through the children, he also hoped to reach the parents and elders, although Gravier also did not fear dividing one generation from another. About his plans for the summer of 1693, Gravier wrote, "As a good many old men and other married people still persist in their infidelity, I have devoted myself, as well as I have been able, to instructing the children and Neophytes until their departure for winter quarters." He taught the catechism and the Bible and guided some of the older children, especially girls, through extensive general confessions. By the winter, Gravier happily reported that he heard children singing hymns and questioning one another about the catechism when he walked among the cabins.

Over the course of the year, the movement seemed to spread beyond the women and children. The leadership of Marie Rouensa and her family played a major role in this development, which amazed Gravier. "What surprises me most," remarked the missionary, "is the assiduous perseverance of the young men of 25, 30, 35, and even those over 40 years of age. . . . The most arrogant become like children at catechism, and not one is ashamed to answer the simplest questions that I put. The fathers and mothers are delighted when I question their children." The fresh enthusiasm for Christianity that Gravier described was greatest among the Kaskaskias.

Gravier hardly made it through even this most successful year without a number of very significant problems, however. The Peorias in particular resisted the missionary's advances. At first, most of the Peorias appeared politely indifferent to Christianity, a reaction that puzzled Gravier. One of the old men explained to the frustrated Jesuit "that his tribesmen had resolved to prevent the people from coming to the chapel to listen to me, because I inveighed against their customs and their juggleries; that they would, however, receive me well, in order to save appearances." Gravier's use of the disparaging term *juggleries* for indigenous ceremonies was actually a sign of the intensity of the cultural contest in which he was engaged. Trouble easily disrupted the superficial harmony he celebrated. A woman grieving for her dead grandson blamed Gravier for the death because he had baptized the child the year before.

She spoke harshly to the missionary and attacked him, pushing him violently out of the cabin where the boy had passed away.

Peoria political and religious leaders also labored to turn the people against the foreigner and his faith. They tried to convince the Peorias to abandon their explorations of Christianity. A young man who had received baptism told Gravier that a Peoria chief planned to hold a feast in which he would bring the neophyte together with "all the old men and all the chiefs of bands. . . . After speaking of our medicines and of what our grandfathers and ancestors have taught us, [the chief would ask,] has this man who has come from afar better medicines than we have, to make us adopt his customs?" In August, when a deadly disease broke out in the villages, many people concluded that Gravier was a sorcerer responsible for the affliction, which was occasionally fatal. Ritual healers opposed the missionary and his work. Parents shielded their children from Gravier's baptismal rites. Only a few bothered to maintain polite appearances with the Jesuit, but even these people purposely interfered with Gravier's program of instruction.[13]

Despite such problems, by 1696, one of Gravier's Jesuit colleagues claimed that the missionary had baptized over 2,000 persons during his six years in the Illinois mission: "[Gravier] says that he is delighted with the fervor of that infant church, . . . [where the people] live in the simplicity and piety of the 1st Christians." Although Christianity attracted a few Peorias, primarily women, the Kaskaskias became the most ardent Illinois Christians. The Kaskaskia conversion was widely recognized as a gendered and generational phenomenon. At the end of the 1690s, several observers commented on the situation at the Immaculate Conception mission. The Jesuit Julien Binneteau joined Gravier in the Illinois country in the second half of the 1690s. According to Binneteau, Illinois healers (usually older men) and young men tended to oppose Christianity, while women and girls formed the core of the Illinois mission. The community seemed sharply divided, with some Christian families offering to take in the children of non-Christian parents. A French trader agreed, writing that girls sometimes mocked Illinois customs and that the men strongly resisted the missionaries. The Jesuits frequently endured taunts and dodged "the pieces of wood, husks of Indian corn, and even the stones" thrown at them by the opponents of the mission during services and instruction.[14]

Gravier's early work with the children may have been less effective with Illinois boys, who became the rebellious young men that so many missionaries complained about. In 1699, after almost a year in the Illinois mission, Gabriel Marest wrote that "but few embrace christianity among the men, especially the young men—who live in excessive licentiousness, which renders them utterly averse to virtue, and incapable of listening to their missionaries. . . . The women and girls, on the contrary, are very well disposed to receive baptism; they are very constant and firm, when once they have received it." According to Marest, some children laughed at the rituals of Illinois healers, and he thought that these traditional practices were "gradually disappearing." The women and children filled the chapel, forcing the Jesuits to build an even larger church to accommodate them. Houses of worship stood on either end of the long, thin Illinois settlement.[15]

Julien Binneteau and many other French observers had much to say about women and gender in Illinois society, the crucial cultural background for the divided reaction to Christianity. In a description typical of European perspectives on Native men and women, Binneteau found that Illinois women were drudges oppressed by disturbingly idle men. He wrote that Illinois women were "continually occupied" in winter quarters, while the men only occasionally left to hunt, spending the rest of their time gambling, dancing, and singing. "They are all gentlemen," Binneteau commented, "the sole occupation of whose lives consists in hunting, in fishing, and in war." In the semipermanent summer villages, the women tilled the soil and grew fine fields of corn. By contrast, Binneteau concluded, "The idleness of the men is the cause of all their debauchery, and of their aversion to the christian religion." Furthermore, the missionary explained with obvious dismay, the women and girls "are the slaves of their brothers, who compel them to marry whomsoever they choose, even men already married to another wife."[16]

On the other hand, in a seemingly contradictory fashion, the French viewed Illinois and other Native women as remarkably independent. The Jesuits frequently lamented this characteristic, particularly when it involved female sexuality. François-Xavier de Charlevoix believed that Illinois women were especially lascivious, and he blamed the Illinois for a supposed decline in the sexual morals of the Indians around the Great Lakes. Another French commentator remarked that "[Illinois] women succumb easily to temptation." The freedom and perceived licentiousness of Native women frightened the Jesuits, who wanted to make women docile and submissive through the institution of Christian marriage. The source of strength and freedom for women in these new arrangements would be their holy relationship with God rather than their traditional status and power in their communities. The missionaries hoped to discipline Native communities through marriage and the accompanying reorganization of social relations.[17]

There is not a great deal of evidence about Illinois social organization, but the information that exists indicates that the patrilineal extended family formed the basic social unit in Illinois communities. These extended families were grouped into linked households that ranged in size from one to four hearths, each fire shared by perhaps two nuclear families. Highly fragmentary evidence suggests that patrilineal clans provided another level of social organization, but the form and function of these clans are obscure. Marriage created important bonds between families. The French trader Pierre Deliette gave the most detailed description of Illinois marriage customs. According to Deliette, men traditionally became eligible for marriage after they had become successful hunters and had made several attacks on the enemy, meaning that they normally married around the age of thirty years. A young man ready for marriage told his father the name of the woman he wished to marry. The father gathered gifts of food, cloth, guns, kettles, or even a slave, according to his means and to the prestige of the woman and her family. The father's female relatives delivered the gifts to the prospective bride's family, which then accepted or returned the gifts according to its decision. If refused, the young man's father might choose to augment the presents and try again. Once the girl's family accepted the gifts, it presented gifts of its own to the family of the suitor. A series of additional gift exchanges formalized the marriage, until eventually the young woman remained with her husband's family. According to the French, polygamy was particularly common with the Illinois. A highly successful man could take additional wives, usually other women in the first wife's lineage.[18]

Deliette's account of Illinois marriage customs indicates that young women did have some influence in deciding whether to accept the marriage proposal, but it is clear that the decision was a family one. There is other evidence too that social restraints considerably restricted female autonomy and that men maintained a significantly higher position of power and authority within the marriage and family. Women did not have complete control of their sexuality. In ideal terms, the Illinois expected unmarried girls to remain modest and chaste and to have little contact with young or even with married men, "in order to be esteemed and married with ceremony." At the same time, Deliette's description of Illinois culture suggests that brothers offered their sisters to other men for sex, even sometimes when they were already married. Deliette also described incredibly harsh treatment for unfaithful wives. According to the French trader, the enraged family of the husband felt compelled to punish adulterous women physically, going so far as to scalp the accused wife or to arrange for a group of men to rape her. "They post some thirty young men on a road by which they know that their wives must pass in going to the woods," Deliette explained. "As soon as they see her, the husband issues from the ambuscade and says to his wife: As I know that you are fond of men, I offer you a feast of them—take your fill. Her cries are futile; several of them hold her, and they enjoy her one after the other." Deliette claimed that over one hundred women, probably not all Illinois, had been scalped during the fifteen years or so that he had spent in the Illinois country before writing his account. "The Miami," he stated, "cut off their noses." Marquette reported about three decades earlier that an Illinois man "boldly kills his wife if he learns that she has not been faithful."[19]

After examining such grim evidence, it would be easy to conclude that Illinois women had limited access to social power and remained vulnerable subjects of a sometimes misogynistic society. In fact, the relative weakness of women, especially in the area of sexual relations, made the actions of female converts like Marie Rouensa that much more remarkable. Although in a general sense male roles and contributions may have outranked those of women, the comparatively distinct daily lives of women and the corresponding complementarity of gender roles in Illinois society supported substantial female autonomy and provided a significant source of power and influence. The Illinois based the standard division of labor on gender differences, with well-defined roles for women and men. Corn formed the foundation for the Illinois diet, for example, and women performed most of the agricultural labor that produced the staple in the rich alluvial soils of the Illinois country river valleys. Women also grew other crops such as melons, beans, and squash in their fields, and they gathered a variety of additional foods in the areas surrounding their villages. Women and men cooperated in their separate roles on communal hunting expeditions in summer and winter. The men conducted the hunts for buffalo and other animals, but women were largely responsible for preparing and hauling the kill. Women also sometimes accompanied men on village marches to attack distant enemies. They could even participate in battle at times, but were restricted to the use of clubs. The bow and arrow was a male weapon. Politics and diplomacy were also in most cases male endeavors. The crucial task of raising children was women's work.

Europeans judged certain aspects of these gender arrangements harshly. They believed that the burden of labor fell inordinately on Indian women, who conducted the agricultural work that supported the community and that in Europe was for the most part the province of men. Indian men in this

Figure 9. *A Sketch of Indians from Several Nations, New Orleans, 1735.* This drawing by Alexandre de Batz shows a group of Illinois Indians in the center, including two male warriors, a woman and child, and a healer (labeled the *dansseur*). Courtesy of the Peabody Museum of Archaeology and Ethnology, Harvard University, 41-72-10/20.

view merely followed the gentlemanly pursuits of hunting, fishing, and war, leaving most of their time free for leisurely socializing, gambling, and dancing. The lives of Illinois women and men actually were quite separate, yet they were intimately interrelated, with each making a vital contribution to the family and community. Women earned status and achieved influence by performing well within their distinctive sphere of activity.[20]

The social separation between women and men extended to ritual life as well. Female spiritual power was distinct from and even dangerously opposed to that of men, and women remained apart when they were in their most spiritually potent states. Girls ordinarily formed a relationship with a personal manitou and thus acquired their primary source of spiritual power at the onset of menstruation, when they left the village to fast for several days in a quest for a significant vision. In the future, during each period of menstruation, the woman would retire to a small hut near her cabin. Only other menstruating women were allowed to enter the hut. Women also gave birth in these huts, away from men and most other inhabitants of the village. Although the sources do not say so explicitly, it is not hard to imagine that during these times of separation women conducted personal rituals to renew connections with their manitous and to refresh their spiritual power. Female spiritual power was tied closely to the cycle of life, to the signs of fertility such as menstruation and birth. The vital economic contribution that Illinois women made through agriculture probably included numerous seasonal rituals to promote fertility and abundance as well. According to Deliette, the distinction between men and women also held at death. When an Illinois woman passed away, other women took responsibility for the corpse, dressing the body as neatly as possible and placing it in a grave with appropriate ceremony.[21]

Female spiritual power held meaning on a personal level and, given its focus on fertility and the life cycle, for the community as a whole. There are numerous instances that demonstrate that the Illinois respected this power. Deliette recounted a story of one girl's vision quest at puberty. He remembered, "I saw a young girl of sixteen who was foolish enough to remain six days without eating or drinking and whom it was necessary to carry back to her cabin . . . because she was not able to stand up." "She made all her relatives believe," he continued, "that she had seen a buffalo, which had spoken to her, and that her two brothers who were leading a party on the warpath against the Iroquois would make a successful attack without losing any life." According to Deliette, the attack was successful, yet one of the brothers was killed. The dream interpreters concluded that the girl's vision was correct but that she simply had not fasted long enough to attain a complete understanding of what would happen. Some Illinois women cultivated this kind of power and used it to become healers and ritual specialists in their communities.[22]

Men feared women's power and its potential effects on male occupations and the power that made them successful. For example, Illinois men blamed contact with their pregnant or menstruating wives for failure in hunting and gaming. Male power and female power were incompatible in many ways, rooted in different sources and aimed toward different goals, and could easily disrupt the effectiveness of the other. At certain times, it was imperative to limit contact between women and men in order to avoid possible interference.

When these periods of necessary separation came to an end, rituals prepared men and women to resume their lives together. The theme of purification is prominent in the set of rituals conducted after the birth of a child, which normally occurred outside the woman's cabin in one of the menstrual huts. According to Deliette's detailed account, after the birth, the woman bathed herself in water and waited for her husband to ready the cabin for her return. "The day when she is to return to her husband's cabin, he has every-thing cleaned, has his furs shaken, and the ashes in the fireplace removed, so that not a speck remains, after which he kindles a new fire with his apparatus and lights it himself. Then he sends word to his wife to enter." Husband and wife could once again live together, but a less severe form of separation con-tinued for a time. Men and women avoided sexual intercourse as long as the woman was nursing the infant. Feeding the child from her breasts, the mother was still in a state of female potency, and her power was potentially disruptive for men.[23]

Christianity appeared as an additional arena for the exploration and ex-pansion of female spiritual power. Once again, older traditions and innovative practices converged in ways that inspired creative adaptations to change. Marie Rouensa sought spiritual strength in isolated prayer, fasting, and self-affliction. She announced her desire to form lasting bonds with Jesus, Mary, and the saints. These activities represented an extension of female ritual practices like menstrual separation and the effort to make and maintain connections to manitous and the medicine they offered. There was considerable continuity in the transition to Christian practice. The structure of personal spiritual experi-ences changed less than the content.

The more dramatic shift in cultural expectations occurred in the re-distribution of social power between women and men in the Kaskaskia com-munity. Rouensa took control of her social identity and her sexuality in her initial refusal to marry Michel Accault. Other Native women used Christi-anity to do the same. The crisis that followed and her role in bringing it to a satisfactory conclusion only increased her influence in the community. Over time, Rouensa's two marriages to French men and her acquisition of personal property added to her authority. Serving as godmother to the children of French men and Indian women also strengthened the social and economic network she constructed.

Marie Rouensa's experience parallels those of the many French women who discovered in religion an acceptable outlet for their spiritual and social energies. French nuns and pious women often pressed at the social barriers that hindered them in their religious roles. Acknowledgment of this effort by religious women to enlarge their sphere of influence is an implicit recognition of the constraints with which they lived. Likewise, the typical social arrange-ments in Native communities set limits on the roles of women even when there was a tendency toward balanced reciprocity in gender relations. The destructive effects of colonization obviously threatened the stability of these indigenous social institutions. Missionaries idealized a patriarchal family model and expected to replace more flexible and equitable Native marriage traditions with lifetime unions, strong husbands and fathers, and pious and subordinate women and children all sanctified and legitimized by the church. Yet, as many Native women realized and some missionaries came to learn, Christianity presented real social opportunities even as it imposed new limits.[24]

Marie Rouensa's labors on behalf of her adopted faith contributed to the emergence of a church community among the Illinois largely dominated by women. Gabriel Marest noted that "the women and girls . . . frequently approach the sacraments; and . . . are capable of the highest sanctity. The number of those who embrace our holy religion increases daily." He called Immaculate Conception "one of our finest missions" despite the fact that so many Illinois men and most of the Peorias remained unconverted and unenthusiastic. Other French commentators also observed that women formed the foundation of the Illinois Christian community. Marest's Jesuit colleague Julien Binneteau wrote that Illinois "women and girls have strong inclinations to virtue . . . there are some among them . . . who prefer to expose themselves to ill treatment rather than do anything contrary to the precepts of Christianity regarding marriage." The French missionaries praised Illinois women and compared them to the most devout and pious women of France. Binneteau exclaimed that some of the Illinois women married to Frenchmen "would be a good example to the best regulated households in France."[25]

For the Illinois women themselves, however, intermarriage and the adoption of Christianity were less about adjusting to French standards for the religious and social behavior of women than they were about adapting to change. Swift and far-reaching transformations created the overriding context for the many conversions of Illinois women in this era. Expanding European trade and economic reorganization, violence and war, migration and increasing intercultural contact, epidemic disease and depopulation placed enormous pressure on the Illinois and forced them to adapt. The Illinois did not experience a total collapse of their communities or way of life at this time, but the interactions in which they were involved and the changes occurring around them nevertheless caused substantial instability and uncertainty.[26]

These strains altered social relations and transformed the social landscape. Deliette reported that the Illinois married at a younger age by the 1690s. Young men who previously waited until they were about thirty years old before seeking a wife, after having established themselves as hunters and warriors, now sometimes married before the age of twenty. Women married under the age of eighteen, as Marie Rouensa did, rather than wait until they were twenty-five as they formerly had. Deliette remarked that "the old men say that the French have corrupted them." The sex ratio in Native communities throughout the Great Lakes region was imbalanced, approaching a ratio of three or four females to each male in some communities, according to observers. The uneven sex ratio probably accounts in part for the prevalence of polygamy. It certainly stimulated the rate of intermarriage with the French, a practice that became increasingly common by the early eighteenth century. Women like Marie Rouensa constructed durable new kinship and economic networks through their marriages to French men and by acting as godparents to the children of these unions. Rouensa had at least eight children baptized in the church, two from her first marriage and six from her second, according to surviving sacramental registers from the Immaculate Conception mission and church. The godparents for her children came from the mixed French, Indian, and métis, or mixed-blood, community. Rouensa, in turn, served as a godmother to at least four children. Such connections extended kinship to more people in the community without the polygamous relationships that the missionaries and many committed Christians found so objectionable.[27]

Conversion, like intermarriage, was part of the natural process of encounter and engagement that occurred in this dynamic cultural environment. Periods of great stress and rapid change produced conditions that encouraged both the examination of new ideas and the conservation of traditional values and practices. The adoption of Christianity was a logical choice for Marie Rouensa and many other Illinois women as well as some Illinois men. The resistance displayed by much of the Peoria community was another equally reasonable choice. Even the rejection of Christianity did not always preclude experimentation with Christian practice. The Illinois healers considered the strongest opponents of the missionaries sometimes sought healing power in Christianity. Likewise, the determination to accept Christianity did not necessarily represent the abandonment of Illinois culture. More often, the incorporation of Christianity exemplified an attempt to locate a point of balance between cultures, to synthesize the old and the new, the experiences of the past with those of the present and possible future.[28]

The pattern of conversion that describes the experiences of so many Illinois women—a quest for spiritual renewal and social power—also explains a number of conversions that occurred among women elsewhere. Beyond the Illinois country, in other places and times, Native women incorporated

Christianity into their own cultural syntheses. Female Christian converts often defied their families and communities. At the Saint Esprit mission that spurred the mass conversion of the Kiskakon Ottawas, Jacques Marquette reported that young women were proud of being Christians and used their attachments to justify their social independence. Marquette cited a young woman whose husband left her, as a spouse had a right to do. The jilted wife refused to remarry despite intense pressure from relatives, until finally Marquette succeeded in reuniting the couple. According to the missionary, the woman became even more zealous in her observance after the events. "She has laid bare her conscience to me," Marquette wrote, "and I am filled with admiration that a young woman has lived as she has." He did not mention the husband's feelings toward Christianity.[29]

Claude Allouez recorded a similar case. He had baptized a girl at Saint Esprit and given her the name Marie Movena. Allouez encountered her again in the Green Bay missions to the west over the winter of 1669–70. His early work there had produced only seven adult Christians. Forty-eight others had received baptism only because they were dangerously ill. Marie Movena was his greatest consolation during the winter. Like the woman Marquette admired, Movena would not consent to a marriage arranged by her relatives. "Her brother has often struck her," Allouez reported, "and her mother has frequently refused her anything to eat,—sometimes reaching such a pitch of anger she would take a firebrand and burn her daughter's arms with it." According to the missionary, "[Movena] willingly made an offering of all her sufferings to God." A few years later, Allouez reported that some Christian girls at the Mascouten and Miami mission carried eagle talons under their robes to ward off the advances of presumptuous young men.[30]

Christianity also offered comfort for some apparently marginal Native women. Some of the first reported Ottawa converts were widows who seemed to have little support. René Ménard established in 1660 a mission to the Ottawas and others settled at Keweenaw Bay. There, he found a widow named Nahakwatkse living in a hovel, "the most miserable cabin of all," according to the priest. In Ménard's account, Nahakwatkse claimed that she found his words full of consolation even if most people did not approve of his teachings. She gave the hungry missionary a dried fish for coming, although she had very little to eat herself. Ménard returned days later, and she was "fully resolved to serve God." Nahakwatkse started attending prayer sessions each morning and evening. She eventually helped bring her brother into the fledgling church. Three of the first six converts Ménard described were widows.[31]

Many of these women must have been attracted to the spiritual potential of Christianity. The premier example of such a woman in the French missions was Catherine Tekakwitha. The Jesuits baptized Tekakwitha at one of their missions to the Iroquois in 1676. Not long after, she fled her village to join the growing Christian Indian community at Kahnawake. In this mission community on the Saint Lawrence River across from Montréal, Tekakwitha became intensely pious and helped create a strong community of Christian women. She modeled her life on the French hospital nuns who worked in the colony, dedicated herself to virginity and refused to marry, and practiced severe self-mortification. The self-punishment took its toll, and Tekakwitha died in 1680. In death, she soon received credit for several miracles, and her tomb became a place of pilgrimage for those in search of spiritual succor and divine inspiration.[32]

In the upper Great Lakes, the Jesuits described a woman who in a similar fashion used Christianity to completely reorient her life. According to her Jesuit chroniclers, the anonymous woman had received some training from the Ursuline nuns of Québec but lived in a Native village on the north shore of Lake Huron in the early 1670s. Her time in Québec may have weakened her communal connections, leaving her somewhat marginalized. She did not participate in the feasts and ceremonies that animated the village and finally decided to live in solitude outside the community. She moved to a small cabin near the adjacent Jesuit mission, where she invited women and girls to pray and to learn about Christianity. The Jesuits reported that she earned the respect of the people in surrounding Native communities. The missionaries saw the influence of God and the operation of grace in the actions of such women. The people in this woman's community more likely feared her possible power in Native terms, wondering whether she had tapped into some potent new source. The woman herself may have discovered an explanation for her spiritual experiences somewhere in between these two divergent conceptions of the world. She completed the connections between cultures that the Jesuits worked so hard to identify and develop and that made Christianity accessible to the region's Native peoples. Overlapping concepts of spiritual power diminished the cultural boundary between the Indians and the French.[33]

*   *   *

If women from the Algonquian-speaking communities of the Great Lakes tended to adopt Christianity in a bid to assert themselves or to gain access to spiritual power, men followed a distinctly different pattern that stressed the links between religion on the one hand and the French alliance, social order, and power of healing on the other. Chief Rouensa of the Kaskaskias certainly hoped to strengthen his relationships with the French. It was most likely a major factor in his support of the marriage between his daughter and Michel Accault. Almost as soon as Rouensa made his very public conversion to Christianity, he started to complain about the problems he had with the French. Gravier related that Marie Rouensa overheard her father say "that the French who had displayed the greatest friendship toward him would not even look at him since he was a christian . . . that he knew not what to think or say of such conduct, unless it were that the French preferred to see him lead the life of a savage rather than that of a christian." If true, this unexpected development must have been quite a disappointment for the Kaskaskia leader.[34]

The missionaries desperately wanted to attract men to their missions and labored hard to do so. They needed men to form complete Christian communities, and they hoped to use the influence of leaders like Rouensa to push others toward conversion. This approach seemed to work with the Kiskakon Ottawas in the late 1660s and to some extent with the Kaskaskias in the 1690s. Ménard and Allouez managed to obtain only a few conversions and to generate only limited interest in Christianity until Kiskakon leaders decided to embrace Christianity and to encourage others to do the same. The evidence suggests that these men intended to revitalize the community with Christianity, strengthening the relationship with the French and restoring communal order in a difficult period of adjustment. The Jesuits were ecstatic with this dramatic shift in attitude and dreamed of reforming the men to produce model Christian husbands and leaders.

More commonly, however, the Jesuits complained of trouble with Native men, as they did among the Illinois, and struggled to bring them into the church. Sébastien Rasles remarked that Illinois men "acknowledge that prayer is good, and they are delighted to have it taught to their wives and children." But when the missionaries tried to persuade Illinois men to join their wives and children in prayer, most were indifferent and merely shrugged off the frustrated priests. Rasles thought the biggest obstacle to their conversion was their continuing attachment to polygamy. Many of Rasles's Jesuit colleagues agreed with the central point of this explanation. The missionaries generally blamed the depth of the well-entrenched male culture for the stiff resistance to Christianity that they met so often with Native men.[35]

Joseph François Lafitau thought that a large part of the problem was that Indian men were simply lazy and enjoyed their pleasurable lives of leisure. Lafitau concluded, "Laziness, indolence, inactivity are to their taste and form the basis of their character so that, having neither learning nor duties, having no longer or scarcely having, the regulated exercises of past times which might hold them in check, they are the idlest people in the world. . . . Almost always they have their arms crossed and are doing nothing except holding meetings, singing, eating, playing, sleeping, and loafing." In Lafitau's sharply negative assessment of Native men and their activities, Christianity demanded a discipline that few men were willing to accept. One of the missionary's primary challenges in converting men was, in this view, to overcome what Rasles labeled "their natural inconstancy."[36]

Many French commentators believed that the problem was especially acute with young men. The missionaries almost universally criticized them for their supposed arrogance and insolence, a generally stubborn attitude that interfered with the establishment of stable Christian communities. Julien Binneteau complained bitterly in 1699 that "the young men are no less opposed to the progress of Christianity than are the jugglers. Among them are monsters of impurity, who abandon themselves without shame to the most infamous actions; this is the reason why we find hardly a single young man upon whom we can rely for the exercises of religion." Intransigent young men often appeared in the tales of adversity the missionaries recounted. The Jesuit Louis André reported trouble with young men at Saint François Xavier on Green Bay. He complained that some young Potawatomi men prepared for a raid against the Dakotas to the west with great feasts, building their fires with the wood of the cross from their village. André believed that God punished the warriors for their terrible treatment of the holy symbol. He claimed that they returned in shame without even attacking the enemy and that in the aftermath of this failure they became more docile.[37]

Another missionary reported a similar incident of disrespect for the cross at the Ottawa mission, a decade after the Kiskakon conversion. In the late 1670s, the Kiskakons participated in a ceremony to venerate a new cross planted at the mission. The large wooden cross was draped with various items to indicate respect. Other nations joined the Kiskakons for the ceremony. A group of men fired two volleys with their guns to honor the cross, but bullets struck the decorations and knocked them to the ground. The missionaries quickly explained the deep disrespect the act had demonstrated, and they abruptly withdrew to their chapel and closed the door in consternation. Representatives of the different nations went to the missionaries to apologize for the insult, saying that the young men were responsible, "that they have no sense." The leaders replaced the decorations and had a palisade constructed around the cross to protect it from future harm. Some Kiskakons ceremoniously presented a belt of wampum for the cross as reparation. According to the description of the episode, many older men in the community, even some non-Christians, seemed interested in promoting order among the rebellious young men.[38]

Indeed, young men in the Algonquian-speaking communities of the Great Lakes were often arrogant and insolent. Even Native leaders sometimes claimed to have little control over the young men in their communities. In one case, elders tried to explain the problem to Allouez at the Green Bay mission. The Indians in the area felt that the French had not treated them well, causing considerable unrest. Allouez attempted to ease the tension with a council. Although the elders seemed largely satisfied with the missionary's plans to improve the situation, they warned him that the young men would not be so easily swayed. These Native leaders "declared that their young men had no sense, and would not listen to the elders, especially as they allowed themselves the license commonly ascribed to Soldiers." In the Ottawa origin story recorded by Nicolas Perrot, the very inception of warfare between the nations arose out of the bellicose behavior of young men. Perrot explained that in the past, diverse nations had been dependent on one another to trade for things they could not produce themselves. Hunters and farmers traded meat for corn. The arrangement encouraged relatively peaceful coexistence. "But eventually the young men," according to Perrot, "through a certain arrogance that is native to all the savages, and no longer recognizing any chief, committed murders by stealth, and incited wars against their allies, who were obliged to defend themselves."[39]

Native communities expected the aggressive behavior of young men, viewing it as part of their social growth, as a necessary step on the path to becoming a man. The major goal in the transition to adulthood was the development of competence in hunting, fishing, and warfare, activities that encouraged and rewarded aggressiveness. As Deliette noted in his discussion of Illinois marriage, the critical "period when a man begins to possess resolution" was his mid-twenties. Traditionally a young man could not marry until he demonstrated the maturity demanded by these essential activities. Although according to Deliette the marriage age declined significantly after contact with the French, the importance of acquiring the quintessential male skills remained and probably even increased with the expansion of trade and with the many conflicts that left the region perpetually unsettled.[40]

The central male occupations required that young men explore the world to acquire and extend the skills that would build a foundation for future success. The quest for a vision and the cultivation of a productive reciprocal relationship with a personal manitou was a process that had an enormous impact on the achievements and prosperity of each man. The first hunting expeditions and raids that a young man participated in strengthened the relationship first formed at puberty and tested the effectiveness of the power that it generated. This process was important not only on an individual basis but on the communal level as well. Male subsistence activities and warfare were generally group enterprises. They mobilized the men and their power in a communal effort, tying them one to another. A practice that Deliette recorded in his description of Illinois warfare is emblematic of the kind of cooperation these projects demanded. Deliette explained that each participant in a war party took the skin of a bird from his medicine bundle and gave it to the leader of the group. The captain then carried all the skins together in a single bundle to pool the power of the party's manitous.[41]

New leaders emerged out of the groups by consistently achieving success, thus demonstrating their skill and power and enhancing their prestige. Instruction, spiritual guidance in acquiring a manitou, and leadership linked generation to generation. The relationships formed in these enterprises cemented ties between young and old. Gifts and the ideal of reciprocity maintained the bonds. Allouez discovered the strength of these religious traditions and intergenerational relationships in his encounters with a Miami captain. The Miami leader had hosted the priest at one time and expressed some interest in Christianity, but he would not make a commitment. Disappointed, Allouez decided to defer the man's baptism. "Although he seemed sufficiently well disposed," the missionary explained, "he could not, on account of his rank as Captain, through courtesy, refrain from involving himself in the superstitions of the Young men." Allouez never did baptize the captain, and presumably the Miami man upheld his alliances with the young men in his community.[42]

The young men engaged in traditional male activities found it difficult to abandon the fundamental cultural practices that ensured success and prosperity at such a crucial and exciting moment in their lives. As Louis André noted, even the young men who had become interested in Christianity and had already started to alter their behavior could not give up their dreams, visions, and manitous when it came to warfare. It was simply too risky, unless there were obvious signs that Christianity could successfully augment or replace the power upon which they had been trained to rely. Identifying areas of convergence between Indian and French cultures created important, and often the earliest, opportunities to experiment with the power of Christianity.

Jesuit Jean de Lamberville described a man at the Sault Sainte Marie mission who encouraged just such exploration. Iskouakite was one of the oldest captains, according to Lamberville, and had fought against both the Dakotas and the Five Nations. Iskouakite encouraged the people in his community to dwell near the mission church. He wanted the women and children to have the protection of the palisade that surrounded the chapel. He called Jesus "the god of war" and suggested that warriors and the community as a whole could draw from the power of the great spiritual being that the missionaries extolled. If Iskouakite was in fact an old warrior who had tasted victory and survived many battles on the strength of his own manitous, his support of Jesus as a new kind of manitou indicated a significant transition. Such exploration pleased the Jesuits, of course, who were more than happy to take advantage of any cultural intersections that appeared.[43]

The missionaries discovered that the best opportunities for conversion frequently arose when men believed that their power failed them. A weakened man searched for new sources of strength and sometimes found one in the rituals, spiritual figures, and symbols of Christianity. Allouez's model Mesquakie convert, Joseph Nikalokita, turned to Christianity during a personal crisis induced by illness and impending death. He survived and regained his health. Nikalokita's coveted rosary beads became a symbol of his recovery and a physical sign of the spiritual power that he credited with saving him. Jacques Marquette shared stories of guardian angels with the neophytes at one of his mission stations to solidify their faith in the protective and healing powers of the Christian God.[44]

The Le Boullenger dictionary described a wise man as *8anantaki met8seni8a*, a reference to a mild-mannered man of peaceful repose. Another expression, from the Gravier dictionary, was *kipa8api8a*, "he is modest, chaste, wise." It took time to reach this stage of life even under the best of circumstances. In the volatile *pays d'en haut* of the seventeenth and eighteenth centuries, developing "sense" and achieving the serenity that came with true wisdom were even more challenging endeavors. Women also sought wisdom, but the journey was very different. The Miami-Illinois language even had at least one special word dedicated to female wisdom, *reb8aca8a*, a term that emphasized modesty and purity in women and girls. These ideals and the social organization that supported them carried through to the encounter with Christianity. The contrast in the experience and meaning of Christianity for men and women, young and old became a prominent feature of the early Illinois Christian community that coalesced in the 1690s. Significant differences remained well into the eighteenth century.[45]

A letter from the Kaskaskia leader Mamantouensa to colonial officials in France vividly illustrates these varied concerns. Chicagou delivered the letter and a belt of wampum to King Louis XV at Fontainebleau in 1725. The message identified some of the problems associated with the influx of French settlers in the Illinois country after the turn of the century. These *habitants* forced Native people out of highly coveted village sites and closed off access to highly productive land. Mamantouensa described in gendered terms the negative consequences of this increasing pressure on the Kaskaskias and other Illinois. He first underscored the depth of the Kaskaskia commitment to Christianity. Mamantouensa explained to the French king that Christianity was an integral part of cultural and social life in Kaskaskia. "My father," the letter read, "I share your prayer, for the Black Robes have instructed me and all my Elders." If the elders were knowledgeable about Christianity and generally content with its role in the community, the young men nevertheless remained on edge. Mamantouensa cautioned that the moves forced by French settlement in the Illinois country "disrupt the prayer [and] upset my young people." Finally, he argued that women and children suffered the most from the shortage of missionaries in the region. The Kaskaskia leader asked for more black robes, so that his own people and the other Illinois nations could benefit from Christian instruction and a more secure alliance with the French. Mamantouensa's statement to the king recognized that Christianity—"the prayer," as he put it—had a distinct purpose and different meanings for the various social groups that made up his community.[46]

Chapter 8

Communities

Indigenous Christianities in the Eighteenth Century

The Jesuit missionary Gabriel Marest arrived in the Illinois country in 1698. Fourteen years later, in 1712, he penned a letter from the mission of the Immaculate Conception at Kaskaskia to a fellow Jesuit in France. The lengthy document sketched a portrait of the Illinois country and its people and described the state of Illinois Christianity in the mission. The Jesuits had labored in the region for four difficult decades. The Kaskaskia conversion was twenty years in the past. In part, Marest wanted to explain just how much had changed during those many years of encounter.[1]

Like so many other missionaries and colonial commentators, Marest reduced Native personalities to a few common characteristics. He told his colleague that, in his estimation, a strong sense of personal independence formed the foundation of the generic Indian character. This perceived independence was not a trait that the missionary admired. Marest believed that it represented a lack of discipline, and he thought it was the ultimate source of all the vices the missionaries hoped to eradicate. "They are indolent, traitorous, fickle, and inconstant," he stated emphatically. "We must first make men of them, and afterward work to make them Christians." In reality, the Jesuits more often worked in the opposite direction, seeking to transform the soul through conversion and then to change the person. In any case, Marest believed that the Illinois, especially the Kaskaskias, were gradually changing. "The Illinois are much less barbarous than other Savages," Marest wrote; "Christianity and intercourse with the French have by degrees civilized them. This is to be noticed in our Village [Kaskaskia], of which nearly all the inhabitants are Christians; it is this also which has brought many Frenchmen to settle here, and very recently we married three of them to Illinois women." In the missionary's opinion, Christianity had "softened" and inspired "docility" in the Illinois.[2]

The missionaries had not completed their jobs, however, and felt they had much left to accomplish. They continued to face resistance in certain quarters. Marest's greatest opponents were the Illinois ritual specialists and healers. Generally, the missionaries no longer worried about the direct intervention of Satan in the activities of Native religious practitioners, but they still considered ceremonial leaders serious obstacles to the firm establishment of Christianity. Marest derisively labeled these religious figures "charlatans" and complained that "to embrace Christianity is to be exposed to their insults and their violence." He mentioned an incident in which a healer threatened to attack a Christian girl because she carried a rosary that the man blamed for the death of his father. "Thank God," Marest exclaimed, "our Village is freed from all these imposters."[3]

Women continued to be the most enthusiastic Illinois Christians. The priest concluded that the heavy work women did for their families and community "humbled" them and made them "more disposed to accept the truths of the Gospel." In a typically disapproving manner, Marest summarized the gendered division of labor: "Hunting and war form the whole occupation of the men; the rest of the work belongs to the women and the girls." Marest was more supportive of the occasional separation of women and men in the daily routines the Illinois followed in Catholic worship and learning. During morning mass, the Christian women sat on one side of the chapel, the men on the other. In the evening, after instruction, a prayer service, and singing, the women and men retired to separate quarters to hold private meetings without the priest. Marest added, "There they recite the Rosary in two choirs, and far on into the night they sing Hymns . . . which are pleasing to them." He did not mention, if he even knew, how different the worship or songs were for each group or whether the men and women organized themselves into distinct religious societies.[4]

The differential pattern of male and female conversion survived as new converts joined the Illinois church, at least in the few specific cases Marest recorded. Women continued to assert their independence through identification with Christianity. Marest described yet another young Illinois woman who refused to marry the man her non-Christian family proposed as her mate. Her brother reportedly threatened to kill her for her persistence in the matter. And men still experimented with the healing power of Christianity.

Marest described a man named Henri, who converted and became a cate-chist when smallpox afflicted him and his family, taking his wife and some of his children. Henri came from "a somewhat inferior family" that did not even live in the village of Kaskaskia. Nevertheless, according to Marest, he "made himself respected by every one" in the community as an instructor and a Christian. He discovered a path from the margins of the community to one of many possible centers. Both men and women could find strength and power in new religious practices.[5]

The members of the Christian Illinois community faced numerous chal-lenges in this and succeeding generations, as did their non-Christian counter-parts. The Fox wars and the Chickasaw wars, the acceleration of depopulation, the small but significant stream of French settlers, more movement and migra-tion, the brandy trade, and an increase in alcohol abuse were but some of the major issues that confronted the Illinois in the eighteenth century. The picture of Illinois Christianity that emerges in this period is fragmented at best, ob-scured by the scattered nature of surviving documentation. Existing evidence suggests, however, that many Illinois assimilated Christianity to form a truly Illinois Christian community that provided an essential source of spiritual guidance, social support, and cultural continuity through the generations.[6]

The missionaries who served this community also encountered a number of serious challenges, not the least of which was that the nature of mission work itself was changing. In his letter to his Jesuit colleague in France, Marest briefly recounted the history of the Illinois mission. He credited Jacques Gra-vier for the solid establishment of the mission of the Immaculate Concep-tion, the most successful Jesuit post in the western Great Lakes. Marest noted that Jacques Marquette had founded the mission during his visits in the 1670s, over a decade before the arrival of Gravier. Allouez had also la-bored briefly in the Illinois field before concentrating his efforts on the Miamis to the north. It was Gravier, however, who first unraveled the intrica-cies of the Illinois language and who directed the conversion of the celebrated Marie Rouensa and the majority of the Kaskaskias.[7]

Marest lived through a major transition in the Illinois mission, becom-ing a vital human link between the pioneer generation of priests and the men who followed. Some observers then and now described a steep and wide-spread decline in the vigor of the Jesuit missions in the eighteenth century, but for the mission and the missionaries in the Illinois country, there was less a decline in fervor or commitment than an evolution of the mission and the religious labor it demanded. The maintenance, consolidation, and nurturing of an already existing Christian community became the primary occupation of the missionaries in the eighteenth-century Illinois mission.[8]

Strenuous, perhaps even monotonous, parish work rather than the more spectacular endeavors of a pioneer mission characterized the experience of French missionaries in this period. The Jesuits did not obtain any more dramatic group conversions in the region. They continued their linguistic studies, but they built on what previous missionaries had already accomplished. The missionaries embarked on few new projects of expansion, although they continued to express a desire to share their message with new peoples, particularly those living west of the Mississippi River. The establishment of formal parish structures beginning in 1719 at the French village of Kaskaskia spread the missionaries thinly between the Illinois and the growing French and métis communities. As the surviving sacramental registers attest, the ebb and flow of marriages, baptisms, and funerals, added to the regular observance of Catholic festivals and the daily routines of the church, shaped an increasingly regimented missionary life.[9]

The expression of Jesuit spirituality in eighteenth-century Illinois took many forms, recalling the Jesuit tradition of martyrs as well as the more mundane spirituality of everyday Jesuit life. Gravier received credit not only for making the Illinois mission a relative success but also for giving his life in service to his mission. Gravier suffered a mortal wound in the Peoria village around 1705. The Jesuit Jean Mermet reported that a Peoria leader named Mantouchensa, already angry with the French, incited his people to resist the missionary, "a person who took notice of everything." In this explosive environment, a Peoria man fired several arrows at Gravier, supposedly in retaliation for perceived mistreatment by the missionary. The man's final shot "pierced [Gravier's] arm above the wrist, and penetrated to below the elbow." The arrowhead lodged in the joint and could not be removed. Severe infection followed.

Mermet celebrated Gravier's calm response to the attack and his bloody sacrifice on behalf of the mission. He wrote that "at the first shots, the father asked the Savage: 'My son, why do you kill me? What have I done to you?'" "He knelt to commend himself to God," Mermet continued, "and at the same time, as soon as the wound was inflicted, the father swam, as it were, in his own blood." Christian women in the village nursed Gravier until some men sent by Chief Rouensa at Kaskaskia rescued the ailing missionary some months later. Gravier left the Illinois country for treatment at the French post of Mobile on the Gulf of Mexico. Mermet wrote that Gravier did so "nevertheless, with the view of returning as soon as he is cured, in order to die on his first battle-field." Such sentiments remained consistent with the Jesuit tradition that praised the persistence and heroism of missionaries like Jean de Brébeuf in New France and the first great missionary of the order, Saint Francis Xavier. Gravier did not survive his wound, however, and the Peorias remained without a missionary for five years.[10]

Hard work and helping souls exhibited a less sensational style of Jesuit spirituality with roots just as deep as martyrdom in the history of the Jesuit order. The Jesuits believed that the daily labor of operating a mission rewarded the missionary in spiritual terms. Conventional Jesuit spirituality emphasized service to God and abnegation of self. Marest highlighted this major element of Jesuit religious culture when he stated with regard to the Illinois missions, "If our Missions are not so flourishing as others on account of a great number of conversions, at least they are precious and beneficial to us, on account of the labors and hardships which are inseparable from them." The physical labor, travel, instruction of neophytes, conduct of the sacraments, care for the sick, study of Native languages, and innumerable other activities enriched the spiritual life of the missionary and, in the Jesuit view, provided an important example for the missionized. Missionary labor displayed a commitment to the mission and its residents. Such dedication also served as a conspicuous example of Jesuit definitions and expectations for diligent work for people the Jesuits so often characterized as lazy and indolent.[11]

Marest died two years after he shared these thoughts in his 1712 account of the Illinois mission. His colleague in the Illinois country, the Jesuit Jean Mermet, wrote an obituary for the priest that revealed the spirituality of service that predominated in the eighteenth century. In traditionally hagiographic style, Mermet praised Marest in the letter announcing his death: "he was a missionary of incomparable zeal, of exceptional charity, and of an ardor to undertake the most extraordinarily difficult tasks; his malady came from an excessive desire to console, relieve, and confess the sick and to administer to them the last sacraments during a widespread epidemic." Mermet reported that two to three hundred people perished in the epidemic during the summer of 1714 at Kaskaskia. Marest died from fatigue, according to Mermet, much to the regret of the Illinois Christian and the French communities. Some people brought gifts and assisted at the funeral for the priest, singing the requiem mass that Mermet said in the departed missionary's honor.[12]

By the time of Marest's death, the missionaries were well entrenched in the Illinois country. A new generation of apostolic workers kept the Indian missions operating and staffed the growing French parishes, although they frequently faced a shortage of personnel. In the time that Gravier and Marest had labored in the missions, the founding generation of Illinois converts helped make Christianity an influential feature of the region's cultural and social mix. Many of the Illinois incorporated Christianity as an integral element of their personal and communal identities while also maintaining numerous links to the traditions and experiences of their Illinois ancestors.

French observers in the late 1710s and early 1720s commented on the strength of Christianity and the extent of cultural change among the Illinois. The commandant at the French post of Detroit, Jacques Charles de Sabrevois, reported in a 1718 memoir on the region that "the French who are settled at this Village [of Kaskaskia] say that it is The most prosperous mission among all The Savages; its people are very devout and an example to the French." Sabrevois noted that the Kaskaskias were relatively affluent, producing corn and French wheat and raising cows, pigs, horses, chickens, and "everything necessary for their subsistence." The division of the village the following year disrupted this productive economy. Charlevoix passed through the region in the fall of 1721 and drew similar conclusions. He found the Jesuit mission at Kaskaskia "flourishing" and determined that almost all of the Illinois were Christians.[13]

Yet even Charlevoix recognized the limits of the transformation and the persistence of Illinois understandings of the world, at least among a portion of the Illinois. He described a chief from the primarily Peoria village on Lake Pimitoui who wore a copper cross and a small image of Mary and the child Jesus around his neck. The chief was not Christian and asked Charlevoix what they represented. The Jesuit explained the meaning of the images and told him that Christians often invoked the Mother of God for protection. Charlevoix related that the chief later requested the intervention of Mary when he was about to be killed in an ambush. The chief survived, miraculously, and, impressed by the apparent power of the Christian saint, from then on always wore the sacred items for protection. According to the account, the Illinois man later had the priest baptize his extremely ill infant daughter. In one of the few overtly spiritual passages in Charlevoix's otherwise mostly descriptive journal, the Jesuit traveler declared, "Should my voyage in every other respect be entirely fruitless, . . . I should not regret all the danger and fatigue I have undergone, since, in all probability, had I not been at Pimiteouy, this child would never have entered into the kingdom of heaven, where I make no doubt but it will soon be. I even hope this little angel will obtain for her father the same grace which he has procured for her." Charlevoix claimed that the chief eventually converted.[14]

Once again, that critical cultural convergence between Illinois and Christian worldviews—the creative connection between power and grace—reduced the conceptual distance that separated Native and missionary. If the account is generally accurate, there were still Illinois, especially among the Peorias, who rejected Christianity, but the process of cultural engagement continued. This experimentation led in a number of directions, from a somewhat selective incorporation of Christian ideas, signs, and practices into a largely Illinois cultural framework to a more thorough transformation and formal adoption of "the prayer."

The account of another French traveler confirms the impression that the Illinois shaped Christianity to their own needs and experiences. Diron d'Artaguiette left a journal of his journey from New Orleans to the Illinois country in 1723. D'Artaguiette was the inspector-general for the Compagnie des Indes, the chartered French company that administered Louisiana at the time. He concluded that the Jesuits "have up to the present failed in their attempts to make [the Illinois] understand that God made himself man and died for us." This skeptical statement does not necessarily contradict the claims of Charlevoix and others that most of the Illinois were Christians. The statement suggests rather that the Illinois had not yet fully assimilated some of the more complex concepts of Catholicism, such as the doctrine of the Trinity. As practiced, Illinois Christianity remained perhaps less than what the Jesuits dreamed it would someday be, but it was still obviously Christian both to the missionaries and to the Illinois themselves. D'Artaguiette by contrast saw more surviving Illinois culture than he did conventional Christianity.

D'Artaguiette contended that customs like polygamy prevented many non-Christian Illinois from fully accepting Christianity. He thought Illinois men did not want to "deprive themselves of the pleasure of having two or three wives." The inspector-general's assertions imply that the integration of Illinois culture with Christianity continued to raise troubling issues for men in particular, even after several decades of missionization. The population imbalance between women and men probably contributed to this ongoing resistance to adopt Catholic marriage patterns. At the same time, D'Artaguiette's conclusions show that the cultural debates over such issues were not completely resolved. The encounters, conversations, and exchanges retained their lively character.[15]

Only two years after D'Artaguiette's brief excursion to Illinois, Kas-kaskia leader Chicagou, during his visit to France, provided additional valu-able insights into the nature of Illinois Christianity. Chicagou emphasized the connection between Illinois Christianity and the French alliance. In the French translation of his speech before officials of the Compagnie des Indes, Chicagou said, "I love prayer and the French. Thus you should love me and my Nation, which has always been allied with the French." He also warned that he had to return with words from the French that would demonstrate their attachment to the Illinois and satisfy the young men in his village. In a later speech, Chicagou thanked his French hosts and reportedly said, "I leave full of satisfaction. . . . I am now entirely French and there are no longer any differences between the French heart and my own. . . . [My nation] will al-ways love prayer and the French." The letter from the Kaskaskia leader Ma-mantouensa reiterated these points. "My father," the letter read, "I share your prayer, for the Black Robes have instructed me and all my Elders."[16]

When Chicagou and Mamantouensa traveled together to New Orleans in 1730, they both demonstrated that the link between prayer and alliance was still vital. The Michigamea chief recalled his trip to France and, accord-ing to the Jesuit Mathurin Le Petit, reminded his listeners that "the king promised me his protection for the Prayer, and recommended me never to abandon it." The Jesuit account suggests that these two men were indeed well instructed in religious matters and that they could also express a sense of piety that went beyond the political concerns of alliance and social order. Le Petit related that the Illinois representatives and their entourage attended mass daily and chanted prayers with knowledge and enthusiasm during their three-week stay. Le Petit concluded that "a great number of our French are not, by any means, so well instructed in Religion as are these Neophytes." The nuns so impressed Mamantouensa that he invited them to instruct Illi-nois women and girls.[17]

The Illinois devotion to Christianity highlighted in the meetings in Paris and New Orleans seems to have weakened somewhat by the middle of the eighteenth century. The Jesuit missionary Louis Vivier wrote two letters in 1750 describing conditions in the Illinois country. The letters appeared in the *Lettres édifiantes*, a series of eighteenth-century volumes that collected accounts of French Jesuit missionary activity from around the world. Vivier's letters con-trast his obvious frustration about the state of the Indian mission with his op-timism for the long-term prospects of the Illinois country as a whole.[18]

"What we have to write of this country is so little curious and so little edifying that it is hardly worth while to take up the pen," Vivier warned his readers before describing the slowly growing colonial region. There were five French villages in the plain between the Mississippi and Kaskaskia Rivers. French settlement had given the area a multicultural character. Vivier estimated that there were 1,100 whites, 300 blacks (most or all of them slaves), and 60 Indian slaves in the French villages. The three Illinois villages in the bottomlands contained around 800 people. There was a fourth, larger Illinois village at Lake Pimitoui. The rich soil, abundant game, fine rivers, and mild climate sustained the population comfortably and without fear of famine. Vivier argued that the Illinois country "is of far greater importance than is imagined. Through its position alone, it deserves that France should spare nothing to retain it." The region provided a critical communications link and essential provisions and natural resources for the distant French colonies of Canada and Louisiana.[19]

Vivier's report on the Illinois mission was not nearly so positive in tone. He explained that there had once been missionaries in all three Illinois villages near the Mississippi. Missionaries of the Séminaire des missions étrangères had charge of the mission to the Cahokias and Tamaroas. There were two missionaries at Kaskaskia, including Vivier. The Jesuits abandoned the third mission, Saint François Xavier at Michigamea, "through lack of a missionary, and because we obtained but scanty results." Almost all of the Kaskaskias were baptized, but Vivier complained that even at Kaskaskia "the harvest does not correspond to our labors. If these Missions have no greater success," he continued, "it is not through the fault of those who have preceded us, for their memory is still held in veneration among French and Illinois."[20]

Illinois culture was in better shape, although this fact was no great solace for Vivier. The Illinois maintained many of their traditions, some of which the Jesuits generally believed were not easily compatible with the regular practice of Christianity. Extended families shared cabins as they always had. The long winter hunts continued, leaving the primary settlements and their chapels virtually empty for months at a time. The gendered division of labor still organized the work life of the community, and like his colleagues before him, Vivier thought the arrangements disgraceful. Women labored in the fields, producing large crops of maize. "As to the men," the missionary grumbled, "with the exception of a little hunting now and then, they lead a thoroughly idle life; they chat and smoke, and that is all."[21]

Vivier cited several reasons for the moribund state of the mission, other than insufficient personnel. Through the decades, the Jesuits wavered in their opinions about the impact, positive or negative, of the French influence on the Illinois mission. At midcentury, Vivier concluded that the French, "who are continually mingled with these people," were a bad example to the Illinois. The missionary also blamed the effects of the brandy trade and the declining Illinois population. Finally, Vivier presented his interpretation of Illinois character, which was typically inconsistent. "Nothing but erroneous ideas are conceived of [Indians] in Europe," he wrote; "they are hardly believed to be men. This is a gross error. The Savages, and especially the Illinois, are of a very gentle and sociable nature. . . . I found in them many qualities that are lacking in civilized peoples." Vivier thought that the personal freedom they enjoyed explained these good qualities, but he also felt that this independence created a major cultural obstacle for missionaries. He attributed the failure of the Jesuits to complete the transformation of the Illinois "above all to their disposition which is certainly opposed to all restraint, and consequently to any Religion."[22]

Vivier's frustration with the Illinois mission was evident, but the lure of distant peoples seemingly untouched by the problems that concerned him still tantalized the missionary's apostolic spirit. He called the vast region drained by the Missouri River, spreading northwest far across the plains to the mountains, "the finest country in the world." Vivier exclaimed, "How many Savage Nations in these immense regions offer themselves to the Missionaries' zeal!" The Jesuits had to wait until the nineteenth century to enter those fields, however, after the return of the Society of Jesus from a lengthy papal suppression. The French colonies in North America were long gone by then, but the French influence persisted in the people, the culture, and the landscape of the Great Lakes region and Mississippi valley.[23]

Marie Rouensa was a leading figure in the encounters that made this influence possible. She forged key social links between the Kaskaskias and the French, and she stimulated the acceptance of Christianity in a large portion of the Illinois community. The amount of significant surviving documentation about her life is relatively large and extremely rare for a Native woman of that era, a result of her dramatic conversion, high social status, marriage to a Frenchman, and subsequent economic success. Although in many ways it appears that Rouensa identified more closely with French culture than with Illinois traditions, she nevertheless maintained at least some connection to her rich cultural heritage. She had her will translated from the

French and read back to her in Illinois. The specific reason is unknown, but the Illinois language invoked the long cultural memory of the Illinois peoples. This small act at the end of her life suggests that she continued to balance a variety of influences in the self-identity she constructed. Rouensa's burial under a pew of the church in French Kaskaskia was a testament to her status and her commitment to Christianity as well as to her ability to confront the realities of a new world and a new age. Her many descendants became prominent in the emerging métis community of the Mississippi valley, weaving together diverse cultural and social strands. In 1792, the sacramental register for Immaculate Conception recorded the burial of Antoine Thomas Rouensa, the seven-month-old son of Antoine Rouensa and Adelaîde Gaspard, who were listed as members of "the nation of the Kaskaskias." The connection between the Kaskaskias and the church continued, at least for some inhabitants of the village.[24]

Marie Rouensa was clearly an exceptional woman. The range of her experiences, the intensity of her encounter and engagement with French culture, and the depth of her influence in the community appear to have been remarkable at least, and possibly unique. It is clear, however, that like Marie Rouensa, a significant number of Illinois women discovered a deeply meaningful way to express their spirituality, to enlarge their sphere of influence, and to adapt to the pressures of change. Women became the foundation of the Illinois Christian community. For Illinois men like Chicagou and Mamantouensa, Christianity was a major component of the Illinois alliance with the French and a way to encourage social order during a period of stressful change. Christianity, along with the marriage of Illinois women to French men, gave Illinois women a role in this critical French alliance. Some men also experimented with the spiritual power of Christianity, seeking a source of healing, subsistence success, or protection from harm.[25]

Within the Illinois and mixed-blood Christian community that emerged in the eighteenth century, the level of Christian practice and piety must have varied a great deal. The evolution of the community and of individuals, the debates over the appropriateness of Christianity for the Illinois, and the decades of dialogue with missionaries made a stable synthesis impossible. There is no way of knowing what Christian Kaskaskia women did in the fields or on long summer hunts on the hot prairies. There is no easy way to measure accurately the commitment of Illinois men to Christian practice. In the eighteenth century, however, Christianity became an integral part of the cultural landscape in the Illinois country. Missionaries became important members of local society. Many Illinois created identities that were both Native and Christian.[26]

*   *   *

The impact of the Seven Years' War finally ended the Jesuit century in the *pays d'en haut*, although the surviving Illinois remained in their homeland until the forced removals of the nineteenth century. On 23 March 1767, an overwhelmed Jesuit priest, Sébastien Louis Meurin, wrote from Kaskaskia to the new bishop of Québec, Monseigneur Olivier Briand, to describe conditions in the rapidly changing Illinois country. The English conquest of New France had unsettled the region. The French had recently ceded the lands east of the Mississippi River to the English. The Spanish now claimed the lands to the west, beneficiaries of a quiet deal with the French. The religious landscape had also been transformed. The Cahokia mission operated by the priests of the Séminaire des missions étrangères was gone, and in 1763, the Jesuits lost their property and their mission in Illinois, leaving the region without any Catholic pastors.

In the letter, Meurin told the bishop that he had obtained permission to resume working in the Illinois country, where he had previously labored as a missionary from the 1740s. He wrote that his commitment to stay was "especially in consideration of the savages," the Kaskaskias having been the primary focus of his mission work in the past. Meurin explained that the people, Indian and French, needed several more priests to prevent a decline in piety. Alone, he divided his time between the French settlements and Native villages on both banks of the Mississippi. The country also required, in Meurin's opinion, someone with the title and power of *grand-vicaire*, or vicar-general. Meurin complained that his lack of a title and clear authority from the bishop inspired insolent behavior in the French communities. His weakness made the situation personally difficult and threatened the continuity of the Catholic communities of the Illinois country.[27]

In another letter to the bishop not even two months later, Meurin seemed absolutely demoralized. Writing from Cahokia, he reiterated the need for priests and warned again of the problems that his lack of authority caused. Meurin complained that he was only sixty-one years old but that twenty-five years of mission labor in the country had ruined his health and carried him close to death's door. "I can no longer meet the spiritual needs of this country," he wrote. To emphasize his point, Meurin told the bishop that he had arrived at Cahokia only three days before but had just been called away to minister to a dangerously sick man at Sainte Genevieve, across the Mississippi, many miles away. "I am forced to leave [Cahokia] with more than three-quarters of the work undone," he lamented.[28]

Bishop Briand informed Meurin in a letter from August 1767 that he had already sent Meurin his powers as vicar-general, making him the bishop's and the church's official representative in the Illinois country, even before he received the first letter detailing "the sad situation" in the Illinois parishes. Briand acknowledged the problems and tried to soothe his priest with thoughts of God, reminding Meurin of the "eternal consolations to which [he] was destined" for his pious perseverance. The bishop indicated that he planned to send two priests to the region the following spring.[29]

Meurin finally received the letters that promoted him to vicar-general, but he claimed to be politically and physically unfit for the demands of the position. He had more complaints for the bishop as well. The priest's appointment had stirred controversy with ecclesiastical authorities in New Orleans. Meurin also bewailed the visible results of the seizure of Jesuit property at Kaskaskia. The forced sale had taken place in 1763, and it perturbed the Jesuit greatly to see the chapel and cemetery being used as a storehouse and garden by the English, who rented the property from the new owner. Meurin shared a little good news, however. The people at Kaskaskia and especially at Cahokia had shown some signs of renewed piety, and a few English Protestants sometimes attended his services.[30]

Another pastor eventually did join Meurin in the Illinois country, but one priest was not enough to alter the pastoral situation dramatically. As usual, Meurin had a list of complaints for the bishop in his correspondence. He thought the new priest, a non-Jesuit named Pierre Gibault, would not last long because of poor health and arduous working conditions. Meurin also could no longer openly visit the settlements on the west bank of the river because, as a Jesuit, he had been banished from the Spanish territories. He worried about the validity of marriages between Catholics and non-Catholics and fretted that people were buried in the cemeteries of Kaskaskia and St. Louis regardless of their standing in the church. Meurin claimed that he was powerless to stop such disorder, but he told Bishop Briand that he also did not validate it by his presence.[31]

Finally, not long before his death in 1777, Meurin admitted to his bishop that his constant complaints had probably painted an excessively gloomy portrait of the inhabitants of Illinois. "The people of this country are no worse than those of Canada," he wrote. "There is even more of the good than of the bad. This is from time to time my consolation," the priest confessed. With Meurin's passing, the Jesuit presence in the Illinois country came to an end.[32]

Although Meurin stated in one of his letters that he wanted to return to the Illinois country primarily to serve its Native peoples, his letters are curiously silent about Indian affairs. There is virtually no information on the Illinois Christians in the period. The Jesuit François Philibert Watrin claimed in a 1764 report on the banishment of the Jesuits from the Illinois country that the Illinois at the Kaskaskia mission wanted Meurin to remain with them and keep his position. Watrin defended the Jesuit record in Illinois, asserting that "despite the inconstancy of [the Illinois], the religion that was long ago established there has been preserved up to the present, the superstition called jugglery having been almost destroyed. Even the unbelievers were zealous in having their children baptized." He considered brandy the most harmful influence on the Christian community.[33]

The Jesuits were unable to stay at the time, however, and even after the return of Catholic clergy, the chapels in the Illinois country remained permanently understaffed. The lack of personnel may have hindered formal Catholic worship, but it also created an opportunity for Illinois Christians. In such an environment, Illinois Christians assumed even greater authority in the Catholic Indian community as lay practitioners and religious leaders. According to Watrin, the Illinois at Kaskaskia obtained permission to maintain the chapel and the missionary's house in their village, "in order that the best instructed person among them might assemble the children and repeat the prayers to them; and that every Sunday and feast-day he might summon those who prayed . . . by the ringing of the bell, to fulfill as well as possible the duties of religion." Family and community became the basis for a truly Illinois form of Christianity. There was simply no other choice.[34]

Christian Ottawas faced a similar dilemma by the 1760s. Since the dramatic Kiskakon conversion a century before, the Ottawas had struggled to maintain a position of strength and regional influence. Most of the Kiskakons and some members of the other Ottawa bands made Michilimackinac their base for revitalization efforts. They had a powerful historical connection to the place that stretched back into mythic times to the origins of the present world. The location was strategically important to trade and diplomacy in the Great Lakes basin and beyond. The Kiskakons in particular also looked to Christianity as one potential source of spiritual renewal and social order.

In the mid-1670s, the Jesuits established a separate mission at Michilimackinac, Saint François de Borgia, for the Ottawas and other Algonquian-speaking peoples in the region. Saint Ignace remained open for the Christian Tionontatis and Wendats at the straits.[35]

A number of challenges tested the Ottawa community at Michilimackinac through the turn of the century. The growing French presence in the Great Lakes created considerable tension. The French maintained Fort Baude at Michilimackinac from 1690 to 1698. Ongoing intertribal rivalries and conflicts periodically erupted into violence. The Ottawas and many other nations strained to piece together an alliance with the French that would regulate affairs in the precarious *pays d'en haut* and alleviate some of these problems.[36]

Two events in 1701 markedly changed the situation. The first was the Grand Settlement of 1701, which established a general peace throughout the Great Lakes region. Several Indian nations cooperated with the French in devastating raids on Haudenosaunee towns in the 1690s, and the Five Nations finally sought peace with the French and their Native allies. Open conflict declined after the settlement, but competition over trade and land as well as persistent interethnic hostility in some quarters continued to generate insecurity. English economic and imperial ambitions in the eighteenth century inserted an additional element of uncertainty. The Ottawa alliance with the French was never entirely stable in this fluid world. It always remained a work in progress.[37] The second major development in 1701 was the establishment of Detroit by Antoine Laumet de La Mothe, Sieur de Cadillac. In part, the French wanted to counter English attempts to gain a hold in the west. The move reoriented the regional fur trade and shifted attention and influence away from Michilimackinac to the new French post. The establishment of Detroit also divided the Ottawas at Michilimackinac, who were forced to decide whether to move or stay.[38]

In 1702, Jesuit missionary Étienne de Carheil reported from Michilimackinac that the missions were in complete disarray. Carheil emphatically denounced the evil influence of brandy in the missions, the lack of support from the French commandants, and the scandalous behavior of French soldiers and traders. "All the villages of our savages are now only Taverns, as regards drunkenness; and sodoms, as regards immorality," he complained bitterly. He even suggested that the Jesuits withdraw from the missions and leave the villages "to the just Anger and vengeance of God."[39]

Although the Ottawas were not completely satisfied with the situation at Michilimackinac, many of them still refused to leave for Detroit, as a number of French officials wanted them to do. The Jesuit missionary Joseph Marest, brother of the Jesuit Gabriel Marest who worked in the Illinois country, related that after three days of deliberation in 1703, "the councillors who were assembled among the Kiskakons told me with one voice that they had resolved to die at Missilimakinak, and that even if they left there they would never go to Detroit; that such was their final resolution." Other Ottawas and most of the Tionontatis did leave, however. Their flock reduced by migration to Detroit, the Jesuits eventually became tired of conditions at Michilimackinac, and in 1706 they left in disgust. The Jesuits returned the following year, probably reestablishing Saint Ignace on the southern shore of the straits, the new site of Michilimackinac, where they concentrated on the remaining Ottawas.[40]

Gabriel Marest described Michilimackinac and the restored mission, where his brother Joseph still labored, in an account of a visit in 1711. Like the Ottawas, Marest thought the location had several obvious benefits. Michilimackinac was "the general resort" of the French and the Indians in the region, and it was still a major center in the fur trade. Although the soil was not great, fish were abundant. Marest's comments on spiritual matters were not so positive, however. "The character of these Savages bears the impress of the climate in which they live," he observed; "it is harsh and indocile." He thought that his brother showed great patience in dealing with them. Marest concluded that few people at the mission truly gave themselves to God.[41]

Many of the Ottawas were probably more concerned with making a living and maintaining stability than with the kind of Christian piety the missionaries longed to see. Joseph Marest reported in a letter from 1712 that the Ottawas at Michilimackinac were upset with the state of their relationship with the French and with the impact of Detroit on their safety and welfare. Sauks, Mesquakies, and Mascoutens had recently attacked Detroit, and the Ottawas feared that yet another round of fighting would engulf them. According to Marest, the Ottawa leader Koutaouiliboe complained: "Formerly, before the establishment of Detroit, we were a powerful nation. All the other nations were obliged to come here to obtain necessaries, and there was no trouble, as there is now. But the most savage and unreasonable of the nations . . . have the power of going on foot to Detroit, in as great numbers as they wish, to buy their powder and trouble their allies. Yet the French desire more than ever to establish Detroit." The Ottawas wanted the French to restore order as quickly as possible, a task that proved virtually impossible in the volatile region.[42]

Other later Jesuit observers did not find much to celebrate at the mission. Charlevoix passed through in 1721 and commented that the post had declined greatly since the establishment of Detroit. He reported that the missionaries were not very well occupied because they had never found the Ottawas that receptive. The continuing importance of the Jesuits came instead from their role as mediators in the alliance system and in their pastoral work for the French residents. Charlevoix did note, however, the enduring significance of the site as a place of history and myth. A little over a decade later, another Jesuit remarked from his post among the Iroquois that the most the missionaries of the Ottawas could accomplish was the baptism of children who were on the point of death. "Those who recover seldom fail later to fall away from the faith," he wrote.[43]

The Ottawa mission may have been struggling from the Jesuit perspective, but the Ottawas did not give up their search for order, and the missionaries continued to participate in that elusive quest. In the early 1740s, the Ottawas at Michilimackinac, mostly from the Kiskakon and Sinago bands, started surveying lands to the southwest, along the shores of the lower peninsula of Michigan. They looked for more productive soil and wanted easy access to good hunting. In 1742, the Ottawas decided in consultation with the French to move to a place called Waugaunaukezee, or L'Arbre Croche, about twenty miles southwest of Michilimackinac. In a speech before the French governor of Montréal, Ottawa leaders outlined their vision of peace and plenty for the new settlement. The rich land at L'Arbre Croche appealed to them. They told the governor that the "fire [at L'Arbre Croche] will never die out; we shall all have the pleasure of warming ourselves there in peace and tranquility with our wives and our Children, And of seeing the Sparks fly up to the Sky . . . we shall take care to live there quietly, and they who come after us will never leave it."[44]

The Jesuits followed, transferring Saint Ignace to L'Arbre Croche and subsequently dividing their time between the Ottawas at the new settlement and the French community at Michilimackinac. At L'Arbre Croche, the Jesuits worked with the Ottawas, operated a farm, and studied the Ottawa language, but Saint Ignace lasted only another two decades. Jesuit dreams of creating an empire of Christian Indians in the Great Lakes ended with the English conquest of Canada. The last Jesuit missionary left L'Arbre Croche around 1764 or 1765, and like the Illinois far to the south, the Ottawas with a connection to Christianity were left on their own.[45]

Although the Ottawas and the Illinois struggled to survive in a difficult colonial environment, their stories are hardly tales of colonial domination. Their histories also do not present a clear linear narrative relating the secure establishment and ever-deepening faith of French Catholic Christianity. There were stops and starts within the Christian communities. The intensity of the attachment to Christianity fluctuated over time and through the generations. Moreover, many Illinois and Ottawas rejected Christianity as a set of foreign, even dangerous cultural practices and renounced the missionaries who promoted the strange ideas as aggressive, antisocial meddlers in Native communities.

Nevertheless, Christianity did become a potent cultural force in the region, and the missionaries emerged as influential religious and political figures. Christianity restructured many Native communities, dividing some in bitterness and acting as a source of solidarity in others. It has been far too easy to associate change in Indian cultures only with loss and destruction and in doing so to discount the creative abilities of adaptation and resilience employed by Native peoples to adjust to new situations, ideas, and environments. Native peoples have always found room within their own societies and cultures and the restrictive circumstances of colonization to maneuver and experiment, to weave peoples into new relationships, to reshape cultures into new forms.

In the *pays d'en haut* of the seventeenth and eighteenth centuries, Native peoples explored Christianity with purpose, testing its spiritual and social capacities. Some of them discovered in Christianity the power to transform themselves and others. Native Christians and French missionaries started with a few favorable cultural convergences to construct a foundation, frustratingly imperfect at times, for mutual understanding. In the process, they created a new Christian culture that contained at least the memory of certain Native spiritual traditions as well as numerous elements of traditional social practice. This engagement transformed missionaries, too. The conversations, exchanges, and conversions were genuine encounters. A more complete historical account must not ignore or dismiss their experiences and influence, as a group or as individuals. The missionaries represented a religious community engaged in a spiritual enterprise, even as they also became an important part of French colonial institutions. They recognized this dual role in North America, but the salvation of souls, including their own, remained their primary objective. While trade and exchange, diplomacy and politics, marriage and kinship all contributed to the complex and contentious French-Indian relationships that emerged in the colonial era, religion and religious change were equally important dimensions of the volatile relationships that reshaped the region.

A nineteenth-century treaty negotiated between the Kaskaskias, allied Illinois bands, and the United States hints at the depth of the impact of these spiritual encounters. Although the Kaskaskias had signed other treaties with the young nation, they made a separate and, for the time, definitive treaty with the United States in 1803. In the agreement, the Kaskaskias ceded most rights to their ancestral lands, maintaining only their village near the town of Kaskaskia and one other tract of land to be determined. The treaty also increased their annuity payments and promised the protection and patronage of the United States. As to religious life, the third article of the treaty stated that "*whereas*, The greater part of the said tribe have been baptised and received into the Catholic church to which they are much attached, the United States will give annually for seven years one hundred dollars towards the support of a priest of that religion, who will engage to perform for the said tribe the duties of his office and also to instruct as many of their children as possible in the rudiments of literature." In addition, the United States agreed to provide three hundred dollars for the erection of a church in the community.[46]

The Kaskaskias had been the most devoted practitioners of "the prayer" among the Illinois since Marie Rouensa's conversion in the 1690s, and they were, not surprisingly, the primary party in the treaty. Joining them in the accord were the remaining Michigameas, Cahokias, and Tamaroas, who also had developed close and lasting ties to the French missionaries in the eighteenth century. Just as significantly, the Peorias, who had opposed the missionaries so much of the time, were not included in the treaty's provisions. This treaty, then, reflects in notable ways the variation in the nature of Illinois encounters with Christianity in the previous century and reveals the persistence of Christian memory and practice among at least a portion of the Illinois people more than a generation after the missions closed.

A Note on Sources and Methods

The *Jesuit Relations* are the most detailed and voluminous source for the history of the Jesuit missions and, more generally, for the religious history of New France in the seventeenth century. The official published *Relations* appeared in France between 1632 and 1673, providing vivid and exciting accounts of Jesuit mission activity in New France. At a time when religious devotion was surging, the much anticipated annual reports became extremely popular with French readers interested in the spread of Catholicism, the piety of inspiring religious figures, and the lands and Native peoples of the New World. From the Jesuit perspective, the volumes provided excellent publicity and attracted powerful patrons and crucial financial support for the Jesuits' work. For more than a century, scholars have mined the *Jesuit Relations* for historical documentation and ethnographic details. The *Relations* are indeed an unparalleled source of such material, but it is imperative to remember that they are also religious texts that document particular historical expressions of missionary spirituality, both as practiced and in ideal terms. A clear understanding of Jesuit spirituality in the early modern era is essential to the analysis of cultural encounters within the mission communities, and such awareness is a major component of the methods that provide the foundation for this study of religious culture. Examining the texts with these thoughts in mind adds additional layers of interpretive insight to the analysis of the people and events described in the documents.[1]

The historical record is unfortunately much more fragmentary for the period after the Jesuits ceased publication of the *Relations* in 1673. The disappearance of this vital source is one reason that scholars have sensed a decline in the vigor of the Jesuit missions at the end of the seventeenth century. Missionary sources for the late seventeenth and the eighteenth centuries do exist, however, providing enough quality material to carry the story of French-Indian religious encounters forward by many decades more than is usual. The "allied documents" in the well-worn Thwaites edition of the *Jesuit Relations* as well as some surviving archival material make such work possible. These post-1673 sources include letters, journals, linguistic manuals, and official documents from the Society of Jesus. In general, the tone of the letters and journals is significantly more personal than the somewhat polished publications that appeared as the actual *Jesuit Relations*. Scholars normally cite both the official *Relations* and the later documents in the same way, often providing neither the author nor the title of the individual piece, because Reuben Gold Thwaites gathered them all into one massive, easy-to-use collection that included the French original and an English translation. The more complete method of citation used for this study is an effort to indicate better the diverse nature of the Jesuit writings and their individual authors.[2]

Scholars also have not generally considered the long history of French missionization in North America. Most studies concentrate on the well-documented Jesuit missions of the first half of the seventeenth century and end with the dramatic destruction of Huronia and the martyrdom of bold Jesuit priests. Scholars have too easily perceived a gradual decline in fervor from this apex of French mission work, a decline that only accelerated in the eighteenth century. The Native peoples of the upper Great Lakes and Mississippi valley, witnessing an influx of missionaries beginning in the 1660s, would hardly have agreed. The end of the Huron mission in 1650 only marked a new phase of Jesuit evangelization. Issues that contribute to the perception of decline include changes in the Jesuit relationship to other colonial institutions, the end of the published *Jesuit Relations* in 1673, and even a failure among scholars to understand core Jesuit spiritual values of apostolic service.[3]

A new periodization for the study of the Jesuits in New France should not neglect later periods and must account for changing goals and historical circumstances. Briefly, while the first half of the seventeenth century was a period of establishment and spectacular martyrdom, the second half of the century saw a dramatic reconstruction of the Jesuit mission network. It was a period that emphasized exploration and expansion. In the eighteenth century, the Jesuits concentrated on maintenance of the existing mission network and on congregational growth and development.

The supreme expression of Jesuit spirituality in the three periods differed greatly. In the pioneer era of the early seventeenth century, martyrdom represented the highest Jesuit ideal. The Jesuit martyrs inspired subsequent generations of missionaries to a spirituality of service to God and Christ, to Native neophytes, and to the Society of Jesus. Constant travel and the opening of new missions, many of them short-lived and unsuccessful, defined Jesuit service in the second half of the seventeenth century. The daily routines of established missions and Christian Indian communities shaped missionary life in the eighteenth century. Much of the hard work of mutual translation took place in this later period. These other forms of Jesuit spirituality based more on dedicated service than on the drama of martyrdom were rooted just as strongly in Jesuit models of apostolic service, abnegation of self, and the salvation of souls.[4]

Rich as they are, the primarily Jesuit sources create serious problems for historical research. The most significant challenges are overcoming missionary bias in the sources and attempting to comprehend Native experiences. Ethnohistorical methods offer guidance in reducing to some degree the impact of these obstacles. In this case, the ethnohistorical analysis relies on a conscious understanding of the French missionary and spiritual context for the documents, an intensive study of Native cultures and histories in the region, and the use of valuable supplementary sources such as linguistic material and oral traditions recorded at the time and occasionally in later periods. Colonial memoirs authored by French officials and traders were not always sympathetic to the missionaries and their projects, and they provide an important opportunity to compare sources. In a very few instances, additional material survives that documents specific Native individuals and groups mentioned in the narrative sources produced by the missionaries.

Individual missionaries also had distinct personalities, varied concerns, and particular approaches to mission work. Piecing together their stories and recognizing their individuality promote an appreciation for the differences in their writings and their perspectives. In addition, the careful consideration of resistance to missionary projects promises a more complete and balanced assessment of the encounters between missionaries and Indians. The missionaries loved to share tales of triumph, but their letters and accounts are also filled with stories of frustrated ambition, bitter disappointment, and genuine debates that they did not always win. The arguments against Christianity and the methods of opposition frequently provide important clues about Native understandings of Christianity and Native perceptions of missionaries, both for those who rejected Christianity and for the most enthusiastic converts.

Coming to terms with the goals and assumptions of missionary spirituality deepens our understanding of the texts the missionaries left behind and stimulates keener insights into Indian experiences of Christianity as well. Indeed, the only way not to perpetuate the Eurocentric approach to mission history is to understand as fully as possible the missionaries who produced these vital documents. A more critical and penetrating analysis of colonial texts, combined with careful study of Indian spiritual concepts and traditions, offers the opportunity to produce an account that treats both missionaries and Indians as creative participants in these cultural encounters. Such an ethnohistory of missions moves beyond the study of missionary ideology and Indian responses to the reconstruction of meaning and shared experience.[5]

The study of conversion in this work, spread over several chapters, shows how these sources and methods can combine to produce a multifaceted understanding of meaning and experience in the conversion process. My investigation began with the delineation of Jesuit assumptions about spirituality and conversion, including an examination of the supreme Jesuit statement on the subject, the *Spiritual Exercises* of Ignatius. It continued with a systematic analysis of seventy-four conversion narratives contained in the *Jesuit Relations and Allied Documents*, highlighting consistent patterns in the experiences of converts and in the expectations of missionaries. Such careful classification of the conversion narratives embedded in Jesuit writings is one way of dealing with the limitations of these frequently formulaic sources (see Tables 1 and 2).[6]

Concepts of Jesuit spirituality and the process of conversion stressed intensive preparation through instruction and interior reflection, the opening of the soul to the operation of God's grace, and the cultivation of personal piety to strengthen the commitment to the will of God. The highest aim was eternal union with God in this life and the next. The narrative analysis demonstrates that the French Jesuits maintained these expectations for their Indian converts. Over 90 percent of the narratives contain evidence of instruction prior to conversion or baptism. Furthermore, just over 70 percent of the descriptions either directly or indirectly detail the operation of grace on the subject, and virtually all of the narratives document the pious behavior the missionaries longed to see. These distinctly religious concerns dominate Jesuit discussions of conversion and cannot be disregarded without distorting the meaning of the texts.

The precise breakdown of conversion narratives also provides significant evidence about Native perspectives on conversion. The results suggest that gender shaped reactions to Christianity, that Native men and women experienced conversion differently. Women were much more likely to exhibit overt defiance toward their families and communities. Around 40 percent of women in these narratives defied the wishes of their families or the standards of their community, as compared to only 27 percent of men. The analysis also offers some confirmation for the assertion that illness was a particularly important feature of the conversion process the missionaries documented for men. A little less than one half of the narratives for both men and women included illness as a prominent dimension of the description. However, men were significantly more likely to die from their illnesses, and the missionaries took great pains to describe these important moments.

Many missionaries commented on the influence of gender in their mission work, and a French trader who authored an important colonial memoir confirmed the presence of the pattern among the Illinois at the end of the seventeenth century. A thorough reconstruction of Illinois gender roles and a consideration of Illinois history in the period contextualize the accounts of these European observers. The lengthy Gravier journal from the Illinois mission relates the dramatic story of the particularly intense conversion and attachment of Marie Rouensa, her family, and the Kaskaskia community. A surprisingly wide variety of sources supports this account, including Marie Rouensa's will and estate inventory, the sacramental registers for the mission, and other appearances of her family and her community in the historical record. Used separately, each of these sources would have been insufficient to draw solid conclusions about the patterns of conversion, but together they offer a fairly comprehensive view of the conversion process and of the meanings of these spiritual and social transformations for the missionaries and for Native individuals and communities.

It is essential that scholars not downplay or disparage these personal and communal choices, for to do so is to devalue or even invalidate the frequently profound experiences of Native people like Marie Rouensa, who found meaning in being both Native and Christian. Scholars must overcome the tendency to assume that the acceptance of Christianity occurred solely by force, under extreme duress, or to meet only political demands or economic needs. It has become too easy for those who study the past to privilege the political, social, and economic over the religious aspects of colonial encounters, when in fact they are all intertwined. Religious experience and understanding may be difficult to access reliably, especially across cultural boundaries, but to abandon the attempt leaves in obscurity an important and influential portion of the already incomplete historical record.[7]

TABLE 1. LIST OF CONVERSION NARRATIVES FROM THE *JESUIT RELATIONS*

Id	Subject	Date	Mission	Nation	Missionary	Sex	Age	Source
1	Nahakwatkse	1660	Notre Dame de Bon Secours	Ottawa	Ménard	F	adult	46: 127–29
2	Plathéhahamie	1660	Notre Dame de Bon Secours	Ottawa	Ménard	F	adult	46: 133–35
3	girl	1660	Notre Dame de Bon Secours	Ottawa	Ménard	F	youth	46: 135
4	widow	1660	Notre Dame de Bon Secours	Ottawa	Ménard	F	adult	46: 135
5	Jean Amikous	1660	Notre Dame de Bon Secours	Ottawa	Ménard	M	elder	46: 129–31
6	Louis	1660	Notre Dame de Bon Secours	Ottawa	Ménard	M	adult	46: 131–33
7	old man	1660	Notre Dame de Bon Secours	Ottawa	Ménard	M	elder	46: 135–37
8	Anne	1661	Notre Dame de Bon Secours	Ottawa	Ménard	F	adult	48: 125–27
9	old man	1661	Notre Dame de Bon Secours	Ottawa	Ménard	M	elder	48: 123–25
10	old man	1661	Notre Dame de Bon Secours	Ottawa	Ménard	M	elder	48: 125
11	old woman	1666	Saint Esprit	Tionontati	Allouez	F	elder	50: 309–11
12	girl	1666	Saint Esprit	Tionontati	Allouez	F	youth	50: 311
13	woman	1666	Saint Esprit	Potawatomi	Allouez	F	adult	51: 37
14	woman	1666	Saint Esprit	Potawatomi	Allouez	F	adult	51: 37
15	old man	1666	Saint Esprit	Potawatomi	Allouez	M	elder	51: 29–35
16	old man	1666	Saint Esprit	Sauk	Allouez	M	elder	50: 309

17	old man	1667	Saint Esprit	uk	Allouez	elder	M	51: 261–65
18	unmarried woman	1668	Saint Esprit	uk	Allouez	adult	F	52: 213
19	old man	1668	Saint Esprit	Ottawa (Kiskakon)	Allouez	elder	M	52: 209
20	Kekakoung	1668	Saint Esprit	Ottawa (Kiskakon)	Allouez	adult	M	52: 209
21	Joseph	1668	Saint Esprit	Ottawa (Kiskakon)	Allouez	elder	M	52: 209
22	old man	1668	Saint Esprit	Ottawa (Kiskakon)	Allouez	elder	M	52: 209–11
23	old man	1668	Saint Esprit	Ottawa (Kiskakon)	Allouez	elder	M	52: 211
24	man	1668	Saint Esprit	Ottawa (Kamiga?)	Marquette	adult	M	54: 171–73
25	young man	1668	Saint Esprit	Ottawa (Kamiga?)	Marquette	adult	M	54: 173
26	young woman	1669	Saint Esprit	Ottawa (Kiskakon)	Marquette	adult	F	54: 179
27	man	1669	Saint Esprit	Ottawa (Kiskakon)	Marquette	adult	M	54: 177
28	man	1669	Saint Esprit	Ottawa (Kiskakon)	Marquette	adult	M	54: 179
29	old man	1669	Sainte Marie du Sault	Ottawa?	Allouez	elder	M	54: 143–45
30	Marie Movena	1670	Saint Esprit	Ottawa?	Allouez	youth	F	54: 239
31	man	1670	Saint Esprit	Ottawa (Kiskakon)	Marquette	adult	M	54: 185
32	old woman	1670	Sainte Marie du Sault	Ojibwa	Druillettes	elder	F	55: 119–21
33	woman	1670	Sainte Marie du Sault	Ojibwa	Druillettes	adult	F	55: 121
34	woman	1670	Sainte Marie du Sault	Ojibwa	Druillettes	adult	F	55: 123
35	young man	1670	Sainte Marie du Sault	Cree	Druillettes	adult	M	55: 123–25
36	young man	1670	Sainte Marie du Sault	Cree?	Druillettes	adult	M	55: 125–27
37	Apican	1670	Sainte Marie du Sault	Ojibwa	Druillettes	adult	M	55: 119
38	healer	1670	Sainte Marie du Sault	Ojibwa	Druillettes	elder	M	55: 127–31
39	healer	1671	Les Apostres	Amikwa	Nouvel	adult	M	56: 97–99
40	young woman	1671	Sainte Marie du Sault	uk	Druillettes	adult	F	56: 109–11
41	old woman	1671	Sainte Marie du Sault	uk	Druillettes	elder	F	56: 111–13
42	old man	1671	Sainte Marie du Sault	uk	Druillettes	elder	M	56: 113

(continued)

TABLE 1. (*continued*)

Id	Subject	Date	Mission	Nation	Missionary	Sex	Age	Source
43	woman	1672	Les Apostres	Amikwa?	Bailloquet	F	adult	57: 243; 61: 101
44	woman	1672	Les Apostres	Amikwa	Bailloquet	F	adult	57: 245–47
45	man	1672	Saint Jacques	Mascouten	Allouez	M	adult	58: 29–33
46	Lazare	1672	Saint Jacques	Mascouten	Allouez	M	elder	58: 35
47	woman	1672	Sainte Marie du Sault	Mississauga	Druillettes	F	adult	57: 215–19
48	girl	1673	Saint François Xavier	uk	André	F	youth	57: 269–71
49	healer	1673	Saint François Xavier	Menominee	André	M	adult	58: 277–79
50	adult	1673	Saint François Xavier	Menominee	André	uk	adult	58: 277–79
51	adult	1673	Saint François Xavier	Menominee	André	uk	adult	58: 277–79
52	woman	1673	Saint Ignace	Tionontati	Marquette	F	adult	57: 261
53	Joseph	1673	Saint Marc	Mesquakie	Allouez	M	adult	58: 45–47
54	captain	1674	Saint Jacques	Miami	Allouez	M	adult	59: 223
55	woman	1675	Saint Ignace	Mississauga	Nouvel	F	adult	60: 225
56	Joseph Nikalokita	1675	Saint Marc	Mesquakie	Allouez	M	elder	59: 225–27
57	brother	1675	Saint Marc	Mesquakie	Allouez	M	youth	59: 229–31
58	brother	1675	Saint Marc	Mesquakie	Allouez	M	youth	59: 229–31

59	old man	1676	Saint François Xavier	uk	Allouez	M	elder	60: 149–51
60	Joseph	1676	Saint François Xavier	Miami	Allouez	M	adult	60: 199
61	Joseph	1676	Saint Jacques	Mascouten	Silvy	M	adult	60: 209
62	man	1677	Les Apostres	Amikwa	Bonneault	M	adult	61: 97–99
63	man	1678	Saint François Borgia	Ottawa (Kiskakon)	Enjalran	M	elder	61: 129–31
64	man	1678	Saint François Borgia	Ottawa (Kiskakon)	Enjalran	M	elder	61: 129–31
65	man	1678	Saint François Borgia	Ottawa (Kiskakon)	Enjalran	M	elder	61: 129–31
66	Joseph Chikabiskisi	1678	Saint François Borgia	Ottawa (Kiskakon?)	Enjalran	M	adult	61: 129–31
67	widow	1693	Immaculate Conception	Illinois	Gravier	F	adult	64: 167–69
68	Marie Rouensa	1693	Immaculate Conception	Illinois (Kaskaskia)	Gravier	F	youth	64: 193–237
69	wife of Chief Rouensa	1693	Immaculate Conception	Illinois (Kaskaskia)	Gravier	F	adult	64: 193–237
70	Chief Rouensa	1693	Immaculate Conception	Illinois (Kaskaskia)	Gravier	M	adult	64: 193–237
71	Antoine	1693	Immaculate Conception	Illinois (Peoria)	Gravier	M	adult	64: 171–77
72	young woman	1712	Immaculate Conception	Illinois	Marest	F	youth	66: 249–51
73	woman	1712	Immaculate Conception	Illinois	Marest	F	adult	66: 251
74	Henri	1712	Immaculate Conception	Illinois	Marest	M	adult	66: 247–49

Sources are listed by volume and page number from Reuben Gold Thwaites, ed., *The Jesuit Relations and Allied Documents* (Cleveland, Ohio: Burrows Bros., 1896–1901).

TABLE 2. ANALYSIS OF CONVERSION NARRATIVES FROM THE *JESUIT RELATIONS*

Id	Subject	GRA	GRI	INS	BAP	BAR	ILL	HEA	DEA	GDD	REF	PTY	MRG	ELT	DEF	ALN	KIN	GRP
1	Nahakwatkse	n	y	y	y	n	n	n	n	n	y	y	y	n	n	n	y	n
2	Plathéhahamie	n	n	y	y	y	n	n	n	n	y	y	n	y	n	n	y	n
3	girl	n	n	y	y	y	y	y	n	n	y	y	n	y	n	n	y	n
4	widow	y	n	y	y	y	n	n	n	n	y	y	y	n	y	n	n	n
5	Jean Amikous	y	n	y	y	y	y	y	n	n	y	y	y	n	n	n	y	n
6	Louis	y	y	y	y	y	n	n	n	n	y	y	y	y	y	n	y	n
7	old man	n	n	y	y	n	y	n	n	n	y	y	n	n	n	n	n	n
8	Anne	n	y	y	y	n	n	n	n	n	y	y	n	n	y	n	n	n
9	old man	y	n	y	y	n	y	n	y	y	y	y	n	n	y	n	n	n
10	old man	y	n	y	y	n	y	n	y	y	y	y	n	n	n	n	n	n
11	old woman	y	n	y	y	y	y	n	y	y	y	y	n	n	n	n	n	n
12	girl	n	n	y	y	y	y	n	y	y	y	y	n	n	y	y	y	n
13	woman	n	y	y	y	y	y	n	y	y	y	y	n	y	n	y	y	n
14	woman	n	y	y	y	y	n	n	n	n	y	y	n	y	n	y	y	n
15	old man	n	y	y	y	y	y	n	y	y	y	y	n	y	y	n	y	n
16	old man	n	y	y	y	n	n	n	y	y	y	y	y	n	n	n	n	n
17	old man	n	y	y	y	n	n	n	n	y	n	y	n	y	n	n	n	n
18	unmarried woman	y	n	y	y	n	n	n	n	n	y	y	n	n	n	n	n	n
19	old man	y	n	y	y	n	n	n	n	n	y	y	n	n	n	n	n	y
20	Kekakoung	y	n	y	y	n	n	n	n	n	y	y	n	y	n	y	n	y
21	Joseph	y	n	y	y	n	n	n	n	n	y	y	n	n	n	n	n	y
22	old man	y	n	y	y	n	n	n	n	n	y	y	n	n	n	n	n	y

23	old man	y	n	y	y	n	n	n	n	n	y	n	n	n	n	n	n	n	y
24	man	n	n	y	y	n	n	n	n	n	y	n	n	y	n	n	n	n	n
25	young man	n	n	y	y	n	n	n	n	n	y	n	n	y	n	n	n	n	n
26	young woman	n	n	y	y	n	n	n	n	n	y	n	n	y	n	n	n	n	n
27	man	y	n	y	y	y	y	y	n	y	y	y	n	y	n	n	n	n	n
28	man	n	n	y	y	n	n	n	n	n	y	n	n	y	n	n	n	n	n
29	old man	n	y	y	y	n	y	n	y	n	y	n	n	n	n	n	n	n	n
30	Marie Movena	n	n	y	y	n	n	n	n	n	y	n	n	y	y	n	n	n	n
31	man	n	n	y	y	y	n	y	n	n	y	y	n	n	n	n	n	n	n
32	old woman	y	n	y	n	y	y	y	n	n	y	y	y	n	n	n	y	n	y
33	woman	y	n	n	n	y	y	n	n	n	y	y	y	n	n	n	n	n	y
34	woman	y	n	n	n	n	y	n	n	n	y	y	y	n	n	n	n	n	y
35	young man	y	n	n	n	y	y	y	n	n	y	y	y	n	n	n	n	n	y
36	young man	y	n	y	y	n	y	n	n	n	y	y	y	n	n	n	n	n	y
37	Apican	y	n	y	y	y	y	y	n	n	y	y	y	y	y	n	n	n	y
38	healer	y	n	y	y	y	y	y	n	n	y	y	y	y	y	y	y	n	y
39	healer	n	n	y	y	y	n	n	n	n	y	y	y	n	n	n	n	n	y
40	young woman	n	y	y	y	n	y	y	y	y	y	y	y	n	n	n	y	n	y
41	old woman	n	n	y	y	n	y	y	y	y	y	y	y	n	n	n	n	n	y
42	old man	n	n	n	n	n	y	n	n	n	y	y	y	n	n	y	n	n	y
43	woman	n	y	y	y	y	n	n	n	y	y	y	y	y	y	n	n	n	n
44	woman	n	n	y	y	y	y	y	y	y	y	y	y	n	y	n	y	n	n
45	man	y	n	y	y	n	y	n	y	y	y	y	y	n	n	n	n	n	n
46	Lazare	n	y	y	y	n	y	n	n	n	n	n	y	n	n	n	n	n	n

(continued)

TABLE 2. (*continued*)

Id	Subject	GRA	GRI	INS	BAP	BAR	ILL	HEA	DEA	GDD	REF	PTY	MRG	ELT	DEF	ALN	KIN	GRP
47	woman	n	y	y	y	y	y	n	y	y	y	y	n	n	n	n	n	n
48	girl	n	y	y	y	y	n	n	n	n	y	y	n	n	n	n	n	y
49	healer	n	y	y	n	n	n	n	n	n	y	n	n	n	n	n	n	n
50	adult	n	y	y	y	n	y	n	y	y	y	n	n	n	n	n	n	n
51	adult	n	y	y	y	n	y	n	y	n	n	n	n	n	n	n	n	n
52	woman	n	n	y	y	y	n	n	n	n	y	y	n	n	n	n	n	n
53	Joseph	y	n	y	y	n	y	n	n	y	y	y	n	y	y	n	n	n
54	captain	n	n	y	n	n	y	n	y	y	n	y	n	y	n	n	n	n
55	woman	y	n	y	y	y	y	y	n	n	y	y	n	n	n	n	n	y
56	Joseph Nikalokita	y	n	y	y	y	y	y	n	n	y	y	n	n	y	n	n	y
57	brother	n	n	y	y	n	n	n	n	n	y	y	n	n	y	n	y	y
58	brother	n	n	y	y	y	n	n	n	n	y	y	n	n	y	n	y	y
59	old man	n	y	y	y	n	y	n	y	n	n	n	y	n	n	n	n	n
60	Joseph	n	n	y	y	n	n	n	n	n	y	y	n	y	n	n	n	n
61	Joseph	n	y	y	y	n	n	n	n	n	y	y	n	n	n	n	y	n
62	man	n	y	y	y	y	y	n	y	y	y	y	n	n	n	n	n	n
63	man	y	n	y	y	y	n	n	n	n	y	y	n	n	n	n	n	y
64	man	y	n	y	y	n	n	n	n	n	y	y	n	n	n	n	n	y
65	man	y	n	y	y	n	n	n	n	n	y	y	n	n	n	n	n	y
66	Joseph Chikabiskisi	n	n	y	y	n	n	n	n	n	y	y	n	y	y	n	n	y
67	widow	n	n	y	y	y	n	n	n	n	y	y	n	n	y	n	n	n

		GRA	GRI	INS	BAP	BAR	ILL	HEA	DEA	GDD	REF	PTY	MRG	ELT	DEF	ALN	KIN	GRP
68	Marie Rouensa	y	y	y	y	y	n	n	n	n	y	y	n	y	y	n	y	y
69	wife of Chief Rouensa	y	y	y	y	y	n	n	n	n	y	y	n	y	n	n	y	y
70	Chief Rouensa	y	n	n	y	y	n	n	n	n	y	y	n	y	n	y	y	y
71	Antoine	n	y	y	y	n	y	y	y	y	y	y	n	n	y	n	n	n
72	young woman	n	y	y	y	y	y	y	n	n	y	y	n	y	y	n	y	n
73	woman	n	y	y	y	y	y	y	n	n	y	y	n	n	n	n	y	n
74	Henri	n	y	y	y	y	y	y	y	y	y	y	y	n	n	n	y	n

GRA: direct mention of the action of grace in the text
GRI: indirect indication of the action of grace in the text
INS: subject provided with at least basic instruction in Christianity
BAP: subject received baptism
BAR: subject requested baptism
ILL: illness reported in the subject
HEA: subject recovered from illness in the process of conversion
DEA: subject died soon after conversion or baptism
GDD: subject described as having experienced a pious Christian death
REF: subject described as having reformed his or her behavior according to missionary standards
PTY: subject exhibited pious Christian behavior
MRG: subject was socially marginal
ELT: subject was a member of a social or political elite
DEF: subject defied social, religious, or political expectations during or after the conversion process
ALN: subject expressed interest in alliance with the French
KIN: conversion occurred as part of a larger family conversion
GRP: subject was part of a large group conversion in a community
y: clearly mentioned in the text or closely related context
n: not mentioned in the text or closely related context

Notes

CHAPTER I

1. Mathurin Le Petit to Louis d'Avaugour, 12 July 1730, in *The Jesuit Relations and Allied Documents*, ed. Reuben Gold Thwaites (Cleveland, Ohio: Burrows Bros., 1896–1901; hereafter, *JR*), vol. 68, 209–11.

2. Ibid., 201–07.

3. Ibid.

4. Jacques Marquette, "Of the first Voyage made by Father Marquette toward new Mexico, and How the idea thereof was conceived," in *JR*, vol. 59, 115.

5. Ibid., 117–19.

6. Ibid., 119–21.

7. Ibid., 121–27; Joseph P. Donnelly, *Jacques Marquette, S.J., 1637–1675* (Chicago: Loyola University Press, 1968), 184–229.

8. Claude Dablon, "Relation of the discovery of many countries situated to the south of New France, made in 1673," in *JR*, vol. 58, 93–109; Richard White, *The Middle Ground: Indians, Empires, and Republics in the Great Lakes Region, 1650–1815* (New York: Cambridge University Press, 1991); Eric Hinderaker, *Elusive Empires: Constructing Colonialism in the Ohio Valley, 1673–1800* (New York: Cambridge University Press, 1997); Kathleen DuVal, *The Native Ground: Indians and Colonists in the Heart of the Continent* (Philadelphia: University of Pennsylvania Press, 2006); W. J. Eccles, *The Canadian Frontier, 1534–1760* (Albuquerque: University of New Mexico Press, 1983); Bernard Lugan, *Histoire de la Louisiane française, 1682–1804* (Paris: Perrin, 1994); Claiborne A. Skinner, *The Upper Country: French Enterprise in the Colonial Great Lakes* (Baltimore, Md.: Johns Hopkins University Press, 2008).

9. Marquette, 89–91 and 161–63; Kenneth M. Morrison, *The Solidarity of Kin: Ethnohistory, Religious Studies, and the Algonkian-French Religious Encounter* (Albany: State University of New York Press, 2002), 59–78.

10. Transcriptions of Illinois words remain as they appear in Illinois language texts from the period. The symbol *8* represents the phonemes *o*, *oo*, and *w*.

11. Marquette, 113–25; Jean Baptiste Le Boulanger [Jean Le Boullenger], [French and Miami-Illinois Dictionary], MS (microfilm copy), Codex Ind 28, 2-SIZE, John Carter Brown Library, Providence, R.I., 33, 63, 102, 116; Jacques Gravier, *Dictionary of the Algonquian Illinois*

Language, MS (photocopy and microfilm copy), American Indian MSS, Watkinson Library, Trinity College, Hartford, Conn., 48, 170, 175, 246; Brett Rushforth, "'A Little Flesh We Offer You': The Origins of Indian Slavery in New France," *William and Mary Quarterly*, 3d ser., 60 (October 2003): 777–808.

12. Pierre Deliette, "Memoir of De Gannes concerning the Illinois Country," *Collections of the Illinois State Historical Library*, vol. 23, *The French Foundations, 1680–1693*, ed. Theodore Calvin Pease and Raymond C. Werner (Springfield: Illinois State Historical Library, 1934), 375–82.

13. Marquette, 129–37; Dablon, 97. On the calumet, consult James Axtell, "Babel of Tongues: Communicating with the Indians in Eastern North America," in *The Language Encounter in the Americas, 1492–1800*, ed. Edward G. Gray and Norman Fiering (New York: Berghahn Books, 2000), 15–29; Colin G. Calloway, *New Worlds for All: Indians, Europeans, and the Remaking of Early America* (Baltimore, Md.: Johns Hopkins University Press, 1997), 128–31; White, 20–23; W. Vernon Kinietz, *The Indians of the Western Great Lakes, 1615–1760* (repr., Ann Arbor: University of Michigan Press, 1965), 190–96; Claude Charles Le Roy, Bacqueville de la Potherie, *History of the savage peoples who are allies of New France*, in *The Indian Tribes of the Upper Mississippi Valley and Region of the Great Lakes*, ed. Emma Helen Blair (repr., Lincoln: University of Nebraska Press, 1996), vol. 1, 308–33; Nicolas Perrot, *Memoir on the manners, customs, and religion of the savages of North America*, in *The Indian Tribes of the Upper Mississippi Valley and Region of the Great Lakes*, ed. Emma Helen Blair (repr., Lincoln: University of Nebraska Press, 1996), vol. 1, 182–88.

14. Le Boulanger, 42. For an emphasis on practice, see Michael D. McNally, "The Practice of Native American Christianity," *Church History* 69 (December 2000): 834–59; Sam Gill, *Native American Religious Action: A Performance Approach to Religion* (Columbia: University of South Carolina Press, 1987).

15. "Conversion," in *Oxford English Dictionary Online*, March 2011. http://www.oed.com.cuhsl.creighton.edu/view/Entry/40773?redirectedFrom=conversion (accessed April 22, 2011); Lewis R. Rambo, *Understanding Religious Conversion* (New Haven, Conn.: Yale University Press, 1993), 3.

16. Thomas A. Tweed, *Crossing and Dwelling: A Theory of Religion* (Cambridge, Mass.: Harvard University Press, 2006), 5, 59, 82, 113, 123.

17. Gilbert J. Garraghan, S.J., ed., *Some Hitherto Unpublished Marquettiana*, reprinted from *Mid-America*, vol. 18, n.s., vol. 7 (1936): 3–5; Claude Allouez, *Relation of 1664–1665*, in *JR*, vol. 49, 241–51; Claude Allouez, *Relation of 1666–1667*, in *JR*, vol. 50, 249–77.

18. Claude Allouez, *Relation of 1669–1670*, in *JR*, vol. 54, 197–207; Claude Allouez, "Sentiments," in *Le Père Pierre Chaumonot de la Compagnie de Jésus: Autobiographie et pièces inédites*, ed. Auguste Carayon (Poitiers: Henri Oudin, 1869), xxi–xxiii. The translation is mine.

19. Allouez, *Relation of 1669–1670*, 227–41.

20. Le Boulanger, 63; Marquette, 129.

21. Jacques Gravier, "Letter by Father Jacques Gravier in the form of a Journal of the Mission of l'Immaculée Conception de Notre Dame in the Ilinois country," 15 February 1694, in *JR*, vol. 64, 171–77.

22. Le Boulanger, 36–37, 43, 48.

23. *Mercure de France* (December 1725): 2827–59, microfilm copy by Bibliothèque nationale de France, 1959. Translations from this source are mine. See also Richard N. Ellis and Charlie R. Steen, "An Indian Delegation in France, 1725," *Journal of the Illinois State Historical Society* 67 (September 1974): 385–405.

24. William James Newbigging, "The History of the French-Ottawa Alliance, 1613–1763" (Ph.D. diss., University of Toronto, 1995).

25. Carole Blackburn, *Harvest of Souls: The Jesuit Missions and Colonialism in North America, 1632–1650* (Montreal: McGill-Queen's University Press, 2000), 3–20; Carol Devens, *Countering Colonization: Native American Women and Great Lakes Missions, 1630–1900* (Berkeley: University of California Press, 1992).

26. James Treat, ed., *Native and Christian: Indigenous Voices on Religious Identity in the United States and Canada* (New York: Routledge, 1996), 9.

27. Joseph Epes Brown with Emily Cousins, *Teaching Spirits: Understanding Native American Religious Traditions* (New York: Oxford University Press, 2001); William A. Young, *Quest for Harmony: Native American Spiritual Traditions* (repr., Indianapolis, Ind.: Hackett Publishing, 2006); Suzanne J. Crawford, *Native American Religious Traditions* (Upper Saddle River, N.J.: Prentice Hall, 2007); Jordan Paper, *Native North American Religious Traditions: Dancing for Life* (Westport, Conn.: Praeger, 2007).

28. For a good overview of the literature, consult Willard Hughes Rollings, "Indians and Christianity," in *A Companion to American Indian History*, ed. Philip J. Deloria and Neal Salisbury (Malden, Mass.: Blackwell Publishers, 2002), 121–38. A number of scholars have started to describe the true complexity of Native encounters with Christianity. Some prominent examples are Rachel Wheeler, *To Live upon Hope: Mohicans and Missionaries in the Eighteenth-Century Northeast* (Ithaca, N.Y.: Cornell University Press, 2008); Emma Anderson, *The Betrayal of Faith: The Tragic Journey of a Colonial Native Convert* (Cambridge, Mass.: Harvard University Press, 2007); David J. Silverman, *Faith and Boundaries: Colonists, Christianity, and Community among the Wampanoag Indians of Martha's Vineyard, 1600–1871* (New York: Cambridge University Press, 2005); Allan Greer, *Mohawk Saint: Catherine Tekakwitha and the Jesuits* (New York: Oxford University Press, 2005); Steven W. Hackel, *Children of Coyote, Missionaries of Saint Francis: Indian-Spanish Relations in Colonial California, 1769–1850* (Chapel Hill: University of North Carolina Press, 2005); Sergei Kan, *Memory Eternal: Tlingit Culture and Russian Orthodox Christianity through Two Centuries* (Seattle: University of Washington Press, 1999).

29. Antoine Silvy, "Relation of 1676–77," in *JR*, vol. 60, 207–9.

30. Ibid.

31. Deliette, 369–71.

CHAPTER 2

1. Jérôme Lalemant, "Journal of the Jesuits," in *The Jesuit Relations and Allied Documents*, ed. Reuben Gold Thwaites (Cleveland, Ohio: Burrows Bros., 1896–1901; hereafter,

JR), vol. 45, 161–63; Jérôme Lalemant, *Relation of 1659–1660*, in *JR*, vol. 46, 65–83. The *donné* system, an innovation in New France, arose in response to the Jesuit need for labor. In the arrangement, a man offered his labor to the Society of Jesus and pledged to live a pious life in return for food, clothing, and care for the remainder of his life. See Peter N. Moogk, *La Nouvelle France: The Making of French Canada—A Cultural History* (East Lansing: Michigan State University Press, 2000), 29–30.

2. Paul Le Jeune, *Relation of 1660–1661*, in *JR*, vol. 47, 115; Helen Hornbeck Tanner, ed., *Atlas of Great Lakes Indian History* (Norman: University of Oklahoma Press, 1987), map 6.

3. René Ménard to Jérôme Lalemant, 2 June 1661, in *JR*, vol. 46, 126–45; Jérôme Lalemant, *Relation of 1662–1663*, in *JR*, vol. 48, 123–43; Jérôme Lalemant to Gian Paolo Oliva, 18 August 1663, in *JR*, vol. 47, 249–53.

4. Heidi Bohaker, "*Nindoodemag*: The Significance of Algonquian Kinship Networks in the Eastern Great Lakes Region, 1600–1701," *William and Mary Quarterly*, 3d ser., 63 (January 2006): 23–52; William James Newbigging, "The History of the French-Ottawa Alliance, 1613–1763" (Ph.D. diss., University of Toronto, 1995).

5. Nicolas Perrot, *Memoir on the manners, customs, and religion of the savages of North America*, in *The Indian Tribes of the Upper Mississippi Valley and Region of the Great Lakes*, ed. Emma Helen Blair (repr., Lincoln: University of Nebraska Press, 1996), vol. 1, 31–37; Bohaker, 31–33.

6. Bohaker, 31–33.

7. Sébastian Rasles to his brother, 12 October 1723, in *JR*, vol. 67: 153–61; Andrew J. Blackbird, *History of the Ottawa and Chippewa Indians of Michigan* (Ypsilanti, Mich.: Ypsilanti Job Printing House, 1887), 72–73.

8. Perrot wrote his memoir for Intendant Claude Michel Bégon, an important French colonial official, with the intention of influencing French policy in the colony during the first quarter of the eighteenth century. See Richard White, "Introduction" to *The Indian Tribes of the Upper Mississippi Valley and Region of the Great Lakes*, ed. Emma Helen Blair (repr., Lincoln: University of Nebraska Press, 1996), vol. 1, 2–3. On Ottawa oral tradition, see Rasles, 153–61; Blackbird, 72–96; W. Vernon Kinietz, *The Indians of the Western Great Lakes, 1615–1760* (repr., Ann Arbor: University of Michigan Press, 1965), 284–303; Melissa A. Pflüg, *Ritual and Myth in Odawa Revitalization: Reclaiming a Sovereign Place* (Norman: University of Oklahoma Press, 1998), 3–12, 66–125; and Charles E. Cleland, *Rites of Conquest: The History and Culture of Michigan's Native Americans* (Ann Arbor: University of Michigan Press, 1992), 1–10.

9. Newbigging, 41–49 and 90–95; Kinietz, 226–307; Cleland, 39–127; Johanna E. Feest and Christian F. Feest, "Ottawa," in *Handbook of North American Indians*, vol. 15, *Northeast*, ed. Bruce G. Trigger (Washington, D.C.: Smithsonian Institution, 1978), 772–77.

10. Perrot, vol. 1, 132–36.

11. Ménard to Lalemant, 137–45.

12. Perrot, vol. 1, 173–74.

13. Ibid., 86–88.

14. Harold Hickerson, "The Feast of the Dead among the Seventeenth Century Algonkians of the Upper Great Lakes," *American Anthropologist* 62 (February 1960): 81–107; Newbigging, 97–98 and 115; Bohaker, 45; Louis André, *Relation of 1670–1671*, in *JR*, vol. 55, 137.

15. Kinietz, 235–42 and 284–97; Cleland, 66–70; Feest and Feest, 774–77.

16. Perrot, vol. 1, 37. On the development of ideas of a separate creation in the eighteenth and nineteenth centuries, see Gregory Evans Dowd, *A Spirited Resistance: The North American Struggle for Unity, 1745–1815* (Baltimore, Md.: Johns Hopkins University Press, 1992), 21–46.

17. Kinietz, 226–32; Cleland, 86; Feest and Feest, 772–74.

18. Newbigging, 1–25 and 80–119; Bruce G. Trigger, *The Children of Aataentsic: A History of the Huron People to 1660* (Montreal: McGill-Queen's University Press, 1976), 353–56; Bruce G. Trigger, *Natives and Newcomers: Canada's "Heroic Age" Reconsidered* (Kingston, Ont.: McGill-Queen's University Press, 1985), 205–7; Cleland, 86.

19. Trigger, *Children of Aataentsic*, chs. 9 and 11; Trigger, *Natives and Newcomers*, 259–81; Daniel K. Richter, *The Ordeal of the Longhouse: The Peoples of the Iroquois League in the Era of European Colonization* (Chapel Hill: University of North Carolina Press, 1992), 50–74; José António Brandão, *Your Fyre Shall Burn No More: Iroquois Policy toward New France and Its Native Allies to 1701* (Lincoln: University of Nebraska Press, 1997).

20. Trigger, *Children of Aataentsic*, 767–840; Tanner, map 7.

21. Kinietz, 227–29; Feest and Feest, 772–73; Tanner, map 6; Perrot, vol. 1, 148–74; Richard White, *The Middle Ground: Indians, Empires, and Republics in the Great Lakes Region, 1650–1815* (New York: Cambridge University Press, 1991), ch. 1.

22. Newbigging, 120–58; Bohaker, 48–49.

23. Claude Allouez, *Relation of 1669–1670*, in *JR*, vol. 54, 201–3; Claude Charles Le Roy, Bacqueville de la Potherie, *History of the savage peoples who are allies of New France*, in *The Indian Tribes of the Upper Mississippi Valley and Region of the Great Lakes*, ed. Emma Helen Blair (repr., Lincoln: University of Nebraska Press, 1996), vol. 1, 283–88; Antoine Denis Raudot, "Memoir Concerning the Different Indian Nations of North America," in W. Vernon Kinietz, *The Indians of the Western Great Lakes, 1615–1760* (repr., Ann Arbor: University of Michigan Press, 1965), 379; Rasles to this brother, 153–61.

24. Sources for this summary of Jesuit mission work in the first half of the seventeenth century include James Axtell, *The Invasion Within: The Contest of Cultures in Colonial North America* (New York: Oxford University Press, 1985), 23–127; Carole Blackburn, *Harvest of Souls: The Jesuit Missions and Colonialism in North America, 1632–1650* (Montreal: McGill-Queen's University Press, 2000), 21–41; Henry Warner Bowden, *American Indians and Christian Missions: Studies in Cultural Conflict* (Chicago: University of Chicago Press, 1981), 59–95; Lucien Campeau, *La mission des jésuites chez les Hurons, 1634–1650* (Montreal: Bellarmin, 1987); Lucien Campeau, "Roman Catholic Missions in New France," in *Handbook of North American Indians*, vol. 4, *History of Indian-White Relations*, ed. Wilcomb E. Washburn (Washington, D.C.: Smithsonian Institution, 1988),

464–71; John Webster Grant, *Moon of Wintertime: Missionaries and the Indians of Canada in Encounter since 1534* (Toronto: University of Toronto Press, 1984), 3–46; Cornelius J. Jaenen, *Friend and Foe: Aspects of French-Amerindian Cultural Contact in the Sixteenth and Seventeenth Centuries* (New York: Columbia University Press, 1976), 41–83; Elizabeth Jones, *Gentlemen and Jesuits: Quests for Glory and Adventure in the Early Days of New France* (Toronto: University of Toronto Press, 1986); Trigger, *Children of Aataentsic*; Trigger, *Natives and Newcomers*, 164–297; Joseph N. Tylenda, *Jesuit Saints and Martyrs: Short Biographies of the Saints, Blessed, Venerables, and Servants of God of the Society of Jesus* (Chicago: Loyola University Press, 1984), 75–83, 206–8, 346–48, 370–76, and 457–62; and Christopher Vecsey, *The Paths of Kateri's Kin* (Notre Dame, Ind.: University of Notre Dame Press, 1997), 3–172.

25. W. J. Eccles, *The French in North America, 1500–1783*, rev. ed. (East Lansing: Michigan State University Press, 1998), 37 and 42–58.

26. Lalemant, *Relation of 1659–1660*, 73–81.

27. Ibid. Jérôme Lalemant, *Relation of 1663–1664*, in *JR*, vol. 48, 275. Ménard was born 2 March 1605 in Paris. "Jésuites missionaires en Nouvelle-France, 1611–1800," GALL. 110 II, Archivum Romanum Societatis Iesu, Rome. Thwaites also gives an alternate date of 7 September and alternate year of 1604 in *JR*, vol. 71, 144.

28. Ignatius of Loyola, *Autobiography*, in *Ignatius of Loyola: "The Spiritual Exercises" and Selected Works*, ed. George E. Ganss (New York: Paulist Press, 1991), 104; John W. O'Malley, *The First Jesuits* (Cambridge, Mass.: Harvard University Press, 1993), 23–36; Tylenda, 241–50; R. Po-chia Hsia, *The World of Catholic Renewal, 1540–1770* (Cambridge: Cambridge University Press, 1998), 26–27.

29. *Constitutions of the Society of Jesus* in *Ignatius of Loyola: "The Spiritual Exercises" and Selected Works*, ed. George E. Ganss (New York: Paulist Press, 1991), 283–84; Hsia, 31; O'Malley, 1–50; Joseph de Guibert, *The Jesuits, Their Spiritual Doctrine and Practice: A Historical Study*, trans. William J. Young (Chicago: Institute of Jesuit Sources, 1964), 1–181.

30. M. Joseph Costelloe, "Introduction: Francis Xavier: The Letters and the Man," in Francis Xavier, *The Letters and Instructions of Francis Xavier*, trans. M. Joseph Costelloe (St. Louis, Mo.: Institute of Jesuit Sources, 1992), xiii–xxiii; Tylenda, 449–57.

31. Pierre Berthiaume, *L'aventure américaine au XVIIIe siècle: Du voyage à l'écriture* (Ottawa: Les Presses de l'Université d'Ottawa, 1990), 238–50; Costelloe, xi; Hsia, 124–25; Gilbert J. Garraghan, S.J., ed., *Some Hitherto Unpublished Marquettiana*, repr. from *Mid-America*, vol. 18, n.s. vol. 7 (1936): 3–5.

32. Francis Xavier, "Prayer for the Conversion of the Gentiles," in Francis Xavier, *The Letters and Instructions of Francis Xavier*, trans. M. Joseph Costelloe (St. Louis, Mo.: Institute of Jesuit Sources, 1992), 210.

33. Francis Xavier, letter, "To the Society of Jesus in Europe," 22 June 1549, in Xavier, *Letters and Instructions*, 280–81; Francis Xavier, letter, "To His Companions Living in Rome," 20 September 1542, in Xavier, *Letters and Instructions*, 51. The italics appear in the original.

34. Francis Xavier, letter, "To His Companions Residing in Rome," 20 January 1548, in Xavier, *Letters and Instructions*, 180. The italics appear in the original.

35. Costelloe, xxii–xxiv; Tylenda, 452–53.

36. The two other new saints were Teresa of Avila and Filippo Neri. Hsia, 122–37; Tylenda, 249–50 and 453.

37. On "colonial hagiography," see Allan Greer, "Colonial Saints: Gender, Race, and Hagiography in New France," *William and Mary Quarterly*, 3d. ser., 57 (April 2000): 323–48, and Allan Greer, *Mohawk Saint: Catherine Tekakwitha and the Jesuits* (New York: Oxford University Press, 2005).

38. "Notice Nécrologique du P. Jean de Brébeuf," in *Monumenta Novae Franciae*, vol. 7, *Le Témoignage du sang (1647–1650)*, ed. Lucien Campeau (Montreal: Les Éditions Bellarmin, 1994; hereafter, *MNF*), 468–69; Joseph P. Donnelly, *Jean de Brébeuf, 1593–1649* (Chicago: Loyola University Press, 1975), 265–86; Tylenda, 75–81; Greer, "Colonial Saints," 333–35.

39. Greer, "Colonial Saints," 333–35.

40. Charles Garnier to Pierre Boutard, 27 April 1649, in *MNF*, 495–97. The translation is mine.

41. Donnelly 291–93 and 304–12; Greer, "Colonial Saints," 333–35.

42. Lalemant to Oliva, 249–53; Lalemant, *Relation of 1662–1663*, 115–51; Perrot, vol. 1, 171–73.

43. Lalemant, *Relation of 1662–1663*, 27–29 and 127–43.

CHAPTER 3

1. 14 June 1671 is the commonly accepted date, although sources disagree. In the colonial bureaucracy of New France, the intendant was "responsible for justice, civil administration, and finance." See W. J. Eccles, *The French in North America, 1500–1783*, rev. ed. (East Lansing: Michigan State University Press, 1998), 75. Accounts of the ceremony are from Reuben Gold Thwaites, ed., *Collections of the State Historical Society of Wisconsin* (hereafter, *CSHSW*), vol. 11 (Madison: State Historical Society of Wisconsin, 1888), 26–29; J. H. Schlarman, *From Quebec to New Orleans: The Story of the French in America* (Belleville, Ill.: Buechler Publishing Co., 1929), 46–48; Claude Dablon, *Relation of 1670–1671*, in *The Jesuit Relations and Allied Documents*, ed. Reuben Gold Thwaites (Cleveland, Ohio: Burrows Bros., 1896–1901; hereafter, *JR*), vol. 55, 105–15; Nicolas Perrot, *Memoir on the manners, customs, and religion of the savages of North America*, in *The Indian Tribes of the Upper Mississippi Valley and Region of the Great Lakes*, ed. Emma Helen Blair (repr., Lincoln: University of Nebraska Press, 1996), vol. 1, 220–25; and Claude Charles Le Roy, Bacqueville de la Potherie, *History of the savage peoples who are allies of New France*, in *The Indian Tribes of the Upper Mississippi Valley and Region of the Great Lakes*, ed. Emma Helen Blair (repr., Lincoln: University of Nebraska Press, 1996), vol. 1, 346–48. See also W. J. Eccles, "Sovereignty-Association, 1500–1783," in *Theories of Empire, 1450–1800*, ed. David Armitage (Aldershot: Ashgate Variorum, 1998), 212–15.

2. *CSHSW*, 28, and Dablon, *Relation of 1670–1671*, 115.

3. Gilles Havard, *Empire et métissages: Indiens et Français dans le Pays d'en Haut, 1660–1715* (Sillery, Quebec: Septentrion, 2003), 115–30 and 681–735.

4. There is not yet an extensive literature on what I call the "geographies of encounter," but there is a rapidly growing and diverse body of work that explores connections between geography, history, and culture. Helpful and suggestive examples include James Taylor Carson, "Ethnogeography and the Native American Past," *Ethnohistory* 49 (Fall 2002): 769–88; Jennifer Reid, *Myth, Symbol, and Colonial Encounter: British and Mi'kmaq in Acadia, 1700–1867* (Ottawa: University of Ottawa Press, 1995); Thongchai Winichakul, *Siam Mapped: A History of the Geo-Body of a Nation* (Honolulu: University of Hawaii Press, 1994); Chris R. Park, *Sacred Worlds: An Introduction to Geography and Religion* (London: Routledge, 1994); David Chidester and Edward T. Linenthal, eds., *American Sacred Space* (Bloomington: Indiana University Press, 1995); Belden C. Lane, *Landscapes of the Sacred: Geography and Narrative in American Spirituality*, rev. ed. (Baltimore, Md.: Johns Hopkins University Press, 2002); Michel Foucault, *Power/Knowledge: Selected Interviews and Other Writings, 1972–1977* (New York: Pantheon Books, 1980); Michel Foucault, "Space, Knowledge, and Power," in *The Foucault Reader*, ed. Paul Rabinow (New York: Pantheon Books, 1984), 239–56; Henri Lefebvre, *The Production of Space*, trans. Donald Nicholson-Smith (Oxford: Blackwell, 1991); Edward W. Soja, *Postmodern Geographies: The Reassertion of Space in Critical Social Theory* (London: Verso, 1989); Keith H. Basso, *Wisdom Sits in Places: Landscape and Language among the Western Apache* (Albuquerque: University of New Mexico Press, 1996); and Hugh Brody, *Maps and Dreams* (New York: Pantheon, 1982).

5. Gregory H. Nobles, *American Frontiers: Cultural Encounters and Continental Conquest* (New York: Hill and Wang, 1997); Richard White, *The Middle Ground: Indians, Empires, and Republics in the Great Lakes Region, 1650–1815* (New York: Cambridge University Press, 1991); Natalie Zemon Davis, *Women on the Margins: Three Seventeenth-Century Lives* (Cambridge, Mass.: Harvard University Press, 1995); Jeremy Adelman and Stephen Aron, "From Borderlands to Borders: Empires, Nation-States, and the Peoples in Between in North American History," *American Historical Review* 104 (June 1999): 814–841.

6. La Potherie, vol. 1, 346–48. On the significance of such symbols, see Heidi Bohaker, "*Nindoodemag*: The Significance of Algonquian Kinship Networks in the Eastern Great Lakes Region, 1600–1701," *William and Mary Quarterly*, 3d ser., 63 (January 2006): 23–52.

7. Reid, 14; Eccles, "Sovereignty-Association," 212–15; Eccles, *French in North America*, ch. 3; Eric Hinderaker, *Elusive Empires: Constructing Colonialism in the Ohio Valley, 1673–1800* (New York: Cambridge University Press, 1997), 1–77.

8. Havard, 209–10.

9. Helen Hornbeck Tanner, ed., *Atlas of Great Lakes Indian History* (Norman: University of Oklahoma Press, 1987), 29–37; Dablon, *Relation of 1670–1671*, 157–67; Antoine Denis Raudot, "Memoir Concerning the Different Indian Nations of North America," in W. Vernon Kinietz, *The Indians of the Western Great Lakes, 1615–1760* (repr., Ann Arbor: University of Michigan Press, 1965), 371–72.

10. Claude Allouez, "Sentiments," in *Le Père Pierre Chaumonot de la Compagnie de Jésus: Autobiographie et pièces inédites*, ed. Auguste Carayon (Poitiers: Henri Oudin, 1869), xvii. The translation is mine. Scholars have paid less attention to French conceptions of

wilderness than to English interpretations: William Cronon, *Changes in the Land: Indians, Colonists, and the Ecology of New England* (New York: Hill and Wang, 1983); Patricia Seed, *Ceremonies of Possession in Europe's Conquest of the New World, 1492–1640* (New York: Cambridge University Press, 1995), 16–40; and Carolyn Merchant, *Ecological Revolutions: Nature, Gender, and Science in New England* (Chapel Hill: University of North Carolina Press, 1989), 1–145. An exception is Carole Blackburn, *Harvest of Souls: The Jesuit Missions and Colonialism in North America, 1632–1650* (Montreal: McGill-Queen's University Press, 2000).

11. Claude Allouez, *Relation of 1670–1671*, in *JR*, vol. 55, 207–19; Pierre Berthiaume, *L'aventure américaine au XVIIIe siècle: Du voyage à l'écriture* (Ottawa: Les Presses de l'Université d'Ottawa, 1990), 256–74; Anthony Pagden, *European Encounters with the New World: From Renaissance to Romanticism* (New Haven, Conn.: Yale University Press, 1993), 7, 160; James Duncan, "Sites of Representation: Place, Time and the Discourse of the Other," in *Place/Culture/Representation*, ed. James Duncan and David Ley (London: Routledge, 1993), 39–45; Peter N. Moogk, *La Nouvelle France: The Making of French Canada—A Cultural History* (East Lansing: Michigan State University Press, 2000), 14, 265.

12. Étienne de Carheil to Louis Hector de Callières, Governor, 30 August 1702, in *JR*, vol. 65, 219–21.

13. Claude Allouez, *Relation of 1666–1667*, in *JR*, vol. 50, 267–69.

14. Ibid., 297–305.

15. Joseph de Guibert, *The Jesuits, Their Spiritual Doctrine and Practice: A Historical Study*, trans. William J. Young (Chicago: Institute of Jesuit Sources, 1964), 109–39 and ch. 13; John W. O'Malley, *The First Jesuits* (Cambridge, Mass.: Harvard University Press, 1993), 4, 372–74; Ignatius of Loyola, *The Spiritual Exercises*, in *Ignatius of Loyola: "The Spiritual Exercises" and Selected Works*, ed. George E. Ganss (New York: Paulist Press, 1991), 129–56 and 389–90.

16. Claude Allouez, *Relation of 1666–1667*, in *JR*, vol. 51, 69.

17. Claude Dablon, *Relation of 1671–1672*, in *JR*, vol. 56, 145; Claude Allouez, "Narrative of a voyage to the Illinois," in *JR*, vol. 60, 165.

18. Jean de Quens, *Relation of 1655–1656*, in *JR*, vol. 42, 225.

19. Claude Allouez, "Relation of 1672–1673," in *JR*, vol. 58, 43. See Allouez, *Relation of 1670–1671*, 191–93, for a similar example.

20. Louise Phelps Kellogg, ed., *Early Narratives of the Northwest, 1634–1699* (New York: Charles Scribner's Sons, 1917), 356–57. Over twenty years later, a French traveler reported that the rock was called Cap St. Cosme after the missionary. See Diron d'Artaguiette, "Journal of Diron d'Artaguiette," in *Travels in the American Colonies*, ed. Newton D. Mereness (New York: Macmillan Company, 1916), 67.

21. A. Irving Hallowell, "Ojibwa Ontology, Behavior, and World View," repr. in *Contributions to Anthropology* (Chicago: University of Chicago Press, 1976), 357–90; Kenneth M. Morrison, *The Solidarity of Kin: Ethnohistory, Religious Studies, and the Algonkian-French Religious Encounter* (Albany: State University of New York Press, 2002); Charles E. Cleland, *Rites of Conquest: The History and Culture of Michigan's Native Americans* (Ann Arbor: University of Michigan Press, 1992), 66–70; Elizabeth Tooker, *Native North*

American Spirituality of the Eastern Woodlands: Sacred Myths, Dreams, Visions, Speeches, Healing Formulas, Rituals and Ceremonials (New York: Paulist Press, 1979), 11–30.

22. La Potherie, vol. 1, 283–88; Raudot, 379–81; Perrot, vol. 1, 31–40; François-Xavier de Charlevoix, *Journal d'un voyage fait par ordre du roi dans l'Amérique septentrionale*, ed. Pierre Berthiaume (Montreal: Les Presses de l'Université de Montréal, 1994), vol. 1, 577–81; Andrew J. Blackbird, *History of the Ottawa and Chippewa Indians of Michigan* (Ypsilanti, Mich.: Ypsilanti Job Printing House, 1887), 72–78.

23. Raudot, 397–99; Pierre Deliette, "Memoir of De Gannes concerning the Illinois Country," in *Collections of the Illinois State Historical Library*, vol. 23, *The French Foundations, 1680–1693*, ed. Theodore Calvin Pease and Raymond C. Werner (Springfield: Illinois State Historical Library, 1934), 303–4; Jean Baptiste Le Boulanger [Jean Le Boullenger], [French and Miami-Illinois Dictionary], MS (microfilm copy), Codex Ind 28, 2-SIZE, John Carter Brown Library, Providence, R.I., 72; Jacques Gravier, *Dictionary of the Algonquian Illinois Language*, MS (photocopy and microfilm copy), American Indian MSS, Watkinson Library, Trinity College, Hartford, Conn., 71; Daryl Baldwin and David J. Costa, *myaamia neehi peewaalia kaloosioni mahsinaakani: A Miami-Peoria Dictionary* (Miami, Okla.: Miami Nation, 2005), 7. For the connection between landscape, narrative, and morality in another Native culture, see Basso, *Wisdom Sits in Places*.

24. Gabriel Marest to Barthélemi Germon, 9 November 1712, in *JR*, vol. 66, 263–65.

25. Pagden, 7.

26. Allouez, *Relation of 1666–1667*, vol. 51, 43–45.

27. Marest to Germon, 221–23.

28. Ibid., 253–65. On the concept of "the gaze" as a disciplinary apparatus, see Michel Foucault, *Discipline and Punish: The Birth of the Prison*, trans. Alan Sheridan (New York: Vintage Books, 1979).

29. Guibert, 26–59, 239–40, and ch. 17; O'Malley, *First Jesuits*, ch. 2; John O'Malley, "Early Jesuit Spirituality: Spain and Italy," in *Christian Spirituality: Post-Reformation and Modern*, ed. Louis Dupré and Don E. Saliers (New York: Crossroad, 1989), 7–8.

30. Claude Dablon, "Account of the Second Voyage and the Death of Father Jacques Marquette," in *JR*, vol. 59, 201–7.

31. Ibid.; Charlevoix, vol. 2, 635–37; "Franquelin's Map of Louisiana," 1684, in *JR*, vol. 63.

32. Jacques Gravier, "Journal of the voyage of Father Gravier, in 1700, from the Country of the Illinois to the Mouth of the Mississippi River," in *JR*, vol. 65, 101–3; Marcel Giraud, *A History of French Louisiana*, vol. 1, *The Reign of Louis XIV, 1698–1715*, trans. Joseph C. Lambert (Baton Rouge: Louisiana State University Press, 1974), 59–61.

33. Jacques Gravier, "Letter by Father Jacques Gravier in the form of a Journal of the Mission of l'Immaculée Conception de Notre Dame in the Illinois country," in *JR*, vol. 64, 171–73.

34. Ibid., 159–63; White, 59.

35. Jean Mermet, 2 March 1706, in *JR*, vol. 66, 53–55.

36. Ibid., 50–65; Marest to Germon, 265–95; White, 74–75.

37. Natalia Maree Belting, *Kaskaskia under the French Regime* (Urbana: University of Illinois Press, 1948), 10–16; Carl J. Ekberg, *French Roots in the Illinois Country: The Mississippi Frontier in Colonial Times* (Urbana: University of Illinois Press, 1998); Winstanley Briggs, "Le Pays des Illinois," *William and Mary Quarterly*, 3d ser., 47 (January 1990): 30–56; Hinderaker, ch. 3.

38. Marcel Giraud, *A History of French Louisiana*, vol. 5, *The Company of the Indies, 1723–1731*, trans. Brian Pearce (Baton Rouge: Louisiana State University Press, 1987), 462–65; Hinderaker, 87–101; Wayne C. Temple, *Indian Villages of the Illinois Country: Historic Tribes* (Springfield: Illinois State Museum, 1966), 40–43.

39. Cornelius J. Jaenen, *Friend and Foe: Aspects of French-Amerindian Cultural Contact in the Sixteenth and Seventeenth Centuries* (New York: Columbia University Press, 1976), 153–89; Jean Delanglez, *The French Jesuits in Lower Louisiana (1700–1763)* (Washington, D.C.: Catholic University of America, 1935), 99–118; Louis Vivier, 8 June 1750, in *JR*, vol. 69, 149.

40. The Fox wars, for example, were a serious threat to the Illinois: R. David Edmunds and Joseph L. Peyser, *The Fox Wars: The Mesquakie Challenge to New France* (Norman: University of Oklahoma Press, 1993) and White, 149–75. On the Kaskaskia division, see Giraud, *History of French Louisiana*, vol. 5, *Company of the Indies*, 461–63; Hinderaker, 87–101; Delanglez, 99–118; Temple, 40–43; Mary Borgias Palm, *The Jesuit Missions of the Illinois Country, 1673–1763* (Cleveland, Ohio: n.p., 1933), 49–55; Charlevoix, vol. 2, 759–76; and D'Artaguiette, 67–75.

41. When the French took possession of the *pays d'en haut*, they did not believe that they had gained actual title to the whole territory. Although French settlements became *le domain du roi*, the rest of the *pays d'en haut* remained Indian country and French law did not even apply there. See Eccles, "Sovereignty-Association," 203–38; Cornelius J. Jaenen, " 'One Cabin, Two Fires': French Sovereignty and Native Nationhood in New France," in *Proceedings of the Seventeenth Meeting of the French Colonial Historical Society, Chicago, May 1991*, ed. Patricia Galloway (Lanham, Md.: University of America, [1992]), 1–11; Cornelius J. Jaenen, "Characteristics of French-Amerindian Contact in New France," in *Essays on the History of North American Discovery and Exploration*, ed. Stanley H. Palmer and Dennis Reinhartz (College Station: Texas A&M University Press, 1988), 88–92; Olive Patricia Dickason, "Old World Law, New World Peoples, and Concepts of Sovereignty," in *Essays on the History of North American Discovery and Exploration*, ed. Stanley H. Palmer and Dennis Reinhartz (College Station: Texas A&M University Press, 1988), 52–78; Giraud, *History of French Louisiana*, vol. 5, *Company of the Indies*, 464; and Briggs, 34.

42. Hinderaker, 36–39; Olive Patricia Dickason, *The Myth of the Savage and the Beginnings of French Colonialism in the Americas* (Edmonton: University of Alberta Press, 1984), ch. 10.

43. *Mercure de France* (December 1725): 2827–59, microfilm copy by Bibliothèque nationale de France, 1959. Translations from this source are mine. See also Richard N. Ellis and Charlie R. Steen, "An Indian Delegation in France, 1725," *Journal of the Illinois State Historical Society* 67 (September 1974): 385–405.

44. *Mercure de France*, 2827–59; Giraud, *History of French Louisiana*, vol. 5, *Company of the Indies*, 465, 489–91; Hinderaker, 36–39; Delanglez, 99–118, 139.

45. White, 50.

46. Delanglez, 99–118, 139.

CHAPTER 4

1. Claude Allouez, *Relation of 1669–1670*, in *The Jesuit Relations and Allied Documents*, ed. Reuben Gold Thwaites (Cleveland, Ohio: Burrows Bros., 1896–1901; hereafter, *JR*), vol. 54, 215–27. On the Mesquakies, see R. David Edmunds and Joseph L. Peyser, *The Fox Wars: The Mesquakie Challenge to New France* (Norman: University of Oklahoma Press, 1993), xviii and 3–54. For the location and name of the village, see Helen Hornbeck Tanner, ed., *Atlas of Great Lakes Indian History* (Norman: University of Oklahoma Press, 1987), map 6. Consult A. Irving Hallowell, "Ojibwa Ontology, Behavior, and World View," repr., in *Contributions to Anthropology* (Chicago: University of Chicago Press, 1976), 357–90, for an analysis of manitous as human and other-than-human persons. Hallowell refers specifically to the Ojibwas in his study, but these spiritual concepts were similar among other Algonquian-speaking peoples in the Great Lakes region, including the Mesquakies.

2. Allouez, *Relation of 1669–1670*, 215–27.

3. Claude Allouez, *Relation of 1670–1671*, in *JR*, vol. 55, 219–25.

4. Allouez, *Relation of 1669–1670*, 227–41.

5. Claude Dablon, *Relation of 1670–1671*, in *JR*, vol. 55, 199–207.

6. For the French as spirits or gods, see Claude Charles Le Roy, Bacqueville de la Potherie, *History of the savage peoples who are allies of New France*, in *The Indian Tribes of the Upper Mississippi Valley and Region of the Great Lakes*, ed. Emma Helen Blair (repr. Lincoln: University of Nebraska Press, 1996), vol. 1, 308. Joseph François Lafitau, *Customs of the American Indians Compared with the Customs of Primitive Times*, trans. and ed. William N. Fenton and Elizabeth L. Moore (Toronto: Champlain Society, 1974), 103–16.

7. La Potherie, *History*, vol. 1, 342–48. La Potherie erroneously gives the year as 1667, but it seems clear from the context that the episode took place in 1671. La Potherie apparently based his accounts of Perrot's activities on Perrot's own unpublished notes. The description indicates that Perrot met Allouez in the Green Bay region just before going to the Miamis.

8. Jean Baptiste Le Boulanger [Jean Le Boullenger], [French and Miami-Illinois Dictionary], MS (microfilm copy), Codex Ind 28, 2-SIZE, John Carter Brown Library, Providence, R.I., 116; Jacques Gravier, *Dictionary of the Algonquian Illinois Language*, MS (photocopy and microfilm copy), American Indian MSS, Watkinson Library, Trinity College, Hartford, Conn., 246.

9. Gravier, *Dictionary*, 246.

10. Hallowell, 357–90. Kenneth Morrison suggests that Person, Power, and Gift are core "existential postulates" in American Indian religious systems and worldviews. See

Kenneth M. Morrison, "Beyond the Supernatural: Language and Religious Action," *Religion* 22 (July 1992): 201–5, for a clear summation of this argument.

11. Cornelius Jaenen, "Amerindian Views of French Culture in the Seventeenth Century," *Canadian Historical Review* 55 (September 1974): 273–78; Cornelius J. Jaenen, *Friend and Foe: Aspects of French-Amerindian Cultural Contact in the Sixteenth and Seventeenth Centuries* (New York: Columbia University Press, 1976), 41–79; James Axtell, *The Invasion Within: The Contest of Cultures in Colonial North America* (New York: Oxford University Press, 1985), 7–19. A good nineteenth-century example of fear of missionaries is Rebecca Kugel, "Of Missionaries and Their Cattle: Ojibwa Perceptions of a Missionary as Evil Shaman," repr. in *American Encounters: Natives and Newcomers from European Contact to Indian Removal, 1500–1850*, ed. Peter C. Mancall and James H. Merrell (New York: Routledge, 2000), 162–75.

12. Louis André, "Relation of 1672–1673," in *JR*, vol. 57, 275–79.

13. Louis André, "Relation of 1673–1674," in *JR*, vol. 58, 283–89.

14. Louis André, "Relation of 1676–1677," in *JR*, vol. 60, 201–3.

15. François Le Mercier, *Relation of 1667–1668*, in *JR*, vol. 51, 259–65; Thierry Beschefer to the Jesuit Provincial, 21 October 1683, in *JR*, vol. 62, 209–11.

16. Olive Patricia Dickason, *The Myth of the Savage and the Beginnings of French Colonialism in the Americas* (Edmonton: University of Alberta Press, 1984); Robert F. Berkhofer, Jr., *The White Man's Indian: Images of the American Indian from Columbus to the Present* (New York: Alfred A. Knopf, 1978), 12–31; Cornelius J. Jaenen, "Characteristics of French-Amerindian Contact in New France," in *Essays on the History of North American Discovery and Exploration*, ed. Stanley H. Palmer and Dennis Reinhartz (College Station: Texas A&M University Press, 1988), 79; William N. Fenton, "Introduction" to Joseph François Lafitau, *Customs of the American Indians Compared with the Customs of Primitive Times*, trans. and ed. William N. Fenton and Elizabeth L. Moore (Toronto: Champlain Society, 1974), vol. 1, li, lxviii–lxxiv; Anthony Pagden, *The Fall of Natural Man: The American Indian and the Origins of Comparative Ethnology* (repr., Cambridge: Cambridge University Press, 1986), 8–9; Peter N. Moogk, *La Nouvelle France: The Making of French Canada—A Cultural History* (East Lansing: Michigan State University Press, 2000), 16–50; James Axtell, "The European Failure to Convert the Indians: An Autopsy," in *Papers of the Sixth Algonquian Conference, 1974*, ed. William Cowan (Ottawa: National Museums of Canada, 1975), 275–76.

17. François-Xavier de Charlevoix, *Journal d'un voyage fait par ordre du roi dans l'Amérique septentrionale*, ed. Pierre Berthiaume (Montreal: Les Presses de l'Université de Montréal, 1994), vol. 2, 677. Translation adapted from the 1761 English edition reproduced in facsimile in Pierre de Charlevoix, *Journal of a Voyage to North America* (Ann Arbor: University Microfilms, 1966), vol. 2, 136.

18. On the dualistic tension in European and French images of Indians, see Berkhofer, 16–31; Jaenen, *Friend and Foe*, 15–34; Cornelius J. Jaenen, " 'Les Sauvages Ameriquains': Persistence into the Eighteenth Century of Traditional French Concepts and Constructs for Comprehending Amerindians," *Ethnohistory* 29 (Winter 1982): 43–56;

Pagden, ch. 8; Moogk, 16–50; W. Vernon Kinietz, *The Indians of the Western Great Lakes, 1615–1760* (repr., Ann Arbor: University of Michigan Press, 1965), 4–9; G. R. Healy, "The French Jesuits and the Idea of the Noble Savage," *William and Mary Quarterly*, 3d ser., 15 (April 1958): 143–67; and Gordon M. Sayre, *Les Sauvages Américains: Representations of Native Americans in French and English Colonial Literature* (Chapel Hill: University of North Carolina Press, 1997), 79–82, 123–29, and 138–43.

19. Carole Blackburn, *Harvest of Souls: The Jesuit Missions and Colonialism in North America, 1632–1650* (Montreal: McGill-Queen's University Press, 2000), 67–69; Jaenen, "Characteristics of French-Amerindian Contact," 79.

20. Pagden, 3–4, 146–98; Luis Martín, "The Peruvian Indian through Jesuit Eyes: The Case of José de Acosta and Pablo José de Arriaga," in *The Jesuit Tradition in Education and Missions: A 450-Year Perspective*, ed. Christopher Chapple (Scranton, Pa.: University of Scranton Press, 1993), 205–14.

21. Dablon, *Relation of 1670–1671*, 207–19.

22. Ibid.

23. For an overview of Illinois culture and history, see Charles Callender, "Illinois," and J. Joseph Bauxar, "History of the Illinois Area," in *Handbook of North American Indians*, vol. 15, *Northeast*, ed. Bruce G. Trigger (Washington, D.C.: Smithsonian Institution, 1978), 673–80 and 594–601. Kinietz, 161–225, contains information on the Illinois and on the culturally and linguistically related Miamis. The tribal groups and bands identified by the French were the Cahokias, Chepoussas, Chinkoas, Coiracoentanons, Espeminkias, Kaskaskias, Maroas, Michigameas, Moingwenas, Peorias, Tamaroas, and Tapouaros. By the eighteenth century, the Cahokias, Kaskaskias, Michigameas, Peorias, and Tamaroas dominated relations with the French. The others were absorbed into these groups or perhaps disappeared from French records because of clarification of their names and status.

24. Claude Allouez, *Relation of 1666–1667*, in *JR*, vol. 51, 47–51; Jacques Marquette, *Relation of 1669–1670*, in *JR*, vol. 54, 185–95.

25. Pierre Deliette, "Memoir of De Gannes concerning the Illinois Country," in *Collections of the Illinois State Historical Library*, vol. 23, *The French Foundations, 1680–1693*, ed. Theodore Calvin Pease and Raymond C. Werner (Springfield: Illinois State Historical Library, 1934), 361–76. For another such perspective, see Nicolas Perrot, *Memoir on the manners, customs, and religion of the savages of North America*, in *The Indian Tribes of the Upper Mississippi Valley and Region of the Great Lakes*, ed. Emma Helen Blair (repr., Lincoln: University of Nebraska Press, 1996), vol. 1, 47–64. On Jesuit perceptions of Indian religion in the first half of the seventeenth century, consult Lucien Campeau, *La mission des jésuites chez les Hurons, 1634–1650* (Montreal: Bellarmin, 1987), 97–112, and Michael M. Pomedli, "Beyond Unbelief: Early Jesuit Interpretations of Native Religions," *Studies in Religion/Sciences Religieuses* 16 (Summer 1987): 275–87.

26. Lafitau, 28, 88–91, 94.

27. Ibid., xlii–lxxxiii, 29–36, 92–116, and 229–59. On natural religion, see Healy, 151–53; Jaenen, *Friend and Foe*, 41–50; John Hopkins Kennedy, *Jesuit and Savage in New France* (New Haven, Conn.: Yale University Press, 1950), chs. 6–8; and James T. Moore,

Indian and Jesuit: A Seventeenth-Century Encounter (Chicago: Loyola University Press, 1982), ch. 2.

28. Charlevoix, *Journal d'un voyage*, vol. 2, 679; Charlevoix, *Journal of a Voyage to North America*, vol. 2, 138.

29. Claude Allouez, "Relation of 1675," in *JR*, vol. 59, 229–31. On Jesuit views of diabolism and shamanism, see Peter A. Goddard, "The Devil in New France: Jesuit Demonology, 1611–50," *Canadian Historical Review* 78 (March 1997): 40–62, and Guy Laflèche, "Le chamanisme des Amérindiens et des missionaires da la Nouvelle-France," *Studies in Religion/Sciences Religieuses* 9 (Spring 1980): 137–60.

30. Le Boulanger, n.p.

31. Ibid., n.p. and 118.

32. Claude Allouez, *Relation of 1664–1665*, in *JR*, vol. 49, 241–51; Claude Dablon to Jean Pinette, 24 October 1674, in *JR*, vol. 59, 64–83; François Le Mercier, *Relation of 1668–1669*, in *JR*, vol. 52, 203–5; Kennedy, ch. 8; Axtell, "European Failure," 288.

33. Thomas A. Tweed, *Crossing and Dwelling: A Theory of Religion* (Cambridge, Mass.: Harvard University Press, 2006).

34. Jacques Marquette, "Unfinished Journal of Father Jacques Marquette, addressed to Reverend Father Claude Dablon, superior of the Missions," in *JR*, vol. 59, 164–83.

35. Claude Dablon, "Account of the Second Voyage and the Death of Father Jacques Marquette," in *JR*, vol. 59, 184–91.

36. Jacques Gravier, "Letter by Father Jacques Gravier in the form of a Journal of the Mission of l'Immaculée Conception de Notre Dame in the Ilinois country," in *JR*, vol. 64, 165–67.

37. Ibid., 159–237.

CHAPTER 5

1. Mathurin Le Petit to Louis d'Avaugour, 12 July 1730, in *The Jesuit Relations and Allied Documents*, ed. Reuben Gold Thwaites (Cleveland, Ohio: Burrows Bros., 1896–1901; hereafter, *JR*), vol. 68, 201–7.

2. Important studies of these processes in different places and periods are Vicente L. Rafael, *Contracting Colonialism: Translation and Christian Conversion in Tagalog Society under Early Spanish Rule* (Ithaca, N.Y.: Cornell University Press, 1988); Louise M. Burkhart, *The Slippery Earth: Nahua-Christian Moral Dialogue in Sixteenth-Century Mexico* (Tucson: University of Arizona Press, 1989); and Pier M. Larson, " 'Capacities and Modes of Thinking': Intellectual Engagements and Subaltern Hegemony in the Early History of Malagasy Christianity," *American Historical Review* 102 (October 1997): 969–1002. See also Edward G. Gray, *New World Babel: Languages and Nations in Early America* (Princeton, N.J.: Princeton University Press, 1999), 30–43; Edward G. Gray, "Introduction," in *The Language Encounter in the Americas, 1492–1800*, ed. Edward G. Gray and Norman Fiering (New York: Berghahn Books, 2000), 1–2; Carole Blackburn, *Harvest of Souls: The Jesuit Missions and Colonialism in North America, 1632–1650* (Montreal: McGill-Queen's

University Press, 2000), 101–4; and James Axtell, *The Invasion Within: The Contest of Cultures in Colonial North America* (New York: Oxford University Press, 1985), 80–83.

3. Few scholars have attempted to analyze such Native language religious texts. Exceptions include John Steckley, "The Warrior and the Lineage: Jesuit Use of Iroquoian Images to Communicate Christianity," *Ethnohistory* 39 (Fall 1992): 478–509; Jeffrey D. Anderson, "Northern Arapaho Conversion of a Christian Text," *Ethnohistory* 48 (Fall 2001): 689–712; Laura J. Murray, "Vocabularies of Native American Languages: A Literary and Historical Approach to an Elusive Genre," *American Quarterly* 53 (December 2001): 590–623; and the impressive collaboration by Luke Eric Lassiter, Clyde Ellis, and Ralph Kotay, *The Jesus Road: Kiowas, Christianity, and Indian Hymns* (Lincoln: University of Nebraska Press, 2002). The manuscripts that form the basis for this study are Claude Allouez, *Facsimile of Père Marquette's Illinois Prayer Book* (Quebec: Quebec Literary and Historical Society, 1908); Jacques Gravier, *Dictionary of the Algonquian Illinois Language*, MS (photocopy and microfilm copy), American Indian MSS, Watkinson Library, Trinity College, Hartford, Conn.; and Jean Baptiste Le Boulanger [Jean Le Boullenger], [French and Miami-Illinois Dictionary], Codex Ind 28, 2-SIZE, John Carter Brown Library, Providence, R.I. Working with the religious texts from the Allouez prayer book and the Le Boullenger dictionary (which includes prayers and other religious writings) would be much more difficult without the outstanding linguistic analysis of Miami-Illinois conducted by David Costa. See David J. Costa, *The Miami-Illinois Language* (Lincoln: University of Nebraska Press, 2003). Daryl Baldwin and David J. Costa, *myaamia neehi peewaalia kaloosioni mahsinaakani: A Miami-Peoria Dictionary* (Miami, Okla.: Miami Nation, 2005) and Daryl Wade Baldwin, "myaamia iilaataweenki (The Miami Language)" (M.A. thesis, University of Montana, 1999), have also been enormously helpful.

4. Claude Allouez, *Relation of 1666–1667*, in *JR*, vol. 51, 47–51.

5. Jacques Marquette, "Of the first Voyage made by Father Marquette toward new Mexico, and How the idea thereof was conceived," in *JR*, vol. 59, 86–163; Claude Dablon, "Account of the Second Voyage and the Death of Father Jacques Marquette," in *JR*, vol. 59, 184–211; Claude Allouez, "Narrative of a Third Voyage to the Illinois," in *JR*, vol. 60, 148–67.

6. The premier study of the linguistic work of the French Jesuits is still Victor Egon Hanzeli, *Missionary Linguistics in New France: A Study of Seventeenth- and Eighteenth-Century Descriptions of American Indian Languages* (The Hague: Mouton, 1969). On Miami-Illinois, see Costa, *Miami-Illinois Language*, 1, and Ives Goddard, "Central Algonquian Languages," in *Handbook of North American Indians,* vol. 15, *Northeast,* ed. Bruce G. Trigger (Washington, D.C.: Smithsonian Institution, 1978), 583–87.

7. Léon Pouliot, "Claude Allouez," in *Dictionary of Canadian Biography*, ed. George W. Brown (Toronto: University of Toronto Press, 1966; hereafter, *DCB*), vol. 1, 57; J. Monet, "Jacques Marquette," in *DCB*, vol. 1, 491; Jacques Marquette, *Relation of 1669–1670*, in *JR*, vol. 54, 185–95; Jacques Marquette to Rev. Father Pupin, 4 August 1667, in *Some Hitherto Unpublished Marquettiana*, ed. Gilbert J. Garraghan, S.J., repr. from *Mid-America*, vol. 18, n.s. vol. 7 (1936): 8–9; Marquette, "Of the first Voyage," 125–27.

8. Gabriel Marest to Barthélemi Germon, 9 November 1712, in *JR*, vol. 66, 245–47; Pierre Deliette, "Memoir of De Gannes concerning the Illinois Country," in *Collections of the Illinois State Historical Library*, vol. 23, *The French Foundations, 1680–1693*, ed. Theodore Calvin Pease and Raymond C. Werner (Springfield: Illinois State Historical Library, 1934), 361. The actual authorship of the Illinois prayer book remains uncertain. See the introduction to the facsimile edition in Allouez, *Illinois Prayer Book*, 7–13; J. Sasseville and John Gilmary Shea, *Notes on the Two Jesuit Manuscripts Belonging to the Estate of the late Hon. John Neilson of Quebec, Canada* (New York: n.p., 1887); and Ives Goddard, "The Description of the Native Languages of North America before Boas," in *Handbook of North American Indians*, vol. 17, *Languages*, ed. Ives Goddard (Washington, D.C.: Smithsonian Institution, 1996), 19–22. For recent analyses of the provenance of Miami-Illinois linguistic material, consult Costa, *Miami-Illinois Language*, 10–12, and Michael McCafferty, "The Latest Miami-Illinois Dictionary and Its Author," in *Papers of the 36th Algonquian Conference*, ed. H. C. Wolfart (Winnipeg: University of Manitoba, 2005): 271–86.

9. Julien Binneteau to another Jesuit father, [January] 1699, in *JR*, vol. 65, 69–71; Le Petit to d'Avaugour, 211; Hanzeli, 25–31; Costa, *Miami-Illinois Language*, 10–2; McCafferty, 271–86.

10. Gray, *New World Babel*, 30–43; Gray, "Introduction," in *Language Encounter in the Americas*, 1–2; Blackburn, 101–4; Margaret J. Leahey, "'Comment peut un muet prescher l'évangile?': Jesuit Missionaries and the Native Languages of New France," *French Historical Studies* 19 (Spring 1995): 105–31; Jane T. Merritt, "Metaphor, Meaning, and Misunderstanding: Language and Power on the Pennsylvania Frontier," in *Contact Points: American Frontiers from the Mohawk Valley to the Mississippi, 1750–1830*, ed. Andrew R. L. Cayton and Fredrika J. Teute (Chapel Hill: University of North Carolina Press), 60–87.

11. Louis André, "Relation of 1672–1673," in *JR*, vol. 57, 269–71.

12. Louis Châtellier notes the importance of the *Pater Noster, Ave Maria*, and *Credo* in European missionary work during the same period in *The Religion of the Poor: Rural Missions in Europe and the Formation of Modern Catholicism, c.1500–c.1800*, trans. Brian Pearce (Cambridge: Cambridge University Press, 1997), 200.

13. Gravier, *Dictionary*, 53 and 145; Le Boulanger, 54, 126, and 136; Baldwin, "Miami Language," 48, 123, 68, and 150; Baldwin and Costa, *Miami-Peoria Dictionary*, 71. Transcriptions of Illinois words remain as they appear in the Illinois language texts. The symbol *8* represents the phonemes *o, oo,* or *w*.

14. Le Boulanger 53 and 157; Gravier, *Dictionary*, 133.

15. Gravier, *Dictionary*, 246; Le Boulanger 78, 116.

16. Spanish missionaries in the Philippines also tried to maintain the purity of some central Christian teachings in a similar manner. See Rafael, 20–21 and 29–30.

17. François-Xavier de Charlevoix, *Journal d'un voyage fait par ordre du roi dans l'Amérique septentrionale*, ed. Pierre Berthiaume (Montreal: Les Presses de l'Université de Montréal, 1994), vol. 1, 448–50. Translation adapted from Pierre de Charlevoix, *Journal of a Voyage to North America* (Ann Arbor, Mich.: University Microfilms, 1966), vol. 1, 300–302.

18. Ibid. On Jesuit complaints about the "poverty" of Native languages and the problems of translation, see Gray, *New World Babel*, 30–43; Gray, "Introduction," in *Language Encounter in the Americas*, 2–4; Cornelius J. Jaenen, *Friend and Foe: Aspects of French-Amerindian Cultural Contact in the Sixteenth and Seventeenth Centuries* (New York: Columbia University Press, 1976), 51–54; Guy Laflèche, "Le chamanisme des Amérindiens et des missionaires da la Nouvelle-France," *Studies in Religion/Sciences Religieuses* 9 (Spring 1980): 139–41; and Lucien Campeau, *La mission des jésuites chez les Hurons, 1634–1650* (Montreal: Bellarmin, 1987), 179–96.

19. Allouez, *Relation of 1666–1667*, 47–51.

20. Gravier supplies the French definitions "chief, captain, lord, duke, king, [and] emperor." Gravier, *Dictionary*, 23. See also Le Boulanger, 40.

21. Marest to Germon, 221; Charles Callender, "Illinois," in *Handbook of North American Indians*, vol. 15, *Northeast*, ed. Bruce G. Trigger (Washington, D.C.: Smithsonian Institution, 1978), 673–80; Margaret Kimball Brown, *Cultural Transformations among the Illinois: An Application of a Systems Model* (East Lansing: Publications of the Museum/ Michigan State University, 1979), 233–45; W. Vernon Kinietz, *The Indians of the Western Great Lakes, 1615–1760* (repr., Ann Arbor: University of Michigan Press, 1965), 161–225; Deliette, 302–96.

22. Gravier, *Dictionary*, 56; Le Boulanger, 10–11 in the prayer manual.

23. Gravier, *Dictionary*, 382–84; Le Boulanger, 68, 95, and 162.

24. Costa, *Miami-Illinois Language*, 353–61. On Native storytelling traditions, see Joseph Epes Brown and Emily Cousins, *Teaching Spirits: Understanding Native American Religious Traditions* (New York: Oxford University Press, 2001), 54–56.

25. Gravier, *Dictionary*, 53; Le Boulanger, 70 and 147.

26. Gravier, *Dictionary*, 178; Le Boulanger, 135.

27. Gravier, *Dictionary*, 145 and 576; Le Boulanger, 43 and 136; Baldwin, "Miami Language," 107 and 135; Baldwin and Costa, *Miami-Peoria Dictionary*, 39.

28. Costa, *Miami-Illinois Language*, 509; Gravier, *Dictionary*, 415; Le Boulanger, 3 and 137. On the Our Father, see Châtellier, 91–183.

29. Gravier, *Dictionary*, 315, 376, and 471; Le Boulanger, 131; Baldwin and Costa, *Miami-Peoria Dictionary*, 28.

30. Gravier, *Dictionary*, 53, 59, 198, 374, and 376; Le Boulanger, 42, 58, 102, 126, 172, and 189.

31. Le Boulanger, 126; Gravier, *Dictionary*, 303; Baldwin and Costa, *Miami-Peoria Dictionary*, 78; Châtellier, 131–37.

32. Deliette, 336–37 and 381–82; Richard White, *The Middle Ground: Indians, Empires, and Republics in the Great Lakes Region, 1650–1815* (New York: Cambridge University Press, 1991), 90–93.

33. Gravier, *Dictionary*, 219–20 and 255; Le Boulanger, 57–58 and 114; Châtellier, 162–83.

34. Gravier, *Dictionary*, 384; Le Boulanger, 95.

35. Jacques Gravier, "Letter by Father Jacques Gravier in the form of a Journal of the Mission of l'Immaculée Conception de Notre Dame in the Ilinois country," 15 February

1694, in *JR*, vol. 64, 211–25. Another term for the process of conversion, *taca8ans8tehe*, may translate loosely as "to refresh the heart." See Gravier, *Dictionary*, 37, and Le Boulanger, 36–37, 43, and 48.

36. Le Boullenger supplies a translation for "to convert" that contains the root for "to give birth." See Le Boulanger, 48. Gravier, "Journal of the Mission of l'Immaculée Conception," 225–37.

37. Marest to Germon, 241–43.

38. Brown and Cousins, 41–56; Sam D. Gill, *Native American Religious Action: A Performance Approach to Religion* (Columbia: University of South Carolina Press, 1987); Lee Irwin, "Native American Spirituality: History, Theory, and Reformulation," in *A Companion to American Indian History*, ed. Philip J. Deloria and Neal Salisbury (Malden, Mass.: Blackwell Publishers, 2002), 103–4; Gravier, *Dictionary*, 250; Le Boulanger, 42 and 70; Christopher Bilodeau, "'They Honor Our Lord among Themselves in Their Own Way': Colonial Christianity and Illinois Indians," *American Indian Quarterly* 25 (June 2001): 352–77.

39. Gabriel Marest to a father of the Society of Jesus, 29 April 1699, in *JR*, vol. 65, 81; Marest to Germon, 231, 241–43, 253–55.

40. Rafael, 21; Le Petit to d'Avaugour, 205.

CHAPTER 6

1. Claude Allouez, "Sentiments," in *Le Père Pierre Chaumonot de la Compagnie de Jésus: Autobiographie et pièces inédites*, ed. Auguste Carayon (Poitiers: Henri Oudin, 1869), xi–xvi. Léon Pouliot notes that a major portion of Allouez's "Sentiments" closely resembles a series of writings included with the *Jesuit Relation of 1635*. It seems Allouez copied some of this material and made his own additions to create a personal written guide for his life as a missionary. See Pouliot, "Claude Allouez," in *Dictionary of Canadian Biography*, vol. 1, ed. George W. Brown (Toronto: University of Toronto Press, 1966), 58. Allouez's apparent model is in Reuben Gold Thwaites, ed., *The Jesuit Relations and Allied Documents* (Cleveland, Ohio: Burrows Bros., 1896–1901; hereafter, *JR*), vol. 8, 168–93. All translations from Allouez's "Sentiments" are mine.

2. Lewis R. Rambo, *Understanding Religious Conversion* (New Haven, Conn.: Yale University Press, 1993); Nicholas Griffiths, "Introduction," in *Spiritual Encounters: Interactions between Christianity and Native Religions in Colonial America*, ed. Nicholas Griffiths and Fernando Cervantes (Lincoln: University of Nebraska Press, 1999), 1–42; Robert W. Hefner, "Introduction: World Building and the Rationality of Conversion," in *Conversion to Christianity: Historical and Anthropological Perspectives on a Great Transformation*, ed. Robert W. Hefner (Berkeley: University of California Press, 1993), 1–44.

3. Pouliot, 57; "Jésuites missionaires en Nouvelle-France, 1611–1800," November 1998, Galliae 110 II, Archivum Romanum Societatis Iesu, Rome; Ignatius of Loyola, *Constitutions of the Society of Jesus*, in *Ignatius of Loyola: "The Spiritual Exercises" and Selected Works*, ed. George E. Ganss (New York: Paulist Press, 1991), 306–7. On the famous

and frequently misunderstood "Fourth Vow," see John W. O'Malley, *The First Jesuits* (Cambridge, Mass.: Harvard University Press, 1993), 298–301.

4. Joseph de Guibert, *The Jesuits, Their Spiritual Doctrine and Practice: A Historical Study*, trans. William J. Young (Chicago: Institute of Jesuit Sources, 1964), 26–59, 239–40, and ch. 17; O'Malley, *First Jesuits*, ch. 2; John O'Malley, "Early Jesuit Spirituality: Spain and Italy," in *Christian Spirituality: Post-Reformation and Modern*, ed. Louis Dupré and Don E. Saliers (New York: Crossroad, 1989), 7–8.

5. Guibert, 109–39 and ch. 13; O'Malley, *First Jesuits*, 4, 372–74; Ignatius of Loyola, *The Spiritual Exercises* in *Ignatius of Loyola: "The Spiritual Exercises" and Selected Works*, ed. George E. Ganss (New York: Paulist Press, 1991), 129, 389–90.

6. Guibert, 282; John Webster Grant, *Moon of Wintertime: Missionaries and the Indians of Canada in Encounter since 1534* (Toronto: University of Toronto Press, 1984), 10–36; James Axtell, *The Invasion Within: The Contest of Cultures in Colonial North America* (New York: Oxford University Press, 1985), 75–77; Louis André, "Relation of 1672–1673," in *JR*, vol. 57, 301; Gabriel Marest to Jean de Lamberville, 5 July 1702, in *JR*, vol. 66, 37–39.

7. Claude Dablon, "Account of the Second Voyage and the Death of Father Jacques Marquette," in *JR*, vol. 59, 184–211. See also Joseph P. Donnelly, *Jacques Marquette, S.J., 1637–1675* (Chicago: Loyola University Press, 1968), 230–66. George E. Ganss discusses the terminology and stages of mental prayer in his editorial notes for Guibert, *Jesuits, Their Spiritual Doctrine and Practice*, 605–9. On hagiography in New France, see Allan Greer, "Colonial Saints: Gender, Race, and Hagiography in New France," *William and Mary Quarterly*, 3d. ser., 57 (April 2000): 323–48.

8. Guibert, 83–85; Ignatius, *Spiritual Exercises*, 130, 146–47; George A. Lane, *Christian Spirituality: An Historical Sketch* (Chicago: Loyola University Press, 1984), 55–56.

9. Ignatius, *Spiritual Exercises*, 166; Lane, 45–50, 55; Guibert, 141–42 and 567–68.

10. Michael J. Buckley, "Seventeenth-Century French Spirituality: Three Figures," in *Christian Spirituality: Post-Reformation and Modern*, ed. Louis Dupré and Don E. Saliers (New York: Crossroad, 1989), 42–43 and 55–57; Guibert, 353–73; Peter A. Goddard, "Augustine and the Amerindian in Seventeenth-Century New France," *Church History* 67 (December 1998): 662–81; Robert Choquette, "French Catholicism Comes to the Americas," in *Christianity Comes to the Americas, 1492–1776* (New York: Paragon House, 1992), 133–41; Allan Greer, *Mohawk Saint: Catherine Tekakwitha and the Jesuits* (New York: Oxford University Press, 2005), 72–77; Cornelius J. Jaenen, *Friend and Foe: Aspects of French-Amerindian Cultural Contact in the Sixteenth and Seventeenth Centuries* (New York: Columbia University Press, 1976), 48–50.

11. Allouez, "Sentiments," xvi–xxii.

12. Claude Allouez, *Relation of 1669–1670*, in *JR*, vol. 54, 207; Allouez, "Sentiments," xvii–xviii.

13. Allouez, *Relation of 1669–1670*, 205–41; Claude Allouez, "Relation of 1675," in *JR*, vol. 59, 225–35. For a description of the Mesquakies and their early encounters with the French, see R. David Edmunds and Joseph L. Peyser, *The Fox Wars: The Mesquakie Challenge to New France* (Norman: University of Oklahoma Press, 1993), chs. 1–2.

14. Allouez, "Relation of 1675," 225–27.

15. A careful analysis of more than seventy conversion narratives embedded in the Thwaites edition of the *Jesuit Relations* (which includes allied documents), covering the period 1660 to 1730 in the upper Great Lakes and Illinois country, confirms the prevalence of this general pattern (see appendix for a detailed explanation). The pattern is similar to the systematic process described for religious conversion in general by Lewis R. Rambo in *Understanding Religious Conversion*. See also Axtell, 116–27, and Peter A. Goddard, "Converting the *Sauvage*: Jesuit and Montagnais in Seventeenth-Century New France," *Catholic Historical Review* 84 (April 1998): 219–39.

16. Allouez, "Sentiments," xxiii–xxiv; Thierry Beschefer to the Jesuit provincial in France, 21 October 1683, in *JR*, vol. 62, 209; Claude Allouez, *Relation of 1666–1667*, in *JR*, vol. 50, 297–305; Claude Allouez, "Relation of 1672–1673," in *JR*, vol. 58, 43.

17. O'Malley, *First Jesuits*, ch. 3.

18. Allouez, "Relation of 1672–1673," 45; Lane, 61–67. Buckley, 55–59; Claude Allouez, *Facsimile of Père Marquette's Illinois Prayer Book* (Quebec: Quebec Literary and Historical Society, 1908), 94–103.

19. Allouez, "Relation of 1675," 231–33.

20. Axtell, 58–127; Choquette, 185–92; Goddard, "Converting the *Sauvage*," 219–39; Goddard, "Augustine and the Amerindian," 662–81; Grant, 30–38 and 47–52; Jaenen, 153–82; Christopher Vecsey, *The Paths of Kateri's Kin* (Notre Dame, Ind.: University of Notre Dame Press, 1997), 23–28.

21. Allouez, "Relation of 1672–1673," 45.

22. Allouez, "Sentiments," xxiv; C. D. [Claude Dablon], letter of 29 August 1690, FCa165, Archives Jésuites de Paris, Vanves.

23. Claude Allouez, *Relation of 1666–1667*, in *JR*, vol. 51, 47–51; Christopher Bilodeau, "'They Honor Our Lord among Themselves in Their Own Way': Colonial Christianity and Illinois Indians," *American Indian Quarterly* 25 (June 2001): 352–77.

24. Allouez, *Relation of 1666–1667*, vol. 51, 47–51.

25. Richard White, *The Middle Ground: Indians, Empires, and Republics in the Great Lakes Region, 1650–1815* (New York: Cambridge University Press, 1991), 25–27.

26. Louis André, "Relation of 1673–1674," in *JR*, vol. 58, 273–81.

27. Jean de Lamberville, "Relation of 1672–1673," in *JR*, vol. 57, 219–37.

28. E. M. Burke, "Grace," in *The New Catholic Encyclopedia*, vol. 6 (New York: McGraw-Hill, 1967), 657–72; Paul Tihon, "Grace," in *Dictionnaire de spiritualité*, vol. 6 (Paris: Beauchesne, 1967), 701–50; Kenneth M. Morrison, *The Solidarity of Kin: Ethnohistory, Religious Studies, and the Algonkian-French Religious Encounter* (Albany: State University of New York Press, 2002), chs. 6–7; Charles E. Cleland, *Rites of Conquest: The History and Culture of Michigan's Native Americans* (Ann Arbor: University of Michigan Press, 1992), 66–70; Elizabeth Tooker, *Native North American Spirituality of the Eastern Woodlands: Sacred Myths, Dreams, Visions, Speeches, Healing Formulas, Rituals and Ceremonials* (New York: Paulist Press, 1979), 11–30; A. Irving Hallowell, "Ojibwa Ontology, Behavior, and World View," repr. in A. Irving Hallowell, *Contributions to Anthropology* (Chicago: University of Chicago Press, 1976), 357–90; Gregory Evans Dowd, *A Spirited*

Resistance: The North American Indian Struggle for Unity, 1745–1815 (Baltimore, Md.: Johns Hopkins University Press, 1992), ch. 1.

29. Claude Dablon, *Relation of 1669–1670*, in *JR*, vol. 54, 141–43; Henri Nouvel, *Relation of 1671–1672*, in *JR*, vol. 56, 125–29; Allouez, *Relation of 1666–1667*, vol. 50, 285–95.

30. Jacques Marquette, *Relation of 1669–1670*, in *JR*, vol. 54, 181.

31. Allouez, "Relation of 1672–1673," 27–33.

32. Axtell, 119–22; Grant, 40–46. Sam D. Gill stresses the importance of performance and action over simple belief in American Indian religions in Sam D. Gill, *Native American Religious Action: A Performance Approach to Religion* (Columbia: University of South Carolina Press, 1987) and Sam D. Gill, *Native American Religions: An Introduction*, 2d ed. (Belmont, Calif.: Wadsworth, 2005). On the connection between ritual, reciprocity, and power among the Montagnais and the Wendats (Hurons), see Morrison, ch. 6, and Lee Irwin, "Contesting World Views: Dreams among the Huron and Jesuits," *Religion* 22 (July 1992): 262–63.

33. Allouez, *Relation of 1666–1667*, vol. 51, 47–51.

34. Lamberville, "Relation of 1672–1673," 239–47.

35. Pierre Bailloquet, "Relation of 1679," in *JR*, vol. 61, 99–101.

36. William James Newbigging, "The History of the French-Ottawa Alliance, 1613–1763" (Ph.D. diss., University of Toronto, 1995), 120–58; Johanna E. Feest and Christian F. Feest, "Ottawa," in *Handbook of North American Indians*, vol. 15, *Northeast*, ed. Bruce G. Trigger (Washington, D.C.: Smithsonian Institution, 1978), 772–74; W. Vernon Kinietz, *The Indians of the Western Great Lakes, 1615–1760* (repr., Ann Arbor: University of Michigan Press, 1965), 226–32; Cleland, 92–98; René Ménard to Jérôme Lalemant, 2 June 1661, in *JR*, vol. 46, 126–45; Claude Allouez, *Relation of 1668–1669*, in *JR*, vol. 52, 205–13.

37. Allouez, *Relation of 1668–1669*, 205–13. For a very different perspective on this event, consult Newbigging, 120–58. Scholars have not generally recognized Christianity as a possible source of cultural revitalization in the Indian communities of this region and time, although they have acknowledged the importance of experiences with missionaries and with Christianity as a background for some revitalization movements in the eighteenth and nineteenth centuries. See Anthony F. C. Wallace, *The Death and Rebirth of the Seneca* (New York: Knopf, 1970); R. David Edmunds, *The Shawnee Prophet* (Lincoln: University of Nebraska Press, 1983); Dowd, *Spirited Resistance*; and Colin G. Calloway, *New Worlds for All: Indians, Europeans, and the Remaking of Early America* (Baltimore, Md.: Johns Hopkins University Press, 1997), 90–91. Two scholars who explain the importance of Christianity in Indian adjustments to colonization are David Silverman in *Faith and Boundaries: Colonists, Christianity, and Community among the Wampanoag Indians of Martha's Vineyard, 1600–1871* (New York: Cambridge University Press, 2005) and Lee Irwin, *Coming Down from Above: Prophecy, Resistance, and Renewal in Native American Religions* (Norman: University of Oklahoma Press, 2008).

38. Jérôme Lalemant, *Relation of 1662–1663*, in *JR*, vol. 48, 123–27.

39. Ménard to Lalemant, 131–35; René Ménard, *Relation of 1663–64*, in *JR*, vol. 48, 267–71.

40. Nouvel, 93–95.

41. Ibid.

42. Allouez, *Relation of 1668–1669*, 205–7. On Jesus instructing his apostles to shake the dust from their feet and move on when they were unwelcome, see Matthew 10:14–15, Mark 6:7–13, and Luke 9:1–5.

43. Allouez, *Relation of 1668–1669*, 205–7.

44. Marquette, *Relation of 1669–1670*, 169–77.

45. Ibid., 181–83; Jean Enjalran, "Relation of 1679," in *JR*, vol. 61, 131–47; Feest and Feest, 773; Axtell, ch. 11; Robert Conkling, "Legitimacy and Social Change in Conversion: The Case of the French Missionaries and the Northeastern Algonkian," *Ethnohistory* 21 (Winter 1974): 1–19.

46. Marquette, *Relation of 1669–1670*, 181–83; Enjalran, 129–31.

47. Allouez, *Relation of 1668–1669*, 209–13.

48. Marquette, *Relation of 1669–1670*, 183–85.

49. Enjalran, 101–47.

50. Dablon, "Second Voyage and Death of Father Jacques Marquette," 201–5. On the Feast of the Dead, see Harold Hickerson, "The Feast of the Dead among the Seventeenth Century Algonkians of the Upper Great Lakes," *American Anthropologist* 62 (February 1960): 81–107; Newbigging, 97–98, 115, and 349–52; White, 102–3; and Theresa M. Schenck, *"The Voice of the Crane Echoes Afar": The Sociopolitical Organization of the Lake Superior Ojibwa, 1640–1855* (New York: Garland, 1997), 38–39.

51. Allouez, "Sentiments," 19.

CHAPTER 7

1. Last Will and Testament of Marie Rouensa, 13 and 20 June 1725, Kaskaskia MSS, 25:6:13:1 and 25:6:20:1, Randolph County Courthouse, Chester, Ill.; Marthe Faribault Beauregard, ed., *La Population des forts Français d'Amérique (xviiie siècle): Répertoire des baptêmes, mariages et sépultures célébrés dans les forts et les établissements Français en Amérique du nord au xviiie siècle* (Montreal: Bergeron, 1984), vol. 2, 77–205; Carl J. Ekberg, trans., "Inventory of the Estate of Marie Rouensa," in Carl J. Ekberg, "Marie Rouensa-8cate8a and the Foundation of French Illinois," *Illinois Historical Journal* 84 (Autumn 1991): 158–60.

2. Last Will and Testament of Marie Rouensa. The translation is mine.

3. Ibid.; Beauregard, vol. 2, 205; Kaskaskia MSS, 28:11:13:1, Randolph County Courthouse, Chester, Ill..

4. Major sources on gender and Christianity in Native North America include Michael Harkin and Sergei Kan, eds., "Native American Women's Responses to Christianity," a special issue of *Ethnohistory* 43 (Fall 1996); Pauline Turner Strong, "Feminist Theory and the 'Invasion of the Heart' in North America," *Ethnohistory* 43 (Fall 1996): 683–712; Nancy Shoemaker, "Kateri Tekakwitha's Tortuous Path to Sainthood," in *Negotiators of Change: Historical Perspectives on Native American Women*, ed. Nancy Shoemaker (New

York: Routledge, 1995), 49–71; Natalie Zemon Davis, "Iroquois Women, European Women," repr. in *American Encounters: Natives and Newcomers from European Contact to Indian Removal, 1500–1850*, ed. Peter C. Mancall and James H. Merrell (New York: Routledge, 2000), 96–118; Carol Devens, *Countering Colonization: Native American Women and Great Lakes Missions, 1630–1900* (Berkeley: University of California Press, 1992); Karen Anderson, *Chain Her by One Foot: The Subjugation of Women in Seventeenth-century New France* (London: Routledge, 1991); Karen Anderson, "Commodity Exchange and Subordination: Montagnais-Naskapi and Huron Women, 1600–1650," *Signs: Journal of Women in Culture and Society* 11 (1985): 48–62; Eleanor Leacock, "Montagnais Women and the Jesuit Program for Colonization," in *Women and Colonization: Anthropological Perspectives*, ed. Mona Etienne and Eleanor Leacock (New York: Praeger, 1980), 25–42; Michelene E. Pesantubbee, *Choctaw Women in a Chaotic World: The Clash of Cultures in the Colonial Southeast* (Albuquerque: University of New Mexico Press, 2005); and Theda Perdue, *Cherokee Women: Gender and Culture Change, 1700–1835* (Lincoln: University of Nebraska Press, 1998), ch. 7. Scholars have not paid the same kind of attention to generational issues. A prominent exception is James P. Ronda, "Generations of Faith: The Christian Indians of Martha's Vineyard," *William and Mary Quarterly* 38, 3d ser. (July 1981): 369–94. On the "gender frontier," see Kathleen M. Brown, "The Anglo-Algonquian Gender Frontier," in *Negotiators of Change: Historical Perspectives on Native American Women*, ed. Nancy Shoemaker (New York: Routledge, 1995), 26–48; Kathleen M. Brown, *Good Wives, Nasty Wenches, and Anxious Patriarchs: Gender, Race, and Power in Colonial Virginia* (Chapel Hill: University of North Carolina Press, 1996); Rámon A. Gutiérrez, *When Jesus Came the Corn Mothers Went Away: Marriage, Sexuality, and Power in New Mexico, 1500–1846* (Stanford, Calif.: Stanford University Press, 1991); and Allan Greer, "Colonial Saints: Gender, Race, and Hagiography in New France," *William and Mary Quarterly*, 3d ser., 57 (April 2000): 323–48.

5. Jacques Gravier, "Letter by Father Jacques Gravier in the form of a Journal of the Mission of l'Immaculée Conception de Notre Dame in the Ilinois country," 15 February 1694, in *The Jesuit Relations and Allied Documents*, ed. Reuben Gold Thwaites (Cleveland, Ohio: Burrows Bros., 1896–1901; hereafter, *JR*), vol. 64, 159–237; Helen Hornbeck Tanner, ed., *Atlas of Great Lakes Indian History* (Norman: University of Oklahoma Press, 1987), map 6.

6. Gravier, "Journal of the Mission of l'Immaculée Conception," 179–237; Susan Sleeper-Smith, *Indian Women and French Men: Rethinking Cultural Encounter in the Western Great Lakes* (Amherst: University of Massachusetts Press, 2001), ch. 2; Richard White, *The Middle Ground: Indians, Empires, and Republics in the Great Lakes Region, 1650–1815* (New York: Cambridge University Press, 1991), 70–75; Eric Hinderaker, *Elusive Empires: Constructing Colonialism in the Ohio Valley, 1673–1800* (New York: Cambridge University Press, 1997), 54–66.

7. On the attractions of Christianity for Illinois women, see Jacqueline Peterson, "Women Dreaming: The Religiopsychology of Indian White Marriages and the Rise of a Metis Culture," in *Western Women: Their Land, Their Lives*, ed. Lillian Schlissel, Vicki L. Ruiz, and Janice Monk (Albuquerque: University of New Mexico Press, 1988), 49–68,

and Sleeper-Smith, ch. 2. On gender relations among the Illinois, consult Pierre Deliette, "Memoir of De Gannes concerning the Illinois Country," in *Collections of the Illinois State Historical Library*, vol. 23, *The French Foundations, 1680–1693*, ed. Theodore Calvin Pease and Raymond C. Werner (Springfield: Illinois State Historical Library, 1934), 328–52; Raymond E. Hauser, "The *Berdache* and the Illinois Indian Tribe during the Last Half of the Seventeenth Century," *Ethnohistory* 37 (Winter 1990): 47–56; Margaret Kimball Brown, *Cultural Transformations among the Illinois: An Application of a Systems Model* (East Lansing: Publications of the Museum/Michigan State University, 1979), 234–43; and W. Vernon Kinietz, *The Indians of the Western Great Lakes, 1615–1760* (repr., Ann Arbor: University of Michigan Press, 1965), 161–225. See Gabriel Marest to Barthélemi Germon, 9 November 1712, in *JR*, vol. 66, 241–45, for the separation of women and men in worship.

8. The most detailed account of female religious practice among the Illinois is Deliette, 352–76.

9. Carl J. Ekberg, "Marie Rouensa-8cate8a and the Foundations of French Illinois," *Illinois Historical Journal* 84 (Autumn 1991): 154; Hinderaker, 110–19.

10. Gravier, "Journal of the Mission of l'Immaculée Conception," 193–213.

11. Ibid., 225–237; Ekberg, "Marie Rouensa-8cate8a," 146–60; Peterson, 49–68; Sleeper-Smith, ch. 2; White, 70–75; Hinderaker, 59–64 and 110–19; Gilles Havard, *Empire et métissages: Indiens et Français dans le Pays d'en Haut, 1660–1715* (Sillery, Quebec: Septentrion, 2003), 625–80.

12. Gravier, "Journal of the Mission of l'Immaculée Conception," 167–69.

13. Ibid., 159–77.

14. Jacques de Lamberville, "Canadian Affairs in 1696," in *JR*, vol. 65, 33; Julien Binneteau to another Jesuit father, [January] 1699 in *JR*, vol. 65, 65–69; Deliette, 361–63.

15. Gabriel Marest to another Jesuit father, 29 April 1699, in *JR*, vol. 65, 79–81; Wayne C. Temple, *Indian Villages of the Illinois Country: Historic Tribes* (Springfield: Illinois State Museum, 1966), 30–31.

16. Binneteau to another Jesuit father, 67–75. See also François-Xavier de Charlevoix, *Journal d'un voyage fait par ordre du roi dans l'Amérique septentrionale*, ed. Pierre Berthiaume (Montreal: Les Presses de l'Université de Montréal, 1994), vol. 1, 582–92; Laura F. Klein and Lillian A. Ackerman, "Introduction," in *Women and Power in Native North America*, ed. Laura F. Klein and Lillian A. Ackerman (Norman: University of Oklahoma Press, 1995), 5–8; Nancy Shoemaker, "Introduction," in *Negotiators of Change: Historical Perspectives on Native American Women*, ed. Nancy Shoemaker (New York: Routledge, 1995), 2–3; Devens, 24–27; Leacock, 26–27.

17. Charlevoix, vol. 2, 617–32; Antoine Denis Raudot, "Memoir Concerning the Different Indian Nations of North America," in W. Vernon Kinietz, *The Indians of the Western Great Lakes, 1615–1760* (repr., Ann Arbor: University of Michigan Press, 1965), 388–97; Anderson, *Chain Her by One Foot*, 55–100; Devens, 24–27.

18. Deliette, 330–35; Kinietz, 204–7; M. K. Brown, *Cultural Transformations among the Illinois*, 234–39; Charles Callender, "Illinois," in *Handbook of North American Indians*, vol. 15, *Northeast*, ed. Bruce G. Trigger (Washington, D.C.: Smithsonian Institution, 1978), 675–76.

19. Deliette, 328–52; Kinietz, 332; Jacques Marquette, *Relation of 1669–1670*, in *JR.*, vol. 54, 185–95. Deliette's memoir was probably written around 1702.

20. Havard, 634–39; Hauser, 47–56; Callender, 674–77; M. K. Brown, *Cultural Transformations among the Illinois*, 233–45; Kinietz, 161–225; Peterson, 55–58; Laura F. Klein and Lillian A. Ackerman, eds., *Women and Power in Native North America* (Norman: University of Oklahoma Press, 1995); Shoemaker, "Introduction," 4–9; Anderson, *Chain Her by One Foot*, 101–61; Leacock, 26–38; Perdue, 1–40.

21. Deliette gives the most complete account of these customs: Deliette, 352–55, 360–61. Other sources include Charlevoix, *Journal d'un voyage*, vol. 1, 582–92; Raudot, 353–97; Joseph François Lafitau, *Customs of the American Indians Compared with the Customs of Primitive Times*, trans. and ed. William N. Fenton and Elizabeth L. Moore (Toronto: Champlain Society, 1974), vol. 1, 178; Nicolas Perrot, *Memoir on the manners, customs, and religion of the savages of North America*, in *The Indian Tribes of the Upper Mississippi Valley and Region of the Great Lakes*, ed. Emma Helen Blair (repr., Lincoln: University of Nebraska Press, 1996), vol. 1, 47–64; Antoine Lamothe Cadillac, "The Memoir of Lamothe Cadillac," in *The Western Country in the 17th Century*, ed. Milo Milton Quaife (Chicago: Lakeside Press, 1947), 41–42, 63; M. K. Brown, *Cultural Transformations among the Illinois*, 242–43; Kinietz, 202–4; and Peterson, 55–58.

22. Deliette, 353–54, 369–71.

23. Ibid., 352–55.

24. Leslie Choquette, "Les Amazones du Grand Dieu: Women and Mission in Seventeenth-Century Canada," *French Historical Studies* 17 (Spring 1992): 627–55; Elizabeth Rapley, *The Dévotes: Women and Church in Seventeenth-Century France* (Montreal: McGill-Queen's University Press, 1990); Natalie Zemon Davis, *Women on the Margins: Three Seventeenth-Century Lives* (Cambridge, Mass.: Harvard University Press, 1995), 63–139. Some scholars have identified Christianity as a serious threat to female authority and autonomy. See Devens, 7–30; Anderson, *Chain Her by One Foot*; Anderson, "Commodity Exchange and Subordination," 48–62; and Leacock, "Montagnais Women." For alternative perspectives that stress opportunities as well as threats, see Harkin and Kan, 563–71; Strong, 683–712; Shoemaker, "Introduction," 9–13; and Davis, "Iroquois Women, European Women," 96–118. On the Illinois case specifically and the attractions of Christianity for Illinois women, see Peterson, 62–63, and Sleeper-Smith, ch. 2.

25. Marest to another Jesuit father, 79–85; Binneteau to another Jesuit father, 65–77; Deliette, 361–63.

26. J. Joseph Bauxar, "History of the Illinois Area," in *Handbook of North American Indians*, vol. 15, *Northeast*, ed. Bruce G. Trigger (Washington, D.C.: Smithsonian Institution, 1978), 594–601; Callender, 677–79; M. K. Brown, *Cultural Transformations among the Illinois*, 227–32; Emily J. Blasingham, "The Depopulation of the Illinois Indians," Part I in *Ethnohistory* 3 (Summer 1956): 193–224 and Part II in *Ethnohistory* 3 (Fall 1956): 361–412.

27. Deliette, 330; Raudot, 388; Beauregard, vol. 2, 107–49; Havard, 625–80; Hauser, 51.

28. Anderson, *Chain Her by One Foot*, 192–223; Anderson, "Commodity Exchange and Subordination," 48–62; Leacock, 36–38; Ronda, 389–94.

29. Marquette, 179.

30. Claude Allouez, *Relation of 1669–1670*, in *JR*, vol. 54, 239; Claude Allouez, "Relation of 1676–1677," in *JR*, vol. 60, 197–99.

31. René Ménard to Jérôme Lalemant, 2 June 1661, in *JR*, vol. 46, 127–45; Jérôme Lalemant, *Relation of 1662–1663*, in *JR*, vol. 48, 123–27.

32. Allan Greer, *Mohawk Saint: Catherine Tekakwitha and the Jesuits* (New York: Oxford University Press, 2005); Shoemaker, "Kateri Tekakwitha's Tortuous Path," 49–71.

33. Jean de Lamberville, "Relation of 1672–1673," in *JR*, vol. 57, 239–47; Vincent Bigot, "Relation of 1679," in *JR*, vol. 61, 99–101.

34. Gravier, "Journal of the Mission of l'Immaculée Conception," 221–23.

35. Sébastian Rasles to his brother, 12 October 1723, in *JR*, vol. 67, 175.

36. Lafitau, vol. 2, 15; Rasles to his brother, 175.

37. Julien Binneteau to another Jesuit father, 67; Louis André, "Relation of 1673–1674," in *JR*, vol. 58, 283–89; Louis André, "Relation of 1672–1673," in *JR*, vol. 57, 275–79.

38. Jean Enjalran, "Relation of 1679," in *JR*, vol. 61, 131–47.

39. Claude Dablon, *Relation of 1670–1671*, in *JR*, vol. 55, 185–91; Perrot, vol. 1, 41–42.

40. Deliette, 330.

41. Ibid., 375–82.

42. Raudot, 355; Claude Dablon, "Relation of 1675," in *JR*, vol. 59, 233–35.

43. André, "Relation of 1672–1673," 275–79; Lamberville, "Relation of 1672–1673," 209.

44. Claude Allouez, "Relation of 1675," in *JR*, vol. 59, 225–27; Marquette, 177–79.

45. Jean Baptiste Le Boulanger [Jean Le Boullenger], [French and Miami-Illinois Dictionary], MS (microfilm copy), Codex Ind 28, 2-SIZE, John Carter Brown Library, Providence, R.I., 162; Jacques Gravier, *Dictionary of the Algonquian Illinois Language*, MS (photocopy and microfilm copy), American Indian MSS, Watkinson Library, Trinity College, Hartford, Conn., 215 and 509.

46. The original account is from the *Mercure de France* (December 1725): 2827–59, microfilm copy by Bibliothèque nationale de France, 1959. Richard N. Ellis and Charlie R. Steen provide annotations and an English translation in "An Indian Delegation in France, 1725," *Journal of the Illinois State Historical Society* 67 (September 1974): 399–400.

CHAPTER 8

1. Gabriel Marest to another Jesuit father, 29 April 1699, in *The Jesuit Relations and Allied Documents*, ed. Reuben Gold Thwaites (Cleveland, Ohio: Burrows Bros., 1896–1901; hereafter, *JR*), vol. 65, 79; Gabriel Marest to Barthélemi Germon, 9 November 1712, in *JR*, vol. 66, 219–95.

2. Marest to Germon, 219–41.

3. Ibid. On changing Jesuit attitudes toward diabolical influences, see Peter A. Goddard, "The Devil in New France: Jesuit Demonology, 1611–50," *Canadian Historical Review* 78 (March 1997): 40–62.

4. Marest to Germon, 241–45.

5. Ibid., 247–51.

6. For the Fox wars and other conflicts, see R. David Edmunds and Joseph L. Peyser, *The Fox Wars: The Mesquakie Challenge to New France* (Norman: University of Oklahoma Press, 1993), and Richard White, *The Middle Ground: Indians, Empires, and Republics in the Great Lakes Region, 1650–1815* (New York: Cambridge University Press, 1991), 142–85. The best sources on French settlement in the Illinois country are Carl J. Ekberg, *French Roots in the Illinois Country: The Mississippi Frontier in Colonial Times* (Urbana: University of Illinois Press, 1998), and Winstanley Briggs, "Le Pays des Illinois," *William and Mary Quarterly*, 3d ser., 47 (January 1990): 30–56.

7. Marest to Germon, 245–47.

8. Scholars who contend that there was a general decline in fervor and in the state of the missions include Susan Sleeper-Smith, "Women, Kin, and Catholicism: New Perspectives on the Fur Trade," *Ethnohistory* 47 (Spring 2000): 425; Robert Choquette, "French Catholicism Comes to the Americas," in *Christianity Comes to the Americas, 1492–1776* (New York: Paragon House, 1992), 185–92 and 213–20; John Webster Grant, *Moon of Wintertime: Missionaries and the Indians of Canada in Encounter since 1534* (Toronto: University of Toronto Press, 1984), 63–67; and Christopher Vecsey, *The Paths of Kateri's Kin* (Notre Dame, Ind.: University of Notre Dame Press, 1997), 3–172. On the changing nature of Jesuit mission work in the eighteenth century, see Pierre Berthiaume, *L'aventure américaine au XVIIIe siècle: Du voyage à l'écriture* (Ottawa: Les Presses de l'Université d'Ottawa, 1990), 274–311; Carole Blackburn, *Harvest of Souls: The Jesuit Missions and Colonialism in North America, 1632–1650* (Montreal: McGill-Queen's University Press, 2000), 41; and John Hopkins Kennedy, *Jesuit and Savage in New France* (New Haven, Conn.: Yale University Press, 1950), 38 and 49.

9. Victor Egon Hanzeli, *Missionary Linguistics in New France: A Study of Seventeenth- and Eighteenth-Century Descriptions of American Indian Languages* (The Hague: Mouton, 1969), 30. The parish was named after the original mission, Immaculate Conception. See Mary Borgias Palm, *The Jesuit Missions of the Illinois Country, 1673–1763* (Cleveland, Ohio: n.p., 1933), 63–73. The sacramental registers for Kaskaskia are reproduced in Marthe Faribault-Beauregard, ed., *La population des forts français d'Amérique (XVIIIe siècle): Répertoire des baptêmes, mariages et sépultures célébrés dans les forts et les établissements français en Amérique du Nord au XVIIIe siècle* (Montreal: Éditions Bergeron, 1984), vol. 2, 71–205.

10. Jean Mermet to the Jesuits in Canada, 2 March 1706, in *JR*, vol. 66, 51–65; Marest to Germon, 265–95; Joseph de Guibert, *The Jesuits, Their Spiritual Doctrine and Practice: A Historical Study*, trans. William J. Young (Chicago: Institute of Jesuit Sources, 1964), 429–39.

11. Marest to Germon, 255; Guibert, ch. 17.

12. Jean Mermet to Father Germain, superior of the Canadian Missions, 25 February 1715, MS copy in the Brotier Collection (GBro 172–04, folio 11 recto/verso), Archives Jésuites de Paris, Vanves. The translation is mine.

13. Jacques Charles de Sabrevois, "Memoir on the Savages of Canada as Far as the Mississippi River, Describing Their Customs and Trade," in *Collections of the State*

Historical Society of Wisconsin, ed. Reuben Gold Thwaites (Madison: State Historical Society of Wisconsin, 1902; hereafter, *CSHSW*), vol. 16, 374; François-Xavier de Charlevoix, *Journal d'un voyage fait par ordre du roi dans l'Amérique septentrionale*, ed. Pierre Berthiaume (Montreal: Les Presses de l'Université de Montréal, 1994), vol. 2, 759 and 776.

14. Charlevoix, *Journal d'un voyage*, 746–49. The translation is from the 1761 English edition reproduced in facsimile in Pierre de Charlevoix, *Journal of a Voyage to North America* (Ann Arbor: University Microfilms, 1966), vol. 2, 212–13.

15. Diron d'Artaguiette, "Journal of Diron d'Artaguiette," in *Travels in the American Colonies*, ed. Newton D. Mereness (New York: Macmillan Company, 1916), 71–75. For brief accounts of the Compagnie des Indes and the administration of Louisiana during this era, see W. J. Eccles, *The French in North America, 1500–1783*, rev. ed. (East Lansing: Michigan State University Press, 1998), 182–84, and Bernard Lugan, *Histoire de la Louisiane française, 1682–1804* (Paris: Perrin, 1994), 78–82.

16. *Mercure de France* (December 1725): 2827–59, microfilm copy by Bibliothèque nationale de France, 1959; Richard N. Ellis and Charlie R. Steen, "An Indian Delegation in France, 1725," *Journal of the Illinois State Historical Society* 67 (September 1974): 385–405.

17. Mathurin Le Petit to Louis d'Avaugour, 12 July 1730, in *JR*, vol. 68, 201–17. On the Natchez wars, see Eccles, 186; Lugan, 116–21; and Daniel H. Usner, Jr., *Indians, Settlers, and Slaves in a Frontier Exchange Economy: The Lower Mississippi Valley before 1783* (Chapel Hill: University of North Carolina Press, 1992), 65–76.

18. On the *Lettres édifiantes*, see Berthiaume, *L'aventure Américaine*, 274–311.

19. Louis Vivier to another father, 8 June 1750, in *JR*, vol. 69, 143–49; Louis Vivier to a father of the same society, 17 November 1750, in *JR*, vol. 69, 201–29. The three Illinois communities were the Kaskaskia, Cahokia, and Michigamea villages.

20. Vivier to another father, 8 June 1750, 149.

21. Ibid., 147.

22. Ibid., 147–49.

23. Vivier to a father of the same society, 17 November 1750, 223–29.

24. Beauregard, vol. 2, 205; Carl J. Ekberg, "Marie Rouensa-8cate8a and the Foundation of French Illinois," *Illinois Historical Journal* 84 (Autumn 1991): 154–57; Susan Sleeper-Smith, *Indian Women and French Men: Rethinking Cultural Encounter in the Western Great Lakes* (Amherst: University of Massachusetts Press, 2001), ch. 2.

25. Jacqueline Peterson, "Women Dreaming: The Religiopsychology of Indian White Marriages and the Rise of a Metis Culture," in *Western Women: Their Land, Their Lives*, ed. Lillian Schlissel, Vicki L. Ruiz, and Janice Monk (Albuquerque: University of New Mexico Press, 1988), 50–55 and 62–63; Michael Harkin and Sergei Kan, "Introduction" to the special issue on "Native American Women's Responses to Christianity," *Ethnohistory* 43 (Fall 1996): 563–71.

26. On the creation of identities that are both Native and Christian, or what Strong calls "hybridized subjectivities," see Pauline Turner Strong, "Feminist Theory and the 'Invasion of the Heart' in North America," *Ethnohistory* 43 (Fall 1996): 696–98.

27. Sébastien Louis Meurin to Monseigneur Olivier Briand, bishop of Quebec, 23 March 1767, in *Documents inédits concernant la Compagnie de Jésus*, ed. Auguste Carayon

(Poitiers: Henri Oudin, 1865; hereafter, *Documents inédits*), vol. 14, 58–64. All translations from this source are mine. The settlements Meurin mentioned were Ste. Genevieve, where he was stationed at the time, and the recently established St. Louis (both on the west bank) and Kaskaskia, Prairie du Rocher, and the French and Illinois villages of Cahokia on the east bank. For French settlement in the Illinois country, see Ekberg, *French Roots in the Illinois Country*, 31–110. On the impact of the Seven Years' War and the end of the French empire in North America, see Eccles, chs. 7–8. For the Jesuits in the Illinois country during this era, consult Palm, 86–97; Jean Delanglez, *The French Jesuits in Lower Louisiana (1700–1763)* (Washington, D.C.: Catholic University of America, 1935), 491–537; and François Philibert Watrin, "Banishment of the Jesuits from Louisiana," 3 September 1764, in *JR*, vol. 70, 211–301. On the Cahokia mission and parish, see John Francis McDermott, ed., *Old Cahokia: A Narrative and Documents Illustrating the First Century of Its History* (St. Louis, Mo.: St. Louis Historical Documents Foundation, 1949), 21–26.

28. Meurin to Briand, 9 May 1767, in *Documents inédits*, 64–66.

29. Monseigneur Olivier Briand, bishop of Quebec, to Sébastien Louis Meurin, 7 August 1767, in *Documents inédits*, 66–67. See also Briand to Meurin, n.d., in *Documents inédits*, 67–70.

30. Meurin to Briand, 11 June 1768, in *Documents inédits*, 70–79. A slightly different version of the letter and an English translation appear in *JR*, vol. 71, 32–47.

31. Meurin to Briand, 14 June 1769, in *Documents inédits*, 84–92.

32. Meurin to Briand, 23 May 1776, in *Documents inédits*, 101; Palm, 93.

33. Watrin, 211–301.

34. Ibid., 269–73. Susan Sleeper-Smith shows that Native women claimed a leading role in fashioning this kind of "frontier Catholicism" in the region. See Sleeper-Smith, *Indian Women and French Men*.

35. Jean Enjalran, "Relation of 1679," in *JR*, vol. 61, 101–47; James Boynton, *Fishers of Men: The Jesuit Mission at Mackinac, 1670–1765* (Mackinac Island, Mich.: Ste. Anne's Church, 1996), 14–26.

36. White, 50–141; Helen Hornbeck Tanner, ed., *Atlas of Great Lakes Indian History* (Norman: University of Oklahoma Press, 1987), map 6.

37. Gilles Havard, *The Great Peace of Montreal of 1701: French-Native Diplomacy in the Seventeenth Century*, trans. Phyllis Aronoff and Howard Scott (Montreal: McGill-Queen's University Press, 2001); William James Newbigging, "The History of the French-Ottawa Alliance, 1613–1763" (Ph.D. diss., University of Toronto, 1995), 230–303.

38. White, 49 and 94–149.

39. Étienne de Carheil to Louis Hector de Callières, Governor, 30 August 1702, in *JR*, vol. 65, 189–253.

40. Joseph Marest to Antoine Laumet de La Mothe, Sieur de Cadillac, 12 May 1703, in *CSHSW*, vol. 16, 217–18; Boynton, 29–31.

41. Marest to Germon, 283–85.

42. Joseph Marest to Philippe de Rigault, Marquis de Vaudreuil, governor of New France, 21 June 1712, in *CSHSW*, vol. 16, 288–92; White, 149–59.

43. Charlevoix, *Journal d'un voyage*, vol. 1, 575–81; Luc François Nau to [Julien?] Bonin, 20 October 1735, in *JR*, vol. 68, 285.

44. A record of the speech appears in *CSHSW*, vol. 17, 372–73. Also see the documents in *CSHSW*, vol. 17, 351–52, 359–60, and 367–69, and Newbigging, 349–62.

45. Boynton, 35–46.

46. "Treaty with the Kaskaskia, 1803," in *Indian Affairs: Laws and Treaties*, vol. 2, comp. Charles J. Kappler (Washington, D.C.: Government Printing Office, 1904), 67–68; Palm, 94; Emily J. Blasingham, "The Depopulation of the Illinois Indians," Part I in *Ethnohistory* 3 (Summer 1956): 213–17; J. Joseph Bauxar, "History of the Illinois Area," in *Handbook of North American Indians*, vol. 15, *Northeast*, ed. Bruce G. Trigger (Washington, D.C.: Smithsonian Institution, 1978), 596–97.

APPENDIX

1. Allan Greer offers a masterful portrait of Jesuit spirituality and Native Christianity in *Mohawk Saint: Catherine Tekakwitha and the Jesuits* (New York: Oxford University Press, 2005). On the history of the *Jesuit Relations*, see Joseph P. Donnelly, *Thwaites' "Jesuit Relations": Errata and Addenda* (Chicago: Loyola University Press, 1967), 1–26, and the introduction in Allan Greer, ed., *The Jesuit Relations: Natives and Missionaries in Seventeenth-Century North America* (Boston: Bedford/St. Martin's, 2000), 1–19. For calls to examine missionary texts as spiritual writings, see Lucien Campeau, *La mission des jésuites chez les Hurons, 1634–1650* (Montreal: Bellarmin, 1987), 11; Pierre Berthiaume, *L'aventure américaine au XVIIIe siècle: Du voyage à l'écriture* (Ottawa: Les Presses de l'Université d'Ottawa, 1990), ch. 4; and Allan Greer, "Colonial Saints: Gender, Race, and Hagiography in New France," *William and Mary Quarterly* 3d ser., 57 (April 2000): 323–48.

2. On the evolution of French Jesuit writings on North America, see Berthiaume, 274–311. The method of citation used throughout this book includes the individual author when authorship is reasonably certain and an English title of the document adapted from the Thwaites collection. Normally, several authors contributed letters and reports to each edition of the *Relations*. A Jesuit editor then organized and edited the material for publication. The *Relation of 1671–1672* was the last of the official published relations, appearing in 1673. For several years thereafter, the Jesuits collected the letters and journals for the relations and sent them to France. Thwaites includes these manuscript relations in his compilation. References to the manuscript relations are in quotations, as in "Relation of 1675," rather than in italics. The Thwaites edition supplies a transcription of the French original and an English translation on facing pages. Although the language is somewhat archaic, the translation is generally good, and it is the basis for all of the quotations from Thwaites in this study.

3. Important works limited to or emphasizing the first half of the seventeenth century include James Axtell, *The Invasion Within: The Contest of Cultures in Colonial North America* (New York: Oxford University Press, 1985), 23–127; Carole Blackburn, *Harvest of*

Souls: The Jesuit Missions and Colonialism in North America, 1632–1650 (Montreal: Mc-Gill-Queen's University Press, 2000); Henry Warner Bowden, *American Indians and Christian Missions* (Chicago: University of Chicago Press, 1981), 59–95; Campeau, *La mission des jésuites*; John Webster Grant, *Moon of Wintertime: Missionaries and the Indians of Canada in Encounter since 1534* (Toronto: University of Toronto Press, 1984), 3–46; Cornelius J. Jaenen, *Friend and Foe: Aspects of French-Amerindian Cultural Contact in the Sixteenth and Seventeenth Centuries* (New York: Columbia University Press, 1976), 41–83; Bruce G. Trigger, *The Children of Aataentsic: A History of the Huron People to 1660* (Montreal: McGill-Queen's University Press, 1976); Bruce Trigger, *Natives and Newcomers: Canada's "Heroic Age" Reconsidered* (Kingston, Ont.: McGill-Queen's University Press, 1985), 164–297; and Christopher Vecsey, *The Paths of Kateri's Kin* (Notre Dame, Ind.: University of Notre Dame Press, 1997), 3–172.

4. On the central themes of Jesuit spirituality and practice, see Joseph de Guibert, *The Jesuits, Their Spiritual Doctrine and Practice: A Historical Study*, trans. William J. Young (Chicago: Institute of Jesuit Sources, 1964) and John W. O'Malley, *The First Jesuits* (Cambridge, Mass.: Harvard University Press, 1993).

5. See Howard L. Harrod, "Missionary Life-World and Native Response: Jesuits in New France," *Studies in Religion* 13 (Spring 1984): 179–92, and the many diverse examples in Joel W. Martin and Mark A. Nicholas, eds., *Native Americans, Christianity, and the Reshaping of the American Religious Landscape* (Chapel Hill: University of North Carolina Press, 2010).

6. Erik R. Seeman advocates a similar kind of systematic analysis of formulaic sources, including the *Jesuit Relations*, in "Reading Indians' Deathbed Scenes: Ethnohistorical and Representational Approaches," *Journal of American History* 88 (June 2001): 17–47.

7. James Axtell discusses the difficulty many scholars have in accepting the validity of Native conversions in "Were Indian Conversions Bona Fide?," repr. in *Christianity and Missions, 1450–1800*, ed. J. S. Cummins (Aldershot: Ashgate Variorum, 1997), 343–67. For a number of modern examples of the struggle to integrate Native and Christian identities, see the enlightening pieces in James Treat, ed., *Native and Christian: Indigenous Voices on Religious Identity in the United States and Canada* (New York: Routledge, 1996).

Index

Acknowledgments

I am grateful to have the opportunity after so many years to thank the people and institutions that offered such generous support for this project. This book came with lasting friendships, memorable conversations, adventures in Paris, Rome, Québec, and Miami (Oklahoma, not Florida), two children, and a wedding. I am thankful for all of this and more.

At Dartmouth College I had the good fortune to begin studying the histories of the Native peoples of North America with three remarkable scholars: Sergei Kan, Colin Calloway, and Michael Green. I continued this work at Arizona State University with Peter Iverson and Al Hurtado. Peter has never wavered in his support of me and his many other fine students. Rachel Fuchs provided more than a guide to the history of France; she became a cherished friend. Susan Gray always pushed in the most positive ways for analytical rigor. Fellow students Jaime Aguila and Andy Fisher became great friends and got me out on the soccer field on a regular basis. Wendel Cox is another of the many friends I value from those years.

Smith College welcomed me for two years as a Woodrow Wilson National Fellowship Foundation postdoctoral fellow in the humanities. The Louise W. and Edmund J. Kahn Liberal Arts Institute at Smith is an innovative site for interdisciplinary scholarship. I still miss my office in the library with its view of the campus (and with Mary Lewis just across the hall). Daniel Horowitz provided opportunities to teach in Smith's excellent American Studies program. Salman Hameed became one of my best friends in my time in Northampton. Our conversations about science and religion continue.

The Department of History has been a supportive home since I arrived at Creighton University. I want to thank my chair, Betsy Elliot-Meisel, for her warmth and spirit. Julie Fox is always a cheerful presence in the department office and someone I have depended on often. John Calvert has been a great friend, hiking partner, and colleague. I suspect that more outdoor adventures and many more debates about history, movies and music, and the contemporary

Middle East are forthcoming. My friends in the Humanities Research Group have strengthened the intellectual environment at Creighton, as has the Kripke Center for the Study of Religion and Society. Nathan Tye displayed his many skills as an undergraduate research assistant in helping me with some last-minute tasks. Participants in the New Mission History Symposium, organized by Joel Martin and Mark Nicholas, came to Omaha for a great weekend of discussion and debate (after a prior productive weekend at the University of California, Riverside). I would like to thank Joel and Mark for inviting me to participate and Ron Simkins of the Kripke Center for funding the event. Other participants in the project were Emma Anderson, Joanna Brooks, Steven Hackel, Dan Mandell, Michael McNally, David Silverman, Laura Stevens, Rachel Wheeler, Doug Winiarski, and Hilary Wyss. I have learned from them all.

I have nothing but praise for the Young Scholars in American Religion Project, organized by the Center for the Study of Religion and American Culture at Indiana University–Purdue University Indianapolis. Philip Goff has a knack for bringing together dynamic groups of people with diverse interests in American religion. John Corrigan and Judith Weisenfeld were the intrepid leaders of our cohort. I had first met John years before at Arizona State University. We have worked together many times since then. He is a model teacher-scholar and a terrific mentor and friend. Courtney Bender, Kathleen Cummings, Sylvester Johnson, and Kristy Nabhan-Warren have become especially good friends from those Indianapolis meetings.

I would like to thank several people who read all or part of this manuscript. Brett Rushforth provided an especially insightful and timely critique. Colin Calloway has seen the manuscript in several stages and offered his advice and support all along the way. Daryl Baldwin and David Costa guided me through the complexities of the Miami-Illinois language material and surely saved me from a number of errors. I also appreciate the opportunities Daryl presented for me to share my work with members of the Miami Nation. Working with Bob Lockhart and Dan Richter at Penn has been a pleasure. I know I made the right decision in bringing the book to them. Steve Warren read some of the book, too. Even more than his helpful commentary, however, I value our friendship and our shared appreciation for the music of Wilco and the novels of Cormac McCarthy.

For generous funding in support of this project, I thank the American Historical Association, Arizona State University, the Creighton University Graduate School, the Phillips Fund for Native American Research at the

American Philosophical Society, and the Society for French Historical Studies. Johns Hopkins University Press provided permission to publish in revised form "Geographies of Encounter: Religion and Contested Spaces in Colonial North America," which first appeared in *American Quarterly*, vol. 56 (December 2004): 913–43. I also received permission from Cambridge University Press to use "'Bad Things' and 'Good Hearts': Mediation, Meaning, and the Language of Illinois Christianity," published in *Church History: Studies in Christianity and Culture*, vol. 76 (June 2007): 363–94, as the basis for chapter five.

Finally, I would like to express my love and admiration for Heather Fryer. She is a wonderful scholar—a great historian and inspirational teacher—and on innumerable occasions I have called upon her expert eye to improve my own work. Yet, it is the love she gives every day that I treasure above all else. Meeting her has been one of the great gifts of my life.